LARGEMOUTH BASS SECRETS

In-Fisherman ®
"Secrets" Book Series

One of the

(F) Fish + (L) Location + (P) Presentation = (S) Success^{SM}

Educational Services

LARGEMOUTH BASS SECRETS

Bobby Murray
Al Lindner
Chet Meyers
Ron Lindner
Billy Murray

TABLE OF CONTENTS

"Three very different environments — yet all hold bass. Would you know how, when, and where to begin?"

"Hopefully this book will help you land a few lunkers, like the one Al Lindner is holding.

CHAPTER 1
The Basics of Bass Behavior

The true bass fishing addict is a strange creature. He moans on brilliant sunny days and rubs his hands with glee when the weather looks dreary and promises rain. He carries a thermometer in his tackle box and will try just about any lure, no matter how strange looking, that might catch a bass. And he reads — everything he can get his hands on that has to do with bass. He knows his quarry inside and out. In many ways he is like the most skilled of hunters. A competent bass angler can wake up in the morning, take one look at the weather, and give you a pretty good idea how, when, and where the bass will be responding on his favorite lake, river, or reservoir. This is what separates him from 99% of all other anglers. Sure, he also has a nice bass boat and probably some fancy equipment, but the key to his success is his knowledge of the creaturely aspects of his quarry.

Most of us have plopped down our money for a new "wonder lure" that promises to solve all our fishing problems, but even as we do so, we know that the real answer to our fishing problems is learning more about Mr. Bass. Because of the wide geographic range and the different types of waters that bass inhabit, we need to understand how bass respond to different habitats and how they are equipped biologically to deal with their watery environment.

Despite their seeming ability to outwit anglers, bass have very small brains and are totally incapable of the high level of thinking that is often attributed to them. But though their brains be small, Mother Nature has more than compensated for this deficiency by providing them with a strong instinct for survival, keen senses, lightning fast reflexes, and a cautionary nature. Bass are captives of an underwater world they can do little to change. All they can do is adapt to changes in their environment. The senses of sight, hearing, and smell are crucial in this day-to-day adaptation and fight for survival.

SENSE OF SIGHT

The wind was calm and the lake surface mirror-like. Though the sun had set some time ago, it was still light as a large female bass made her way up the point and into the shallows in search of food. Suddenly she sensed a noise in the distance. An overexuberant field mouse had fallen from its perch in an old boat house and its splash attracted the bass's attention. She swam around in a search pattern until her lateral line picked up the sound vibrations more clearly. Then she began to zero in on her quarry. Soon she saw the small creature struggling in the water. She didn't recognize this particular type of "bug," but quickly inhaled it and continued her search for food.

Bass, along with most other gamefish, are very nearsighted. This means that, just like the bass in the preceding situation, they often rely on their senses of hearing and smell to first direct them to their prey. Only when they are in the immediate area of prey do they rely on their eyes for the final strike. Biologists are not sure how far bass can see underwater, but even in clear water their vision is probably limited to 10 or 15 feet. And even at that distance, they cannot clearly distinguish objects. Though handicapped by this nearsightedness, bass have almost microscopic close-up vision. The implications of all this for anglers are twofold.

When fishing for bass we usually rely on two general approaches: (1) *tempting* the fish to take live bait or a simulated live bait, or (2) *triggering* an instinctual strike through the rapid retrieve of an artificial lure. Realizing that bass have excellent close-up vision, when we are using the first approach, we should use light line, small hooks, and no terminal tackle (i.e., leaders, swivel snaps, etc.). A good suggestion when trying to tempt bass with live bait or a plastic worm is to make our presentation look as natural as possible. When a bass is directly eyeballing our bait it can quickly tell if something is unnatural. Of course some fishing conditions may dictate heavier line, as when fishing plastic worms in flooded timber, but a good rule of thumb is to use as light a line as possible.

When we are trying to trigger an instinctual strike, we do not have to be quite so careful. Usually in these instances we are casting a rapid retrieve lure, like a crankbait. The fish hears the approaching sound, turns on a dime, and slams into our presentation. Of course it is important to make sure that our lures are running correctly, but we can often get by with heavier line and even with a swivel snap without lowering our chances. One caution, however — be sure to read the directions that come with your lure, as some types of swivels and snaps do not help the action of a lure. Most lures are tested to operate correctly only under certain conditions. Sometimes they should be tied directly to the line and other times they come with a snap or split ring attached. In either case, you don't have to worry about the bass's microscopic vision. Just make sure the lure is working properly and that you are presenting it near one of Mr. Bass's hangouts.

Another interesting aspect of a bass's sense of vision is the position of the eyes. Bass have an extremely wide range of vision. Their eyes are so positioned that they can see not only straight ahead, to the side, and partially behind, but also downward and overhead. This means that bass can actually see above the water level when the conditions are right. This "periscope effect" is particularly important when the water is a flat calm and when anglers are fishing shallow water bass. On a calm day in shallow water, bass can see an angler move along a bank or stand up in a boat. Often the simple movement of a cast will spook these fish. Bass instinctively spook at the sign of a quick movement overhead, because as young fry many of their predators take the form of fish-eating birds such as kingfishers or herons. Of course at a distance bass cannot tell what is making the movement, but they know to avoid it and to head for deep water or available cover.

The implications of the "periscope effect" should be obvious. If we are fishing from the shore, it is wise to avoid quick movements, to wear clothing that blends into the natural background, and to stand well back of the shoreline when making our casts. Boat anglers might consider wearing light colored shirts that will blend with the sky and should also avoid quick or unnecessary movements. Another hint that will help any angler fishing shallow water bass is to wear a pair of polaroid sun glasses. Not only will these save wear and tear on the eyes, they will also help you see your quarry. Polaroids cut down on surface glare and help you see below the surface. You can often tell the feeding mood of bass just by observing how they react to your presentation. If you see fish darting off when you make a cast, realize that these fish are in a skittish mood and proceed with caution.

"Polaroid glasses will not only save wear and tear on your eyes, but also help you see shallow water bass when the water is calm."

Can Bass See Color?

A number of studies have indicated that fish in general, and bass in particular, can distinguish colors. In one experiment, bass were trained to respond to different shades of purple plastic worms. Researchers discovered that the fish could even detect color variations that humans had trouble identifying. Many anglers argue that lure color makes a big difference in their fishing success. All of us have probably experienced times when one color out-produced another. This can be true, so it is important to have a few different colors of your favorite lure in your tackle box. Most of the time, however, color is not a crucial variable. The depth, speed, and action of the lure are much more important.

Of course some diehards will continue the color debate as long as someone else will listen. Plastic worms anglers love to discuss the pros and cons of different colors, lengths, and even flavors. One angler thinks he has resolved this debate for once and for all. "You know," he said, "there is just a lot of plain baloney about different colors and sizes of plastic worms. As far as I'm concerned just about any plastic worm made will catch bass . . . as long as it's purple and six inches long."

Sensitivity to Light

A few years ago, there were a number of theories circulating about fish and their sensitivity to sunlight. The early structure fishermen were convinced that light was "the enemy." While there is some truth to this statement, we now know that different species are affected differently. Some fish, lake trout for example, actually develop cataracts on their eyes if exposed to direct sunlight for extended periods of time. Bass, on the other hand, seem to suffer no ill effects. They can lie for hours over a shallow spawning bed, with the sun directly overhead. But, like most fish, when they have the option, bass will avoid the sun. They do this not because light hurts their eyes, but because they associate the absence of light with security. Small bass fry are constantly trying to avoid becoming someone else's dinner. Therefore, they instinctively avoid lighted areas and seek cover under weeds, rocks, or trees, or in deep water.

The late Bob Underwood, author of *Lunker* (another excellent bass fishing book), took his research so seriously that he actually had an eye doctor examine a bass to clear up this question of sensitivity to light. He discovered that although bass do not possess eyelids, they can limit the amount of light that enters their eyes by contracting or expanding the pupil or by moving their eye lens forward and backward. Underwood also discovered that bass are about five times more sensitive to light than are humans. This means that under very dim light conditions bass can see quite well. Bass typically make shallow water movements in the evening. As the amount of light decreases with the setting sun, bass will simply drop down closer to the bottom so they can use the available light to silhouette their prey against the surface.

Competitiveness

There is one final factor related to a bass's sense of vision that should interest anglers. When bass begin to actively feed, the action can become fast and furious. Bass are naturally competitive. If one fish grabs a large minnow, other fish will actually try to take it away. This explains those strange occasions when two bass are caught on the same cast. Skin divers have observed two or three bass following a hooked fish and trying to strike at the protruding lure. Though your fellow anglers might not appreciate it, it often makes good sense to cast right where a friend has hooked a bass. This can cause some confusion, but can also add a number of fish to your stringer. Of course, if your buddy has on the lunker of a lifetime you would be best advised to hold off. Try this sometime. Bass are so competitive that they just can't leave well enough alone, and the smart angler will use this greed to his advantage.

SENSE OF HEARING

Last year, while doing a test netting in a small Florida lake, a biologist came up with a seven-pound largemouth bass. Nothing strange about that, except this particular bass was blind in both eyes, and from the evidence of the scar tissue, had been blind for a few years. The bass was in excellent health and had just eaten a few shiners. While this may seem a rare instance of survival, it does emphasize the importance of the sense of hearing, for it is this very keen sense that enabled that particular bass to survive.

Bass hear, i.e., pick up sound vibrations, through two separate organs, the inner ear and the lateral line. Each of these organs functions separately and for different purposes. The inner ear is used to detect distant noise while the lateral line is used for nearby sound.

The inner ears of a bass are not directly exposed to the water, but are buried under the skin on each side of the fish's head. Sounds are transmitted from the water through the skin, muscle, and bone to the inner ear. This probably explains the inner ear's lack of sensitivity to close noise. It is used to detect noises that come from a distance, approximately 25 feet and further. Through this sense the bass can detect the presence of a sound but is not aware of its direction. Just how far away can a bass hear noises? This naturally depends on the intensity of the sound. But consider this. A bass's sense of hearing is much keener than a human's, and water transmits noise about five times better than air. Chances are that if you literally "throw out the anchor" near your favorite fishing hole, you alert every fish within a radius of one hundred yards.

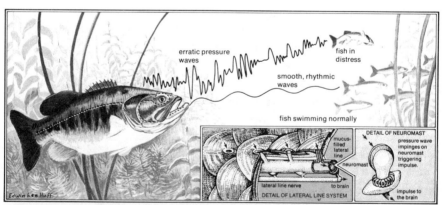

Bass often hear their prey before they see it. The lateral line serves as a directional sonar and is effective up to distances of 20 feet.

To determine the actual direction of a sound, bass rely on their lateral line. The lateral line is a series of open nerve endings that run the length of the body from just behind the gill cover to the base of the tail. At ranges of less than 25 feet a bass can tell exactly where a sound originates. In fact, in a recent experiment, bass were blindfolded with special plastic discs and released in a large aquarium with some minnows. Though they had some trouble, the bass did manage to track down their prey without using their eyes.

This may sound like interesting tidbits of bass biology, but what does it have to do with fishing? Actually quite a bit. Being aware of the sensitivity of a bass's hearing may explain why some of us fail to catch fish. As far as anglers are concerned there are just two classes of noise: those that attract fish and those that scare fish. Sadly, many of us are quite good at making the latter type of noise.

Sounds That Repel

Bass are very aware of sounds that are a normal part of their environment — the sound made by a school of baitfish, the sound of an approaching predator (the distinctive thump of a northern pike's tail), the sound of small insects falling into the water, etc. They are also aware of sounds that are foreign to their watery world, and these sounds will alert them to the angler's presence. Dropping an anchor over the side of a boat is equivalent to setting off a small depth charge. Lesser noises may not scare fish away, but they will alert fish that you are around, and once alerted a bass is much more difficult to catch. Metal stringers clanging against the side of a metal boat don't help. Any shuffling of feet or movement in a boat will also advertise your presence, especially when fishing shallow water. Bob Underwood did an experiment while fishing over a small school of bass. He simply stood up in a carpeted bass boat — didn't kick over the minnow bucket, thump his feet, or bang an oar — he just stood up. According to his diver, every bass within twenty feet turned to look at the source of the noise. The diver didn't hear anything, but those bass sure did.

Perhaps the biggest culprit of boat noise is the tackle box. One hint that helps to avoid opening and closing this noise-maker is to attach a small strip of styrofoam to the inside of your boat. Get out all the lures you think you will use that day and hook them into the styrofoam. Then put your tackle box under the seat and don't touch it for the rest of the day.

What about motors, paddles, and oars? In fairly deep water, over ten feet, fish are aware of these sounds but are not bothered by them. In shallow water it's a different story. In one study researchers learned that a gas motor will drive most bass out of shallow water into deeper water. An electric motor, on the other hand, had little negative effect. The fish were aware of its presence and some even swam up for a closer look, obviously undisturbed. This means that if you plan to fish shallow water bass you should cut your gas motor some distance from your actual fishing spot and use an electric motor to move in closer.

You might think that paddles or oars would be even less disturbing than an electric motor, but the same study concluded differently. Apparently there is something about the currents produced by an oar or paddle that bothers fish. The oar doesn't even have to be squeaky; just its current puts fish on the alert and makes them skittish. Canoers and rowers might want to consider a small electric motor on their favorite lake to see if this improves their fishing success.

One final suggestion also has to do with fishing shallow water bass. When casting to shoreline objects like boat docks, stumps, and clumps of lily pads, many anglers like to impress their friends by placing their lure exactly where they

"An electric motor disturbs shallow water bass less than a canoe paddle or gas motor."

expect the fish to be holding. Dropping a quarter-ounce spinnerbait right next to an old stump is just like throwing a small rock at it. It will probably spook the fish. Always try to cast beyond where you think the fish is located so that you won't frighten it. Then, on your retrieve, try to bump that stump or dock piling with the lure. "Bumping the stump" will pay a lot more dividends than "splashing the bass."

Sounds That Attract

One of the great joys of angling is hearing the soft "plop" of a surface lure interrupted by the explosion of a bass trying to make a meal of it. Small, non-threatening noises, even though they are unfamiliar to bass, will often pique a bass's curiosity. And surface lures like the Jitterbug or Crippled Minnow have been slaying curious bass for decades. There are just two problems with this type of fishing: (1) it's addictive — you may not want to use any other approach, and (2) it's usually limited to shallow areas when the water is calm. Still, for some anglers, surface fishing for bass is the only way to go.

While we don't know exactly what noises will trigger a bass to strike, we do know that sound-producing lures are particularly important when fishing in dark or murky water. Of course all lures create some type of sound as they move through the water; even plastic worms send out some vibrations. But in murky water, noisemaker lures like spinnerbaits or crankbaits with rattles inside will be more effective because bass will rely heavily on their sense of hearing. We also know that what triggers a response one day may not work the next. Bass pros often make minor modifications, such as putting a slight bend in the blade of a spinner, to change the action of a lure. One of our friends likes to take a balsa minnow, like the Rapala, and put a slight crimp in the middle with a pair of long-nosed pliers. He says this gives the lure a strange action that sometimes drives bass crazy. No lure manufacturer has yet developed a surefire noise that will always work, so go ahead and experiment on your lures. It's not only fun, but may put a few extra bass on the stringer.

SENSE OF SMELL

The largest part of a bass's brain is dedicated to the sense of smell, so it is not surprising that this is the keenest of its senses. Bass use this sense not only to locate prey and to detect the presence of predators, but to select a mate and perhaps to locate certain types of vegetation. Like most freshwater gamefish, bass have two nostrils, one on either side of their snout. A special arrangement allows water to be forced over the sensory nerve endings quickly. This means that once a smell is even faintly detected, bass can quickly zero in on its source. Scientific experiments conducted on coho and chinook salmon demonstrated that these fish could detect less than two hundredths of a drop of seal (a natural predator) extract in a 23,000 gallon swimming pool. Now that's a sensitive sniffer. No formal studies have been conducted on bass, and their noses may not be quite so sensitive as a salmon's, but the fact that bass can locate prey in murky water and at night tells us they too have a keen sense of smell. Knowing how extremely sensitive a bass's nose is should help anglers with their fishing tactics.

Odors That Repel

Perhaps it is because our own human sense of smell is so poor that we often underestimate how well fish can smell and, therefore, often make mistakes while fishing. Care should always be taken when handling live bait. Gas and oil from a boat motor can easily be passed to minnows and crawlers, and a crawler tainted with gasoline is sure to make bass shy away. Make sure if you are running the motor to clean your hands before reaching into the bait bucket. You don't have to go so far as wearing gloves, but carrying a small bar of soap and occasionally washing your hands will certainly help.

Another odor that repels bass is the smell of a predator. This of course applies to lakes where muskies or northern pike are present, and not to southern waters where bass are at the top of the food chain. We once watched two small lads fishing for crappies in a Minnesota lake. Both boys were literally catching fish on every cast using small feathered jigs. Soon one boy, bored with all his success, moved down the shore and directly landed a small pike. After a few minutes, he returned to his friend for a few more crappies. His buddy continued to catch fish, but he struck out completely. Obviously some slime from the northern got on his jig and was keeping those crappies at arm's length. Consider this the next time you are bass fishing and happen to land a pike. Rinse off the lure completely or tie on a new one, and be sure to clip off about three feet of line. Often pike like to roll when they are hooked and slime can get all over the fishing line.

One odor that definitely disturbs bass is that given off by another bass that has been injured. Scientific studies have proven that many species of fish give off an alarm substance, called *schreckstoffen,* when they are injured. This substance always has a negative effect on fish of the same species. In experiments when an injured bass was released, it instinctively tried to return to its school and the other fish became nervous, ceased feeding, and left the area. Minor injuries to the mouth area do not, however, cause the release of this substance. But any fish that has been seriously injured or is bleeding should not be released, as it will probably die anyway and, if released, will put an end to fishing in that immediate area. Also, be sure to wipe off your hands and rinse your lure when you have handled an injured fish. A plastic worm tainted with the blood of an injured bass will catch few fish.

Odors That Attract

Though lots of magic fish scents have been bottled and sold, no one yet has come up with a potion that always attracts bass. Plastic worms have been marketed in just about every conceivable flavor or smell. And, while anglers have their favorites, there is no evidence that bass prefer strawberry over watermelon. What bass do like is the smell of baitfish. They are particularly sensitive to the odor of an injured baitfish. While the alarm substance of another bass is bad news, the alarm substance of a shiner minnow can trigger a feeding frenzy. One old timer we know puts this knowledge to work for him. He uses a nail clipper to take off part of one fin of the baitfish. He then hooks the baitfish to a bobber rig, and the erratic swimming motion works like magic on bass and northerns.

In dark or murky water, the use of live bait alone, or in combination with a lure, will increase odds of enticing a bass. Many anglers think of artificial lures and live bait as mutually exclusive and fail to realize how well they often work together. Northern anglers have been using the jig and minnow combination for years as a deadly tactic for walleyes, northerns, and bass. For some strange reason the jig and minnow or jig and crawler have never caught on in the southern part of our country. We have found that this is one of the best methods for taking bass. Redtail chubs, fathead minnows, or even small sucker minnows coupled with a slow dropping jig are unbeatable as a cold-water bass tactic. River anglers like to use a jig with a small piece of nightcrawler as a combination for smallmouth bass. The added enticement of a natural prey odor can sometime spell the difference between success and failure.

INFLUENCE OF WATER TEMPERATURE

One final aspect of bass biology that anglers should appreciate is a bass's sensitivity to changes in water temperature. We will take an in-depth look at this subject in Chapter 3, but a few comments are appropriate now. The activity level of bass, as cold-blooded creatures, is a function of water temperature. Unlike humans, bass do not maintain a constant body temperature and their metabolism must adjust to the temperature of their watery environment. It is therefore not surprising that bass can detect extremely small changes in water temperature.

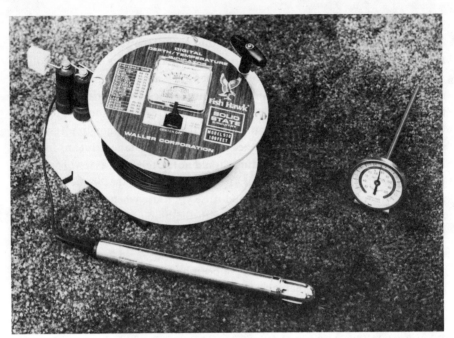

"Water thermometers come in different styles and price ranges. Knowing water temperature is an important part of bass fishing, particularly in the spring and fall."

Some changes have predictable effects. A quick drop in temperature has a negative effect on bass activity. It causes them to cease active feeding and requires an adjustment time before things get back to normal. A sharp rise in temperature, however, does not have such an adverse effect and often will send bass on a feeding spree. Since most rapid fluctuations like this occur in the spring and fall, it's a good idea for anglers to carry a thermometer and to keep track of daily changes. A careful monitoring of water temperature often provides valuable clues to the activity level and feeding moods of bass.

The range of survival temperatures for most members of the bass family is from 33°F to about 90°F. While it is often noted that the "preferred" temperature of bass is in the mid 70's, the term "preferred" is a misnomer. If bass actually prefer 72°F water, then we are tempted to conjure up images of schools of shivering bass in icebound northern lakes, waiting expectantly for ice-out and the first warm rains of spring. Bass really don't prefer any water temperature, within reasonable limits. They do, however, probably function best when water is in the 70° range. Experiments done in large aquariums, where the water temperature could be manipulated, proved that, as temperatures increased, bass became more active and fed more often. This trend continued up to about 85° F, at which point the bass fed almost continuously. Temperatures over 90° F proved lethal.

Appreciating how water temperature affects bass activity is important to the bass angler. One example should suffice. Let's say you are planning a visit to a southern reservoir for some early spring fishing. You've heard that the bass are really moving and want to get in on the action. In talking with some anglers that just brought in a nice string of two- to five-pound bass you learn that they caught the bass at the backs of coves on spinnerbaits. Great news! You head out with high hopes and, after fishing the back end of coves with spinnerbaits for over five hours, haven't seen a bass. What happened? Well, what those lucky anglers didn't tell you, because you forgot to ask them, is just what coves they were fishing. On a large sprawling reservoir in the early spring the coves at the furthest distance from the dam site are the first to warm up. A large reservoir can have more than a hundred coves, and the water temperature in each of them will vary. As the diagram below indicates, the temperature in the coves near the original river

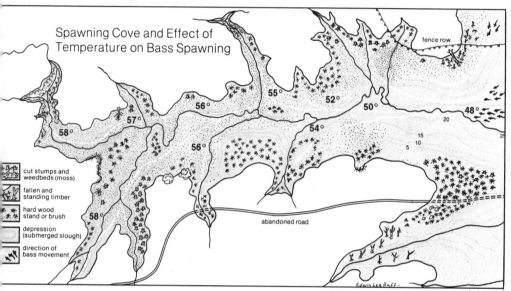

This diagram illustrates a typical reservoir spawning cove and the wide range of water temperatures present. Bass in the back of the cove are well into the pre-spawn calendar period, while bass in the main-lake still are in a cold water attitude. This explains why pre-spawn bass come into the shallows in "waves" as the water begins to warm.

system might be 58° F, a perfect temperature for pre-spawn largemouth. These coves are warmer because the water is shallower at this end of the reservoir and because warm spring rains are entering from the river systems. The bass in these coves are probably in two to six feet of water and are in an aggressive mood. The coves near the main marina, the ones you were fishing, are in much deeper water and are about 51° F. At this temperature the bass are tightly schooled in water 12 to 20 feet deep, are much less active, and probably could only be tempted with a jig and eel. Spinnerbaits would be a poor choice. All your hopes and dreams blown out of the water because you didn't take time to consider the temperature of the water and how it can affect your presentation.

SUMMARY

As you can see from this brief review of bass biology, even though the bass is not an intelligent creature, its creaturely instincts and responses to changes in its environment cannot be taken for granted. Too often anglers put their faith and money into expensive sophisticated fishing tackle and equipment instead of taking time to study the creature they are investing all this money in. In the chapters that follow, we will continue to focus on the creaturely habits of the bass and see how these dictate bass location in different bodies of water. When we put together these basic aspects of bass biology with the different types of water that bass inhabit, bass location ceases to be a mystery and the appropriate choice of tackle and lures becomes a matter of common sense.

CHAPTER 2
The Largemouth, Smallmouth, and Spotted Bass —
Similarities and Differences

There are six members of the bass family in North America. Naturally, there are differences in range, habitat preference, and body coloration, but the different species share many similar traits. All members of the bass clan have the same short, almost truncated, body shape. This physical makeup allows for excellent maneuverability, but does not lend itself to the speed and stamina of open water pursuit that the pike and muskie enjoy. For this reason, bass are best equipped to take their prey from ambush. You will often find bass using some type of structure — be it weedbed, boat dock, rocky dropoff, or sunken timber — as cover while waiting to pounce on their prey. Of course, the particular environment in which the bass lives will dictate the availability of this cover. Also, the predator-prey relationship will determine which zones bass will use for resting or seeking prey. In northern waters, where pike or muskie patrol the open waters, bass are often forced inside the weedline to satisfy their survival needs. In some southern lakes and reservoirs, on the other hand, there is no toothy predator to feed on bass; therefore, bass may roam open water in search of shad or other types of open water baitfish. As you will discover throughout this book, bass location and movement are always a function of the larger ecosystem in which they live.

A decade ago, when fishing was a younger science, it was fairly easy to make blanket statements like "all bass relate to the edge of brush or the weedline," or "all bass are by nature schooling creatures." While there is still much truth to these statements, we are discovering exceptions to the rule almost daily. Recent studies have been conducted using radio telemetry to follow bass movements, and some of the findings may shock old time bass addicts. In one study, conducted by Jim Winter, three bass were studied throughout the summer on a small lake. The territorial ranges of these bass differed significantly.

A similar tracking study was conducted by Mike Lembeck on large California impoundments and, though the environment was quite different, the results were strikingly similar. Both studies indicated that different groups of bass exhibit different behavioral patterns. Some fish are roamers, while others like to stay close to home. Some bass spend most of their time in large schools, some live in small bands, and others are loners.

Not only do locational patterns differ, so do bass personalities. In a small Minnesota lake, Al Lindner has been tagging and releasing largemouth bass for over four years. During this tagging study, some bass were caught time and time again. They are innately aggressive and just can't seem to resist those tempting spinnerbaits. Other bass would be caught, released, and never caught again. And some fish that were spotted while spawning and bore distinctive body marks appeared immune to artificial lures. What does all this tell us? Maybe that bass have different personalities, just like human beings. This is both good news and bad news. The bad news is that we can no longer make simple statements about bass behavior. The good news is that there are probably always a few aggressive bass hanging around, ready to accept our new-fangled lures.

These studies may first sound confusing, because it becomes difficult to predict what fishing will be like if different groups of bass have different habitat preferences and different feeding attitudes. But these studies also bear out some of our longtime knowledge of how bass behave. In any given body of water, bass will exhibit certain patterns of feeding behavior that most anglers can recognize. That is, bass activity does not occur randomly, without rhyme or reason. Though all smallmouth in a Canadian lake may not relate to the same bottom conditions, there will be types of rocks and dropoffs that *most smallmouth will prefer*. Though all largemouth in natural northern lakes do not relate to the weedline, *the weedline is usually a good place to begin prospecting for fish*. And, finally, although all bass, regardless of their species, do not hide under rocks, brush, or logs, *most bass will take their prey from some sort of cover or ambush point* if they have the opportunity. With all this in mind, let's take a closer look at the habitats and habitat preference of the largemouth, smallmouth, and spotted bass.

THE LARGEMOUTH BASS

When the European colonists first invaded the North American continent, the largemouth bass was already the most widely distributed game fish. Originally, old bucketmouth called nearly the entire eastern half of the United States home. He was native to most of the nation's glacially-formed lakes east of the great plains region. But he was absent from the waters of the Canadian Shield, a few rocky cold water areas of Michigan and northern Minnesota, the entire western part of the country, and the northern portion of the eastern seaboard. Throughout the south (where natural lakes are rare), the black bass was a fish of the rivers. Until the reservoir building boom, you either fished largemouth bass in the north or in Florida lakes, or chased him in the southern rivers. Today, as a result of massive stocking programs, the largemouth bass can be found, except for some "high" country trout waters, in almost every corner of the continental United States and Hawaii.

Old bucketmouth inhabits all stages of eutrophic, mesotrophic, and some oligotrophic natural lakes. He swims in the waters of canyon, highland, hill-land, flatland, and lowland reservoirs, and is found in adult, middle aged, old, and tidal rivers. Largemouth bass have also been stocked in strip pits, stock ponds, and even in concrete agriculture irrigation channels. Within the confines of these bodies of water, you'll find all varieties of water quality, bottom content, and

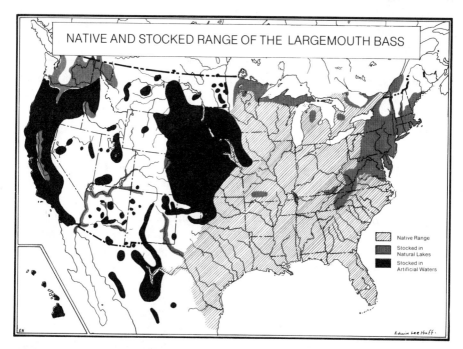

NATIVE AND STOCKED RANGE OF THE LARGEMOUTH BASS

Native Range

Stocked in Natural Lakes

Stocked in Artificial Waters

depth ranges. Different combinations of predator/prey relationships are numerous and affect bass location significantly. In short, the largemouth bass in America must adapt to and contend with the widest range of aquatic conditions to be found in the world.

It continues to amaze both biologists and bass anglers how adaptive the largemouth is to different watery environments. One of the more pleasant surprises has been the tremendous growth of largemouth in certain lakes and reservoirs of California. A few years ago, a 20-pound-plus bass was caught in Lake Miramar near San Diego, California. Many anglers are convinced that the next world record bigmouth will come from one of these California impoundments.

Another exciting development has been the introduction of Florida bass to other parts of the country. While it is a true largemouth, the Florida bass is a separate strain and exhibits fantastic growth patterns. As more and more Florida bass are successfully stocked outside their native range, more anglers will enjoy the thrill of hooking and landing real lunker bass.

Even the folks in Hawaii are now enjoying the thrills of largemouth fishing. Though other, more exotic, species of fish are native to this tropical paradise, it didn't take long for some enterprising anglers to convince biologists in the Department of Natural Resources to explore stocking bass in some of the small highland lakes. The largemouth adapted successfully and is now at home in a new environment and doing quite well.

Physical Characteristics

It might sound foolish to say that the one thing that distinguishes the largemouth from other bass is its large mouth, but that's the way it is. There is enough difference in coloration and patterning to distinguish the smallmouth from the largemouth, but most novices still have trouble distinguishing the largemouth from the spotted bass. The burr-like tooth on the tongue of the spotted bass is absent in the largemouth, and the lobes of the spotted bass's tail are more forked than on the largemouth.

It is difficult to make generalizations about actual color shading because shading depends on habitat. A largemouth bass out of the weeds and cruising over sand turns a light tan, and its dark horizontal stripe almost disappears. In clear highland reservoirs, schools of bass chasing shad in open water actually become silvery, while in murky water they turn a light milky greenish-white. In other waters "old linesides" lives up to his name; the body is a dark greenish-black with a pronounced dark horizontal bar running the entire length.

"A largemouth bass, churning through the lily pads, brings fond memories to any bass angler."

A nest builder, like all bass, the largemouth seeks out sheltered bays or channels, usually on the leeward side of prevailing winds, when constructing its saucer-shaped nest. In the midwest, anglers typically look for bays on the northwest side of lakes. These areas get the first morning rays of the sun and are the first to warm in the spring. Northwest bays also offer protection from the prevailing winds, which are often strong and come with regularity in this windswept area of our country. If bass nested on a windward shore, they would literally be blown off their nests and their eggs scattered, with little likelihood of hatching.

The weight of a largemouth bass naturally depends on the length of the growing season and the amount and type of prey present. It might take a New York state bass six years to reach a length of fifteen inches, while a Florida cousin could be that big before the end of its second year. Of course, bass size will always be relative. In Vermont a five-pounder will always be a lunker, while in Texas only eight-pounders qualify as lunkers. The world record largemouth is one of the older freshwater fishing records and has stood since 1932 at 22 pounds, 4 ounces. But just wait. It won't be long 'til some southern lake or California reservoir produces a new world record.

Habitat Preference

Because of its adaptability and extensive geographical range, it is almost impossible to make simple statements about the largemouth's preferred habitat. The spotted bass and smallmouth are much easier to understand, simply because their range is so limited. An adult largemouth bass, on the other hand, is a fish that is at home in a variety of ecological niches. In the clear, rocky, deep-water canyon reservoirs like Lake Powell in Utah, bass are taken in over 60 feet of water. At the same time, they are equally at home in a tepid weed-choked bayou in Louisiana, where they may spend their entire life cycle in less than six feet of water.

The implications of this adaptability are enormous to the angler, and the truly versatile fisherman must be familiar with different types of lakes, reservoirs, and rivers to consistently locate and catch bass. Any generalizations about large-mouth, such as "it is a fish of shallow water habitat," without qualification as to the type of body of water, are misleading. As the case studies in the following chapters will illustrate, largemouth are extremely adaptable, and this often causes difficulties for anglers who leave their home turf to pursue bass in unfamiliar environments. One brief example should help make this point.

A few years ago some friends of ours, who are pretty good bass fishermen on northern lakes, took a trip south to Table Rock Reservoir in Arkansas. They were greeted by a body of water so different from the sandy, mesotrophic lakes they usually fished that they just about went crazy. Table Rock has thousands of acres of flooded timber, and our "Yankee" friends had never fished in a flooded forest before. The bass were in the trees and there wasn't a shallow reed bed for hundreds of miles. They eventually learned how to catch "tree top" bass but not without a lot of pain and frustration. Before they left Arkansas for the "friendly" northern lakes of Minnesota, our friends decorated that sunken timber with a variety of Yankee bassin' lures. A little prior research on fishing reservoirs could have made their trip a lot more enjoyable.

The broad location of bass in different bodies of water isn't difficult to determine. But just knowing where the fish might be is only part of the problem. Even if you are presenting your bait very near, or even right next to the fish, they will not always pounce on it — even when hungry. And when they are not hungry, the process becomes infinitely more involved. There are important factors such as subtleties in location, timing, and choices in presentation that are essential to know. If you are going to take on the largemouth in different parts of our country, you are going to have to be a versatile and adaptable angler. There just isn't any other way.

THE SMALLMOUTH BASS

Like its cousin the spotted bass, the smallmouth was originally a river fish. But this river bass soon made a very successful adaptation to certain northern lakes and southern reservoirs. The original range of the smallie was limited to the middle and northeastern United States. It flourished in the upper Mississippi River, the Great Lakes, and the St. Lawrence River system. In the late 1800's, and on through the depression, smallmouth were stocked in numerous lakes of the Canadian Shield. Fish were often transported in large metal milk cans and followed the railroads, as the railroads followed the lumber camps northward. During the Depression, with the creation of the Tennessee Valley Authority (T.V.A.), smallmouth were introduced to some of the larger, deep-water impoundments. They demonstrated not only that they could survive in southern climes, but that they could thrive in the deep rock-ledge waters where both crayfish and shad abounded.

Throughout the Depression years, the stocking of smallmouth in the Canadian Shield region continued. Little Vermillion Lake, near Sioux Lookout in Canada, was privately stocked in the mid-1930's by a tourist outfitter, and the species

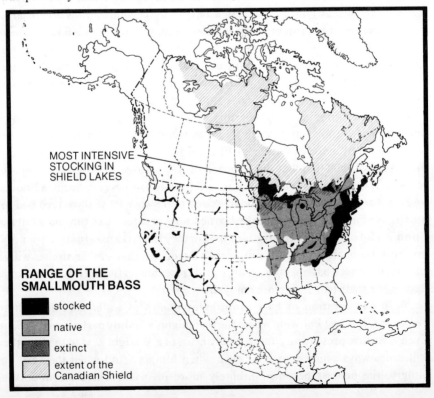

MOST INTENSIVE STOCKING IN SHIELD LAKES

RANGE OF THE SMALLMOUTH BASS

- stocked
- native
- extinct
- extent of the Canadian Shield

quickly became established there. Through the efforts of such "Johnny Appleseeds" of the fishing world, the smallmouth spread to Big Vermillion, Maskinonge, and Hooch Lakes.

About 1946, the wreck of a train carrying smallmouth bass west of the Ghost River forced the crew to release the surviving fish into that waterway. From there, the bass spread to Abram, Minnitaki, and Pelican Lakes. A smallmouth population of unknown origin is found in Pakwash Lake, south of Red Lake. They were most probably transplanted by fishermen. Today, a number of lakes north of the known established range of the smallmouth also contain the species.

Many of the waters in the western Thunder Bay, Rainy River, and southern Kenora districts now support smallmouth bass, due to numerous public and private plantings. Natural dispersal has further spread the species' range.

Because of these plantings, however, bodies of water such as Lake of the Woods, Rainy, and Vermillion were never the same again. After the smallmouth took hold and reproduced naturally, they had a definite impact on the natural walleye population in many waters.

In some areas of the north central United States and Canada, the smallmouth has become the dominant gamefish, much to the dismay of walleye fishermen. In fact, some of the best smallmouth fishing in the world can be found in the clear-water lakes of the famed Boundary Waters Canoe Area, where lakes like Lac La Croix and Basswood offer unexcelled fishing for the bronzeback. Perhaps the most untapped smallmouth fisheries of all remain the river systems that originally spawned this handsome battler. Generally rivers and streams are underfished, and many of them throughout the east and midwest teem with smallmouth that have never seen a lure.

Physical Characteristics

The classic way to distinguish a smallmouth from its cousins is to draw an imaginary vertical line through the middle of the fish's eye, down through the jaw. If the end of the jaw does not extend beyond this line, you've got a smallmouth. A much simpler test is to assess the fish's fighting ability when it's hooked. It was Dr. James Henshall, "the father of black bass fishing," who said of the smallmouth, "I consider him, inch for inch and pound for pound, the gamest fish that swims." Another distinguishing characteristic is the wide range of coloration that the smallmouth exhibits, from a dusky orange-brown to an almost green-black. Vertical coloration bars also help distinguish the smallie from the largemouth and spotted bass, whose coloration patterns usually exhibit a horizontal pattern.

Another interesting characteristic of the smallmouth has to do with the range of water temperature that it will tolerate. The body of water in which a smallmouth can survive is limited by its summer water temperature range. The bronzeback needs water no lower than 60 degrees and usually no more than about 80 degrees to function successfully. Lethal temperature has been calculated at about 95 degrees, but generally oxygen depletion and other factors will bring about a smallmouth's demise much sooner. Despite the smallmouth's many non-specialized attributes, much of its diet and seasonal movement is influenced by a strong impulse to remain in its preferred temperature range. This single factor of temperature tolerance largely dictates the smallmouth's survival pattern.

Although the smallmouth and largemouth both spawn within the same water temperature range, between 62° F and 70° F, more bronzebacks are likely to spawn at the upper end of this range. While many largemouths are on their spawning beds by the time water temperature is 65° F, smallies are just starting to spawn at the same temperature. Another difference between the spawning activity of these two fish is the depth at which they build their nests. While most largemouth nesting in natural lakes occurs in two to four feet of water, we have seen smallmouth lying over nests in 12 to 15 feet of water. The gin-clear water that exists in many Canadian smallmouth waters allows for deep water spawning. Even in fifteen feet of water, the sun's rays can still provide the necessary warmth to incubate the eggs. The actual nest of the smallmouth is similar to the largemouth's, although smallies often fan out a smaller area and drop their eggs behind a large rock or log. For this reason, smallmouth nests often lack the beautiful symmetry of the "spawning saucers" that largemouth create.

Though most anglers readily agree that a smallmouth can outclass a largemouth on rod or reel, smallies seldom reach the tremendous size that bigmouths do. The world record smallmouth is only 11 pounds, 15 ounces, but can you imagine hooking into 11 pounds of fighting smallmouth? It staggers the imagination.

Habitat Preference

The smallmouth is the most territorially-minded fish among our five major warm-water, inland game fish. With acceptable living space at a premium on a lake, this territorial imperative is vividly demonstrated. The better areas are occupied seasonally by a resident family group year after year. The smallmouth is a homebody and localized populations are the rule. In fact, many smallmouth return to within 200 feet or so of their previous year's spawning nest. In years of adequate food, more fish of a "clan" can utilize a given site. In lean years, "colonizers," or strays, migrate to new sites.

One explanation for the smallmouth's territorial nature has to do with its choice of prey. Both in Canadian Shield lakes and in southern impoundments, the smallmouth has a particular fondness for crayfish. A compilation of ten studies completed on different lake types showed that the average smallmouth bass relies on crayfish for over 50% of its diet. This heavy reliance on one type of prey explains the mysterious behavior of smallies on many crystal-clear Canadian lakes.

The first few years we fished smallmouth in Lake Vermillion, a typical oligotrophic lake of northern Minnesota, we were perplexed by our inability to catch many bass in water deeper than 20 feet. In fact, most of our fish came out of water less than 15 feet deep. Now, with the sun beating down on gin-clear water, we naturally expected all the bass to head for deeper water. We looked for those nice deep-water sunken rock piles that "top-out" at 25 or 35 feet. We found plenty of rock piles in deep water but could only catch walleyes over them. Except for a few stragglers, smallmouth bass were noticeably absent. At first we thought this was due to a territorial battle between walleyes and smallmouth; but as we continued our study, we discovered a more likely reason. Observations from our skin divers, and talks with biologists, confirmed that the reason smallmouth are usually not found much deeper than 20 feet on these lakes is that there aren't many crayfish at this depth. Without its favorite food supply, the smallmouth is restricted to a rather limited diet and feeding zone. As far as the bright sun was concerned, those large glacial boulders afforded plenty of cracks and cubbyholes for Mr. Smallmouth to avoid sunstroke.

Naturally, the behavior of smallmouth on southern reservoirs is different from that of these northern cousins. Smallmouth on southern impoundments still feed on crayfish, but they have also adapted to pursuing open-water baitfish like gizzard shad. There are open-water baitfish on northern lakes, but the presence of both walleye and northern pike in this open water zone forces the smallmouth to feed almost exclusively on crayfish.

All this discussion of smallmouth and crayfish may lead anglers to believe that rock piles and smallies are the only sure combination. And, while it's always a

"Mr. Smallmouth sizes up his favorite dinner fare."

good bet to check out rocky areas for smallmouth, these fish also relate to a weedline, just like the largemouth, provided a food source is nearby. In some middle-aged natural lakes, where weed growth is abundant, we have often taken smallmouth in cabbage or coontail beds using a leech or minnow as bait. Smallmouth will also suspend off rocky cliffs in southern reservoirs, as do spotted bass, and feed on baitfish instead of crayfish. So, if you want to play the percentages, crayfish, rocks, and smallmouth are a good combination. Just don't restrict yourself to this combination exclusively. Fish may be "where you find them," but finding them depends on the available food source and the habitat that Mother Nature has provided.

THE SPOTTED BASS

At one time, anglers viewed the "spot" as a hybrid cross between the largemouth and the smallmouth. While it shares some characteristics of both these fish, the spotted bass is a fish in its own right — a distinct species. Perhaps the most distinguishing characteristics of the "spot" are its rather limited geographical range and its particular habitat preference.

The ecological niche the spotted bass inhabits has been described by some biologists as a compromise between that of the smallmouth and largemouth bass — a narrow slot where neither of these fish functions well. In the northern part of its native range, the spotted bass is typically found in the larger pristine streams and rivers that are slightly too fast and too cool for largemouth, but just a bit too slow and warm for smallmouths.

In the south, where the waters are generally warm, the spotted bass is found predominantly in the smaller streams with moderate gradients — waters that are clear and often spring-fed. In the Gulf states, the spot is especially suited to those rivers with abundant alternating riffles and pools, the kinds of waters that have smallmouth up north, where the water is a bit cooler.

The native range of the spotted bass originally encompassed all of the central and lower portions of the Mississippi River drainage system, as well as Gulf Coast drainage areas of the Chattahoochee River of Georgia and the Guadalupe River in Texas. Stocking has expanded the range very little. The fish has, however, been introduced into some central portions of Missouri and parts of southern Texas, as well as specific areas in Virginia and California.

Attempts to introduce the spot in the cooler natural lakes of the north have met with failure. Although thought of as a cool-water critter, the spotted bass is actually less tolerant of cold temperatures for spawning purposes than either the largemouth or the smallmouth. It is notably absent in rivers and lakes that are subjected to prolonged winter weather and/or ice cover. On the other hand, largemouth and smallmouth bass do quite well in these waters. Even though spots can be quite active in cold water compared to their bassy cousins, their hardiness extends only to a certain point. They are unable to survive the long harsh winters common up north, so their potential range is limited.

While the spotted bass is native to the Mississippi River drainage system, it does not do well in the Mississippi River itself. It is particularly absent from the delta area and from coastal tidal rivers due to the water's turbid quality. The spot has a definite preference for clean, clear water.

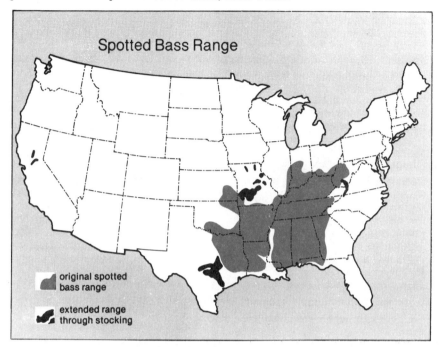

As a result of the artificial impoundment-building boom in states like Arkansas, Tennessee, and Kentucky, the spotted bass has made an accommodation to lake living. As some of the highland rivers were dammed, spots became trapped in the resulting artificial lakes. They have flourished in bodies of water exhibiting fair water clarity, relatively cool summer water temperatures, and minimum turbidity. These waters fall into our highland reservoir classification. Their bottom is usually red clay and/or rock, and they are generally very deep and clear, with an overall water temperature that is quite cool, considering how far south they are located.

Where are these lakes located? The so-called "Kentucky belt" cuts a path about 250 miles wide and stretches from the Atlantic Coast to slightly past the Mississippi River. It begins in Virginia and the Carolinas; crosses Kentucky, Tennessee, and Georgia; and includes parts of northern Alabama, northern Arkansas, and southern Missouri. Most of the good spotted bass reservoirs are found in this region. Some prime examples are Lake Sidney Lanier in Georgia; Table Rock in Missouri; Bull Shoals, Quachita, and Greer's Ferry in Arkansas; Smith Lake in Alabama; Cumberland in Kentucky; Smith Mountain in Virginia; and Center Hill and Dale Hollow in Tennessee.

Physical Characteristics

There are some obvious physical differences between a spotted bass and a large or smallmouth bass. The spot has a number of dotted lines just above its belly. It has a pronounced forked tail and its eye lines up with the back of the lip. With the largemouth, the lip extends behind the eye, and with the smallmouth, the lip ends in front of the eye.

Perhaps the most distinguishable characteristic is the spotted bass's burr-like tooth on its tongue — something that's absent on other black bass. This additional piece of hunting equipment allows this creature to prey very effectively on crayfish. The burr, along with strong jaws, can crush a "craw's" shell in short order. Although crayfish constitute a great portion of its diet, the spot does forage seasonally on small shad and aquatic insects when they are easily accessible. But most of the time it's crayfish the spot is after.

Besides physical differences, the spot has a shorter life span than either the smallmouth or largemouth bass. For this reason, it does not grow as large. While the species is known to live as long as seven years, four years is more common, a much shorter span than the largemouth (10-16 years) or the smallmouth (10-14 years).

The spotted bass is not noted for rapid growth; the world record is only 8 pounds, 10½ ounces. This fish was taken from Lewis Smith Reservoir in Alabama in 1972. Most spots, however, do not exceed three pounds. As a rule, growth is more rapid in reservoirs than in streams, and is better in the large rivers than in smaller tributary streams. Whatever the case, a four-and-a-half or five-pound spotted bass is considered a very big fish.

Habitat Preference

Though originally a river fish and not much sought after by anglers, the popularity of the spot has grown as it has adapted to the developing reservoir system of the Tennessee Valley and neighboring states. It is these highland reservoirs that are the present stronghold of the spotted bass. And because these reservoirs also contain both largemouth and smallmouth, the spot has its own particular patterns of location.

As far as behavioral patterns are concerned, the spot occupies a niche in reservoirs (as it did in rivers) different from that of a large- or smallmouth bass. In Norris Reservoir of Tennessee, for example, spots have been found at considerable depths in summer, generally greater than those selected by the smallmouth bass. In one study, spotted bass were taken at 100 feet. At the same time the smallmouths were found no deeper than 60 feet and the largemouths were near the surface. Naturally, the deeper the water, the colder it became. This spread indicates that the spot is a fish that can remain active in water temperatures lower than either the smallmouth or largemouth can.

What kinds of areas do spots use? It's really very simple. The entire life of the spotted bass in these reservoirs revolves around vertical rock walls. These bluff banks are the home of the crayfish — the spot's major source of food. As long as there is suitable spawning water nearby, a family of Kentucky bass never has to leave the bluff areas. They often spend their entire lives in a fairly restricted area,

"Here you can see the irregular longitudinal stripe and series of dark spots on the belly that help distinguish a spotted bass from the largemouth."

making location very easy. And since spotted bass live close to these vertical bluffs, they suspend a lot in relation to them.

Given the spot's limited ecological niche, it is obvious that typical top-water tactics that often work on largemouth will not be successful. In Chapter 8 we will explore in depth a few presentations that help anglers dredge up spotted bass from these deep-water hangouts.

SUMMARY

From this brief introduction it should be clear that the three species we are studying have different ranges of adaptability. Because of its limited ecological niche, the spotted bass can be readily psyched-out on reservoirs, once the angler has had an introduction. The largemouth, on the other hand, has such a wide range of adaptability that anglers can't make simple statements about its location and behavior. A spotted bass addict can survive, knowing a few basic presentation tactics. The largemouth afficionado must be much more versatile, particularly if he likes to travel the country and fish largemouth in a variety of lakes, reservoirs, and rivers.

The bulk of this book will take a case study approach to investigating fish behavior in different types of habitat. In this case study approach, we will take a close look at lures, baits, and different methods of presentation. Hopefully, this approach will provide the basics for following all three species throughout the United States. Before we do that, however, there is one more concept that we need to understand: the seasonal movement and feeding attitude of bass.

CHAPTER 3
The Calendar Periods and
Seasonal Fish Movement in Natural Lakes

The story is classic and is reinacted every year throughout the fishing world. You stop to talk with an angler who is casting for bass from the shore. It is mid-July and hot as blazes. The man is fishing in three feet of water. You inquire about his luck and he tells you that he hasn't gotten anything yet; but in April he pulled in a four-pound bass from the exact same spot. In all likelihood that man will continue to fish that spot throughout the year and probably won't see another bass until *next* April. Why? He simply hasn't learned that fish move around in lakes and rivers and that his "hog hole" is a spawning area that is used just a few weeks out of the year. Though bass do not exhibit the dramatic migration patterns of salmon, they do move around in tune with their own yearly calendar, and the angler who sits in one spot all the time might as well relax and take along a good book . . . he may be fishing, but he's not going to do much catching.

The concept of a fishing calendar, different from our human calendar, has long been understood by anglers who appreciate Mother Nature's yearly cycles. It was not, however, given a more concrete form until a cold, wintry morning in 1973 when Bill Binkleman, Ron Lindner, and Al Lindner got stranded in a snowstorm. While waiting for the storm to lift, the three men hammered out a rough outline for a fishing calendar, based not on days and months, but on water temperature and the developing food chain in a body of water. It wasn't an easy task. The spawning season for largemouth bass in Florida occurs two or three months earlier than it does in northern climes. If such a calendar was to be an aid to fishermen throughout the country, it would have to be flexible.

They began talking with other anglers. While Binkleman and the Lindners knew intimately the lakes and rivers of the upper midwest, Bobby and Billy Murray understood the reservoir systems of the south. Slowly the pieces began to fall together and a calendar emerged. Mother Nature's web of life is complex, but certain factors seemed to dictate how and why the calendar periods worked. Two of the most important were water temperature and the developing ecosystem of a given body of water.

1. *Water temperature* not only controls a bass's overall metabolism and feeding activity, it also triggers the annual spawning urge. The yearly calendar for all fish begins with the movement to the spawning grounds. For bass this is a springtime event. And while this spawning activity is fairly predictable within a given geographic region, it can vary from

year to year, depending on how soon or late spring arrives. Bass could care less about our human designation of March 21 as the first day of spring. If weather is overcast and cool, bass will simply wait until the waters warm. Rising water temperature is pretty much a function of the amount of sunshine, nighttime temperatures, and cool or warm rains. Knowledgeable anglers will keep a close eye on the weather and check water temperatures with a thermometer as a guide to when the spring spawn should be underway.

Water clarity will also have an effect on the calendar periods. Lakes with clear water do not warm as quickly as those with stained or murky water. Once again, radiant energy from the sun is the key. Dark water simply absorbs more of the sun's rays. This means that two lakes, side by side, can be in different calendar periods if their water clarity is sufficiently different. The bass in a dark, tamarack-stained lake can be through spawning and into their summer pattern, while in a clear lake bass may be just moving into the spawning bays.

2. *The developing food chain and weed growth* also play a tremendous role in determining the calendar periods for a body of water. Once the spring spawn is completed, where bass will locate in a body of water depends on the type of cover available and the prey they must feed on. It's actually the little minnows, insects, and forms of crustacea that determine where the "hawg" bass will be. As this food supply varies from lake to lake, so do the locational patterns of the bass. Reservoir bass following a school of open-water shad can move incredible distances in one day. On the other hand, bass feeding on crayfish in a natural lake might relate to the same area of shoreline for the entire summer period.

In natural lakes, where weed growth can often be a key to bass location, the types and amount of weeds available are an important factor. Weed growth is usually not fully developed until the summer calendar period. Before weed growth is at its maximum, bass will often relate to those weedbeds that develop most quickly. In the cold-water period, when weeds are dying off, fish will abandon dead weedbeds and relate to the few remaining green ones.

Understanding how water temperature and the natural ecosystem of a body of water interact is really what the calendar periods are all about. They help us understand that fish movement is seldom random — if fish are in a given area there is a good reason for it. The calendar periods also help us understand why fish are easier to catch at some times than at others. The early summer often sees a flurry of feeding activity. The reason is that fish are active, but the lake's food chain has not fully developed, i.e., there is little for bass to feed on. In the summer, bass are even more active but they are harder to catch. This is because there is an abundance of natural food available to the bass. Why try to eat a spinnerbait when there are lots of tasty shad to feed on? With these initial clues in

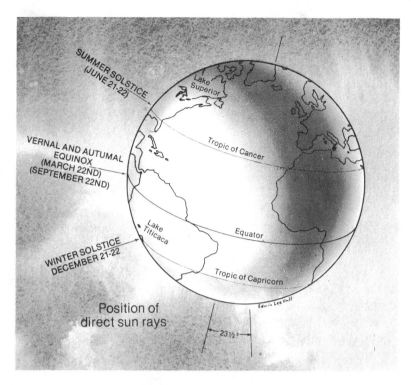

SUMMER SOLSTICE (JUNE 21-22)

VERNAL AND AUTUMAL EQUINOX (MARCH 22ND) (SEPTEMBER 22ND)

WINTER SOLSTICE DECEMBER 21-22

Lake Superior

Tropic of Cancer

Lake Titicaca

Equator

Tropic of Capricorn

Position of direct sun rays

23½°

This drawing indicates the official dates for the changing of the seasons. The different calendar periods for gamefish will depend on how late or early the seasons actually arrive. By learning to identify clues on land, such as the arrival and departure of songbirds, or by observing when certain trees and plants bloom, you can stay in tune with what is happening underwater. The "natural" calendar periods of bass are always synchronized with animal and plant patterns on land.

mind, let's take a look at the calendar periods and see what else is happening in that underwater world. In so doing, we will examine the calendar periods as they exist in natural lakes. There will be minor modifications of this calendar when we look at the case studies on rivers and reservoirs. In most natural lakes, depending on geographical range, there are either nine or ten basic activity periods. They are:

1. Pre-Spawn
2. Spawn
3. Post-Spawn
4. Pre-Summer
5. Summer Peak

6. Summer
7. Post-Summer
8. Fall Turnover
9. Cold Water
10. Frozen Water

Some of these periods are shorter than a month; others might last two or more months. The timing and length of each period depends on water temperature, geographic location, and other natural influences that affect fish behavior.

In northern Canada, the first nine periods can take place in four months. In the south, on the other hand, periods four through nine might last nine months and

"Ron Lindner fishes a small channel that teems with largemouth bass during the pre-spawn but is devoid of fish by mid-summer."

the tenth period would never occur. But though the length of these periods vary from region to region, fish behavior for each period is rather typical.

PRE-SPAWN: This period occurs when fish are on the way to, or in the vicinity of, their spawning areas prior to actual spawning. During this stage, there can be a lot of feeding activity and heavy "grouping." Fishing can be very good but will depend on water temperatures. Springtime fluctuations in water temperature can be as much as eight or nine degrees in one day. A quick drop in temperature will move bass out of shallow-water spawning grounds and into deeper water. When this occurs, fishing activity drops off dramatically.

SPAWN: This brief period is directly linked to the range of preferred temperatures for spawning of each species of bass. Generally, feeding activity is minimal, non-existent in most cases. Remember, within this period, all bass DO NOT spawn at one time. Some will have finished spawning, while others can still be actively spawning. In northern natural lakes, we do not encourage fishing for bass when they are actually on their spawning beds.

POST-SPAWN: The length of this period is highly variable, depending on lake or river conditions, the species of fish, and even the sex of the fish. Male fish tend to be more responsive than females, which often return to their deeper haunts shortly after spawning. Females remain difficult to catch for some time. Although generally slow, fishing tapers off even more toward the end of this period.

PRE-SUMMER: This is a "catch-up" or transition period. The fish will be in the process of establishing themselves in their respective summer patterns. Fishing can be tough and sporadic as the fish go through this time of adjustment. This Pre-Summer period usually arrives just before a body of water is comfortable for swimming. Naturally there are some exceptions. Some Canadian lakes never get warm enough for "comfortable" swimming. This period is pre-thermocline. As you might expect, fish are at various depths and "scattered." Locating *concentrations* of biting fish is difficult. Fishing often goes into a slump.

SUMMER PEAK: This is a short period that may last only 10 to 14 days. By now the fish have moved into their normal summer locational patterns, but the food system of the lake is just beginning to produce. The females have recuperated from spawning and both males and females are active. This can be one of the best times of the year to go fishing. One key to the summer peak is that it usually occurs just after the first real hot spell of the summer.

SUMMER: Fish will hold to the location patterns which they established in the Summer Peak. But algae blooms, cold fronts, increased natural food supplies, and many other factors make fishing difficult. This is usually the longest of the calendar periods and may last for two months in northern climes to over four months in the south. Fish are very active, but with an overabundance of natural food in most lakes and reservoirs, fishing can be tough. Patterns of feeding become stable, with daily weather conditions playing an important role. Often there will be heavy feeding movements towards dawn and dusk.

POST-SUMMER: This period takes place during the tail end of any region's summer and can mean about a week or slightly more of terrific fishing! Days can heat up to 90° F, but nights are still cool. This period often is marked by several dead-calm days with bait fish breaking the surface. All fish feed actively. Sadly, many anglers miss out on this period of super fishing because they have put away their fishing gear and are preparing for hunting season.

FALL TURNOVER: This is a three- to four-day period when the lake is in turmoil. A mixing or "turning over" of the water takes place as cold surface water settles and warmer water from below rises. This turnover HOMO-GENIZES lakes that have thermoclined (layered according to water temperatures) in summer and reoxygenates the water. At times, you can actually smell the dead bottom water after it rises to the surface. You might even see dead weeds and other bottom debris floating on the surface. Fishing is poor at this time. Note: Some bodies of water never actually thermocline. But they all go through a similar period.

COLD WATER: During the cold-water period, water temperature once again becomes crucial to fish feeding activity. Our experience tells us that 55° F is a pivotal temperature for most members of the bass family. When water temperature drops into the low 50's, fish activity takes a real nose dive. There will still be short, even active, periods of feeding, but these periods will be much further apart than in the summer. Water temperatures can fluctuate in this period as they did in the spring. A warm sunny day can draw bass into the shallows for a real flurry of activity, and a cold rain can shut them down completely. Presentation is important, with slower retrieves and live bait producing best in cold water.

When fish are active, locational patterns can be quite different. Some fish may be working the shallows (if waters have warmed), while others may be active near deep water dropoffs.

FROZEN WATER: For a brief time, in bodies of water that freeze, all water is 39° F. Then the surface water cools and eventually ices up, while the deeper water remains at 39° F. (This is the opposite of what occurs during PRE-SPAWN.) Fish of the same species might be found at vastly different depths. Stragglers are much more common now than in any other period. Sometimes, there is a brief, one- or two-day feeding binge just before freeze-up.

Strange as it may seem, during this transition between the cold-water and frozen-water period, smallmouth bass "shut down" before largemouth. One would think that, because smallmouth usually inhabit cooler waters, the opposite would be true; but winter anglers fishing in open water below dams on midwest rivers, report that while every once in a while a largemouth ends up on their stringers, smallmouth are almost never seen.

"Most anglers put away their fishing gear in the fall, but for those willing to bundle up in warm clothing the fishing can be unsurpassed.

In areas of the country where waters freeze over, there is very little bass fishing. We have talked with few anglers who catch largemouth through the ice, but this is a rare breed of angler.

As you can see from the description of the various calendar periods, life in any

"On natural lakes, anglers need to recognize the more important weed types that large-mouth may prefer (l. to r., broadleaf cabbage, curly cabbage, and coontail)."

body of water is far from static. Movement is the rule rather than the exception. The first three calendar periods are determined by the biological urge to spawn, the appropriate water temperature, and the availability of adequate bottom conditions. The summer periods depend on the developing food chain and the availability of weed growth or other kinds of cover. Towards the end of the calendar periods, fish location is determined by water temperature and limited amounts of natural food.

If we lived under water, the seasonal movements of gamefish would become obvious as the food chain developed and moved through its paces. We would see signs of it everywhere — emerging vegetation, schools of minnows and baitfish following their food source, and growing numbers of developing insect larvae and crustacea. But since the surface of a body of water is all that most of us ever see, we need to become aware of other clues to these changes.

Learning to Recognize Mother Nature's Clues to Calendar Periods

Most of us are aware of the seasonal changes that occur on land, particularly if we live in the northern or central regions of our country. Those crisp fall mornings and the brilliant reds and golds of the maple tree leave no doubt that change is on its way. In the south, changes are not so dramatic, but flowering citrus trees and the migration patterns of songbirds and waterfowl provide clues to changes in Mother Nature's cycles. The reason underwater seasonal cycles remain a mystery to most people is that they can't visualize what is happening beneath the surface. It is easy to recognize the changing colors of autumn, but few of us are aware of developing underwater vegetation. Even fewer of us are willing to slip on a diving suit to check out these underwater developments. Luckily this is not necessary, for we can look to nature's clues above water to tell us what is happening in the world of the bass. In the midwest, for example, lilacs begin to bloom just as the bass are moving onto their spawning beds. The arrival of flocks of coots in the fall is a sure sign that the cold-water period has begun.

While these signs may vary from region to region, the perceptive angler learns to recognize nature's clues and changes his location and presentation accordingly. Here is where a log book proves crucial. The next time you hit a "peak time" on your lake, river, or reservoir, take a look around at the surrounding countryside. What is going on that can give you a clue? Is a particular plant just coming into bloom? Have you just seen the first robin of the year? How about an insect hatch or the budding of some kind of aquatic weed-growth? By recording these external clues in your log book, you will quickly begin to recognize the calendar periods on your particular body of water. It is amazing how consistent these patterns will be, once you learn to identify and recognize them.

Water temperature, of course, is one important factor, and taking constant readings is a way to keep in touch with many of the calendar periods. The patterns you see developing on land are a function of the same weather conditions that determine the underwater patterns. Some old-timers are well aware of these cycles; this is one source of folk wisdom that is usually right on target. Experienced anglers are instinctively able to see, smell, and feel a calendar period arriving, leaving, or holding.

Recognizing the Prey That Bass Feed On In Your Body of Water
There are plenty of good technical fisherman who have mastered a number of forms of presentation but who still fail to understand how the predator/prey relationship relates to the calendar periods. Consequently, they run into recurrent problems. Our experience through the years has been that the key to successful angling is understanding baitfish movements and movement patterns of other forms of prey. Strange as it seems, those ferocious predators are actually at the mercy of the prey they feed on. When the prey move the predators have to follow. Similarly, baitfish and other prey are responding to the movement of smaller life forms they feed upon.

The force that controls the overall pulse of this complex aquatic world is the intensity and duration of light. This, of course, relates to the sun's yearly orbit. Changing water temperatures affect each organism, from the lowest form of algae to the highest species of fish. Insect eggs hatch to larvae, and larvae in turn become insects. Snails and aquatic worms move seasonally from zone to zone. Plankton periodically blooms, is consumed, and dissipates in a complicated cycle of life.

Naturally, fish movement, in response to these changes in the food chain, depends on the different life systems in different types of water. The important thing to remember is that fish movement throughout the calendar periods IS NOT RANDOM. If you understand what bass feed on, their movements begin to make a lot of sense. In reservoirs, where bass feed on open water prey like shad, their patterns of movement are quite different from Yankee bass. In natural lakes

The Building Blocks of Aquatic Life

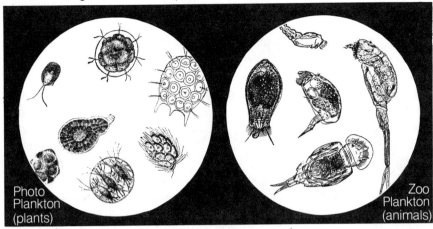

Photo Plankton (plants)

Zoo Plankton (animals)

These little critters, almost invisible to the eye, are the beginnings of the food chain and play an important role in the calendar periods.

where the fall signals a sudden migration of frogs from the swamps back to the lakes, bass will quickly move close in to feast on frog legs. In rivers where smallmouth feed on crayfish, location patterns are usually simple because this prey seldom moves around much.

Most state departments of natural resources do regular test nettings, so information on the important baitfish and prey in most lakes, rivers, or reservoirs is available. By understanding how prey movements dictate gamefish movements, we can eliminate much guesswork and begin to understand the reasons for fish locale and attitude in each of the calendar periods.

There is another aspect of the food chain that it is important to understand if the calendar periods are to be placed in their proper perspective. It would appear that the best time to fish would be when the water temperature is such that the fish's metabolism would be highest, causing it to feed the most. But it doesn't always work that way. Usually when predator fish are eating the most, food is also plentiful. So the angler finds himself in stiff competition with the natural order. Thus, prime water temperature for a species *does not* necessarily mean it is a time when the fish is easiest to catch. On the other hand, an adverse water temperature does not always mean fish are hard to catch. There is more to it than that. The available food supply, the timing of the feeding movements, overall population levels, competition among predators, and seasonal density of cover all play an important role in angling success. These are the kinds of factors that were taken into consideration in the development of the calendar periods.

Changing Lures and Baits with the Calendar Periods

Methods of presentation will vary throughout the calendar periods. Once you have learned to identify how bass react during the calendar periods in your body of water, it will become evident that by varying your presentation you can be more successful. Sometimes presentation calls for fast movement, while at other times a slow retrieve is best. Sometimes presentation is more effective on the bottom, while at other times a surface approach is best.

While confidence in a particular lure or bait is a big part of fishing success, too many anglers stick to their favorite lure under totally inappropriate circumstances. For instance, let's say an angler insists on using a jig and minnow with a regular open hook in a lake that has no cabbage beds but enormous growths of coontail, a weed that is tough to "rip through." Naturally, he is going to get hung up on weeds most of the day. In this situation and in this calendar period, a Texas-rigged plastic worm would be one of the more sensible presentations for bass.

During the summer periods when weed growth is at its greatest, some forms of presentation that did well in the early spring might not work. This means not only a change in lures, but a change in tackle. The same bay you fished with ultralight tackle last spring might be so weed-choked in August that baitcasting equipment and 17-lb.-test line is in order. Water clarity also changes during the calendar periods, and this can make a difference in presentation.

Not only do different lake conditions dictate different presentations, but gamefish actually seem to prefer certain kinds of lures and baits throughout the various calendar periods. Top-water baits for bass are effective in the summer calendar periods, but are no great shakes in the fall cold-water period.

Spinnerbaits are usually a fantastic lure for pre-spawn largemouth, but during the summer period are only average.

The reasons behind these varying preferences have to do with both the developing food chain in a body of water and the metabolic activity of the species pursued. It's probable that a bass's normal preference for minnows in the Pre-Spawn, Spawn, Post-Spawn, and Cold Water periods has to do with general lack of baitfish of preferred size during these particular calendar periods. As a body of water begins to produce numbers of minnows of a size that bass can feed on, maybe a switch in presentation to crawlers and leeches will trigger fish. With all of those baitfish around, a leech or crawler might be a welcome change from the routine.

Finally, the water temperature has a predictable effect on fish metabolism. Fishing for smallmouth bass during the cold-water period, for example, requires slow presentation. Smallmouth slow down a lot when the water temperature dips below 50° F. A fast-moving crankbait that might be super all summer long will not produce, while a jig and minnow worked slowly might just turn the trick when the cold-water period sets in.

Summary

In the final analysis, the only way to understand the different calendar periods on any body of water is to spend enough time there so that you begin to identify these patterns. A water thermometer will help, but a keen eye to Mother Nature's clues is even better. Comparing notes with other anglers will also help you get a grasp of the calendar periods. And, of course, keeping a daily log of weather and water conditions, as well as fish feeding patterns, will help considerably. Often a review of last year's fishing log during a cold winter night provides not only a glimmer of past fishing glories but also an insight into some seasonal fishing patterns that you never noticed before. Remember, fish movement and feeding patterns may not always be predictable. But you can learn the seasonal circumstances that trigger the fish to respond and the locational patterns resulting from them. Combine this knowledge with the right presentation and you will have reached that fishing plateau that separates the expert angler from the average.

CALENDAR PERIODS IN SUMMARY

PERIOD	DESCRIPTION	KEY FACTORS
Pre-spawn	Fish activity varies, depending on water temperature. Movement from late winter location to the spawning areas. Some heavy groupings and super fishing at times.	Water Temperature Hormone Levels
Spawn	A short period, but all bass do not spawn at the same time. Look for nests in areas protected from prevailing spring winds. Fish not actively feeding.	Water Temperature Hormone Levels Bottom Conditions
Post-spawn	Recuperation period for females. Males usually guard nests and may be catchable, but fishing is typically slow. Gradual dispersal away from spawning areas.	Physical Condition of Females
Pre-summer	Movement to summer locations. Bass begin to regroup. Fishing is slow with patterns difficult to pinpoint.	Developing Food Chain
Summer Peak	Fish are grouped and active, but food chain is just beginning to develop. Excellent fishing for one to three weeks.	Developing Food Chain Available Cover
Summer	Natural food chain is in high gear. Fish have plenty of natural food to choose from. Patterns are established and identifiable. Daily weather conditions are important. Some deoxygenation may occur at lower levels of some reservoirs and lake.	Developed Food Chain Developed Weed Beds Available Cover Weather Conditions Lack of O_2 in Some Areas
Post-summer	Prior to actual arrival of first cold fall weather. Diminishing sunlight slows down the food chain. Fish active, but less food available. Fishing excellent.	Food Chain Slows Down Daily Weather Conditions
Fall Turnover	First really cold nights cause top layer of water to sink and general mixing of water. Fish disoriented, schools break up and fishing is terrible for 7-14 days.	Water Temperature Homogenization of Lake Waters
Cold Water	Bass action tends to be spotty, with feeding periods sporadic and of short duration. If you can locate fish that are active, fishing can be excellent.	Water Temperature Lack of Natural Food
Frozen Water	Time to clean and repair tackle. For the adventurous, a time to experiment with winter lures and baits. Bass are comatose.	Water Temperature Lack of Natural Food

CHAPTER 4
Classifications of Natural Lakes

Every body of water has its own personality, a personality characterized primarily by overall physical structure. Reservoirs are classified according to the original topography of the land that has been flooded. Rivers are characterized by the bedrock they flow over and by their gradient, or speed of flow. And lakes are classified according to their geological age and structure.

No two lakes are alike. The dynamics of predator/prey relationships, amounts and types of aquatic vegetation, and numerous structural considerations assure their uniqueness. To bring some order out of this seeming chaos, lakes have been classified very broadly in terms of three geological types: oligotrophic, mesotrophic, and eutrophic. In common parlance we often simplify these scientific terms and refer to lakes as young, middle-aged, and old. As complicated life support systems, lakes are always undergoing change. Some of these changes are short term, like the seasonal patterns we discussed in the last chapter. Others, such as the aging process, take place very slowly and are measured in hundreds, or thousands, of years. This process of aging is called "eutrophication," and it is natural and inevitable. Generally speaking, geologically "young" lakes are rocky and have deep, clear water; "old" lakes have mud bottoms and are shallow with murky water.

It is the fate of virtually all lakes to fill in with sediment and become swamps, and, eventually, dry land. The initial stages may take thousands of years, but the final states can happen quickly, sometimes in less than 100 years. Many small lakes found on turn-of-the-century maps no longer exist.

As lakes age, their character changes and so do their fish populations. Certain lakes in this country supported good populations of lake trout and whitefish at the turn of the century. Their waters were crystal clear with very little weed growth. Today some of these lakes contain bass, perch, and walleyes. Their waters are less clear and weed growth is abundant. Not only do the species of fish change as a lake ages, but the locational patterns of fish alter dramatically. Often the key to locating largemouth bass in a middle-aged lake is to find the outside edge of the deep weeds, which may occur in 15 feet of water. In an old lake, on the other hand, the water clarity may be so poor that deep-water weeds are nonexistent and bass will be found under lily pads and thick mats of vegetation in only two or three feet of water.

Characteristics of Young Lakes
Geologists use the term "oligotrophic" to refer to lakes that are youngsters at the earliest stages of the aging process. Actually these lakes may be thousands of

years old, but geological age is measured in terms of fertility and water quality, not years. Oligotrophic lakes are characterized by their low level of nutrients (mineral richness) in ratio to the total volume of water. In most cases the surrounding terrain of these lakes is rocky and quite free of organic soils. Their water sources are springs, streams, or rivers, also low in nutrients.

Young lakes also are characterized by having dissolved oxygen in their deepest levels. This lake type does not thermocline (stratify into separate temperature and oxygen layers). The shape, bottom content, and structural configuration combine to allow equal distribution of dissolved oxygen throughout the lake's system, from shallow water to deep.

Sharp, steep drop-offs allow for little organic sediment to settle in shallow water areas, and most of the lake's upper basin is composed of rock. Aquatic plant seeds have a tough time taking root. Therefore, there is a low density of plant life in the surface water, but non-rooted (free-floating) plant life in the form of algae occurs at many different levels.

Oligotrophic lakes tend to be quite deep. Often more than half of the lake basin will be over 50 feet in depth. Maximum depths in these young lakes range from 80 to 120 feet. Most shoreline drop-offs are sharp and abrupt. Long, slow-tapering flats are rare, and even rocky reefs pop up and then suddenly drop off. The actual amount of water 10 feet and less is but a fraction of the lake's total surface area. Oligotrophic lakes are generally found north of the 42nd parallel, but there are exceptions in high plateau areas, as with Lake Tahoe in California. A few eastern lakes are right on the border line.

Largemouth and spotted bass are not found in natural oligotrophic lakes, and only toward the later end of this lake stage does the smallmouth appear on the scene. The boundary waters of Canada and northern Minnesota are typical of these late-stage oligotrophic lakes that support populations of smallmouth bass. While smallmouth can thrive in this type of lake, their range of movement is often quite limited. Because walleyes and northern pike patrol the deep open-water zone, and because northerns will feed on smallmouth, the smallie spends most of its time in water 15 feet deep or less. It is on shallow tapering shelves and rock piles that the smallmouth encounters the prey that makes up the largest part of its diet, the crayfish. This locational pattern of smallmouth often confuses anglers.

Because the water is so clear in these lakes and there is so little vegetation, most anglers expect to find bass in water 20 feet or deeper. While a few bass may exist in this zone, fishing there is generally a waste of time. Over 90% of the smallies do quite well in the shallow, rocky water by using rock slabs and boulders as hiding places and ambush points. On one trip to Whiteshell Provincial Park in Manitoba, we took a good catch of bass from an area with a maximum depth of three feet. We could see every detail of the bottom, but what we couldn't see were the bass. They were hiding on the shady sides of rocks or down in the cracks between the boulders. One deadly tactic under these conditions is simply to toss out a leech on a small hook and split shot. Throw it close to a crevice or on the shady side of a rock and just let it lie there. If you try to retrieve it you are sure to

41

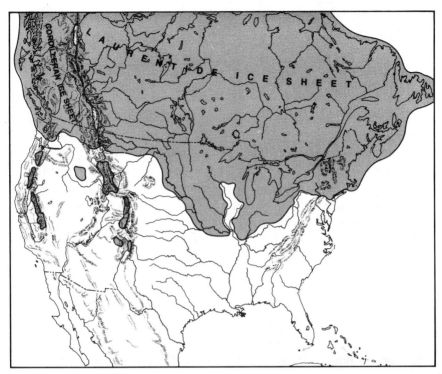

This map shows how far south glaciers advanced during the last ice age. As they retreated, glaciers left behind the vast majority of our natural lakes. At the turn of the century, all inland fishing — except for Florida and a few isolated regions — was restricted to lakes, rivers, ponds, and backwaters created by glaciers. The great number of manmade reservoirs is responsible for the bass finishing boom in the south, central, and western part of our country.

get hung up. Watch your line carefully and, when you see it move, set the hook. Then hang on. Smallmouth love to jump and then dive back among the rocks. There is no "horsing-in" these clear water battlers, but a tight line and constant pressure will usually keep them out of the rocks. Landing a smallmouth from crystal clear Canadian lakes is one of the greatest joys of angling. It's a fight you'll long remember and the fish's beautiful color and excellent taste are just icing on the cake.

Characteristics of Old Lakes

To better understand the mesotrophic, or "middle-aged," lake type, which is difficult to pin down, we now jump to the other extreme — the geologically old, or eutrophic, lake.

In the last stages of a lake's aging process the distribution of dissolved oxygen declines to a point where fish cannot exist. Just before this occurs, however, you have what we call a "bullhead" or "carp" lake. This body of water has filled in with sediment, is shallow, and has a muck bottom. The water color is very murky and weeds grow only to a depth of one or two feet.

The richness of the water produces an abundance of free-floating plant life —

green or blue-green algae — on the surface. It resembles thick pea soup. This effectively blocks out the sunlight and reduces the oxygen in all but a thin "ring" around the shoreline. Biologically, this lake is very, very "old" and about to die. Here, the food chain is not very complex. Plants and simple animal organisms are consumed directly by bullheads or carp. Such lakes do not support game fish.

The largemouth bass is the last game fish to survive the eutrophication process. It can survive long after walleye, smallmouth bass, northern pike, and muskellunge have disappeared from a body of water.

Most eutrophic lakes that support largemouth bass are shallow with an average depth of less than 20 feet. Their maximum depth is about 35 feet, but some may be 50 feet in depth. The deeper lakes thermocline while the shallower ones usually do not. Yet both types have very low oxygen counts in mid-summer and mid-winter. These lakes usually do not have sharp shoreline drop-offs. Instead, they often taper out for a distance, then make one break toward the basin. Long, shallow weed-covered flats or points are common. The smaller lakes (500 acres or less) generally do not contain sunken islands and the shoreline-to-the-drop-off area constitutes most of the "fishable" water.

Some larger lakes contain both visible and submerged islands. Around these, the drop-offs are usually slow and tapering. Weed growth varies from extensive mats of rooted "junk" weed and shallow, weed-choked lily pad bays to sparse, deep weeds.

Any angler who regularly fishes natural eutrophic lakes for largemouth must learn to fish in the weeds. Floating and submerged vegetation is the key to fish location, and learning to recognize the weed types in eutrophic lakes will help in the identification of fish feeding patterns. Weed beds also provide clues to the seasonal movements of bass. In the middle to late spring, fish begin to move away from their spawning grounds and will relate to the first developing weed beds. Summer locations on eutrophic lakes depend on the shape or contour of the weeds, as well as their location with regard to nearby deep water. In the fall, bass abandon those weed beds that begin to die off and relate to the few remaining green weeds. By becoming aware of types and growth patterns of aquatic vegetation on a eutrophic lake, you can soon learn to "psych out" its fishing potential.

Characteristics of Middle-aged Lakes

If the "bullhead" or "carp" lake is at one end of the spectrum and the "lake trout lake" on the other, there is obviously a vast range in between. In fact, most natural lakes in the United States fall into this "middle" category.

Mesotrophic lakes extend from the Canadian prairies into the Dakotas and portions of Minnesota, Wisconsin, Michigan, Indiana, Ohio, New York, and other states. A mesotrophic lake is much harder to describe than the two other categories. It can be deep and thermocline, or shallow and not thermocline. Some have rock outcroppings, others sand and reeds. Some have sharp, steep drop-offs, but usually not as sharp as oligotrophic waters. Other lakes may have long, tapering shoreline flats with visible and/or sunken islands, or none at all. They can be round or spiderlike in shape. The weed growth varies in amount, types, and depth.

Not only do mesotrophic lakes have great structural variety, they also support the largest variety of fish populations. Both largemouth and smallmouth bass exist and can thrive in middle stage mesotrophic lakes. Spotted bass, primarily a river and reservoir fish, are one of the few freshwater species not common to these middle-aged lakes.

Fish-holding structure in mesotrophic lakes is as varied as the lakes themselves. Classic largemouth locations range from the outside edge of the deep weeds toward the shore. If there are no natural predators, such as pike or muskie, bass will even locate ouside the weedline.

A number of lakes in northeastern states exemplify such a food chain, where largemouth bass are the predominant predator. Beside the typical food sources such as perch, bluegill, and crayfish, these lakes support a baitfish known locally as "sow bellies." The sow belly spends much of its time suspended, and the largemouth has quickly adapted to life outside the weedlines as it feeds on this open-water prey. Though not typical of largemouth location patterns on natural lakes, this is a good illustration of why it is so important to understand the predator/prey relationship. If an angler from Wisconsin traveled to the northeast and spent all his time fishing bass inside the weedline, he would probably be missing a lot of fish.

In upper midwestern mesotrophic lakes, where the northern pike sits on top of the food chain, largemouth bass spend most of their time inside the weedline. Smallmouth bass will relate to the remaining rocky bars and sunken islands and, when these are not available, move into the weeds. A good approach to fishing these lakes is to cast a jig and minnow, or jig and eel, parallel to the outside edge of the weeds and slowly work it back to the boat. Inside the weedline, a jig and eel or slip-rigged plastic worm can be worked up and down through cabbage beds. One particularly deadly tactic for springtime bass is to work a diving lure, like a crankbait, over the tops of newly emerging weeds. Just tickling the tops of the cabbage beds can often result in a fantastic haul of springtime bass.

Mesotrophic lakes often have extensive reed flats. These areas can host a considerable population of largemouth all summer long. Naturally, weather conditions dictate when bass will be active in the reeds, as do the different types of reeds and their location in relation to other weeds and deep water. We will take a look at reed fishing in depth in Chapter 5-C, but for now we will mention that spinnerbaits and plastic worms are hard to beat as a presentation on these reedy flats.

How Different Lake Types Affect Fish Location and Fishing Tactics

Understanding the aging process in natural lakes is crucial not only in the location of gamefish but in the selection of proper fishing tactics. But before we

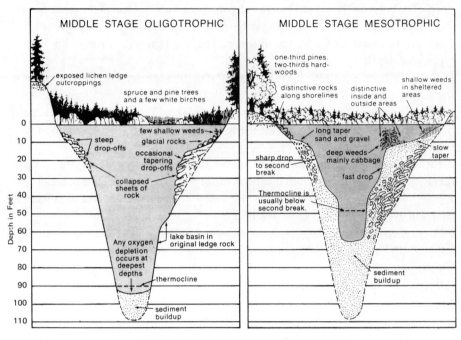

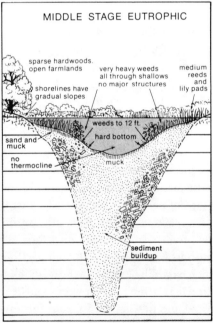

These diagrams illustrate the natural aging process that all lakes experience. As lakes ages, both fish populations and fish-holding structure change.

discuss tactics, one word of warning. The three lake types are simply typologies, generalizations, examples. Any particular lake will fall somewhere in between. It may not *exactly* resemble the types we have outlined. Also, there may be sections of large lakes that are older or younger than the main body of water. For example, large eutrophic bays often occur in young, oligotrophic, Canadian shield lakes. These muddy bottom, weedy bays may look like some of the small lakes found in southern Illinois or Ohio. In some of the larger mesotrophic lakes, one section may harbor most of the smallmouth population, while another, more eutrophic, section will be the stronghold of the largemouth. These seeming contradictions need not be confusing, for large lakes do not go through the aging process uniformly. When you run into a lake like this, simply divide it into manageable sections and treat each section as if it were a separate lake — in many instances it is.

Whether your lake is large and complicated, with different age zones, or small and rather consistent throughout, there are two aspects of the aging process that will help in the selection of appropriate fishing tactics:

1. Water Clarity
2. Fish-holding Structure

Importance of Water Clarity

Water clarity is one of the most important personality traits of a body of water. We often think of murky water as polluted and less desirable than crystal clear water. Not so. Water can be stained by mineral or vegetable matter (like the tea-stained water that drains out of tamarack swamps) and still be clean enough to support healthy populations of gamefish. Changing water clarity is inevitable and just another part of the aging process. Usually the young oligotrophic lakes have crystal clear water and old eutrophic lakes are pretty murky.

Changes in water clarity often mean changes in the weight line and type of tackle we use. Young, clear lakes usually demand lighter line and, probably, smaller lures, in order not to spook the fish. Bright shiny lures will also be more useful in young lakes because fish can see better in these lakes than can their brothers and sisters in murky water lakes. An ultralight rod with four-pound test may sound flimsy to many anglers, but, when fishing for smallmouth bass on Canadian shield lakes, it is more than adequate. Remember, these young lakes have very few weeds to tangle the angler's line, and, in open water, four-lb. test can handle just about any smallmouth around. Light line is particularly crucial in this crystal clear water with a live bait approach, such as the leech and split-shot combination we mentioned earlier. Once those bass start using their microscopic vision to eyeball your presentation, you want it to appear as natural as possible, and light line and small hooks are the key to natural presentation.

As a lake begins to age, its water clarity usually decreases, and light line is not as essential as it is in the gin-clear waters of oligotrophic lakes. In older, murkier lakes, bass have decreased visibility, so anglers can often use heavier line without hindering their chances. In murky lakes it also makes sense to use sound-producing lures, such as spinnerbaits, and to use live bait in combination with lures whenever possible. Decreased vision means that fish must rely more heavily on their senses of hearing and smell to track down a meal.

Another aspect of older lakes that dictates a change in fishing tackle is the presence of extensive aquatic vegetation. When fishing around lily pads, reeds, and other forms of deep-rooted vegetation, you may need a sturdy baitcasting outfit and 15-to-20-lb.-test line. Some anglers may object to this and argue that such heavy duty tackle isn't fair when the bass may only weigh two or three pounds. If this were an open water situation, that might be true, but under super weedy conditions it is just plain stupid to use light spinning tackle. The question of what is or is not fair should be rephrased to, "What is appropriate tackle under these circumstances?"

The first time Chet Meyers fished this weedy "slop" with Al Lindner, Al was using a baitcasting outfit with a 20-lb.-test and a stiff graphite rod. Chet had a spinning reel with ten-lb.-test on a medium action rod. The results were predictable. Al boated two bass to every one of Chet's, though both men had the same number of strikes. Chet's spinning outfit simply couldn't turn the bass and keep their heads out of the weeds. The results? Lots of lost fish and plenty of broken line. Al's outfit, on the other hand, could literally skip those bass across the lily pads and then play with them when the fish hit open water. So when fishing dark, weedy water, don't be a "light tackle purist." Use the tackle necessary to get the job done properly.

Though most of our weedy lakes have darker water and most clear lakes are relatively weed free, there are some exceptions. And when you find this combination of crystal clear water and extensive weeds, get ready for tough fishing. Some spring-fed lakes do not easily fall into our lake classification system. They don't have the rocky makeup of most oligotrophic lakes, they have plenty of weeds, and yet they aren't true eutrophic lakes. One rather depressing fishing tale can illustrate what anglers are up against when fishing in clear weedy lakes.

A few years ago some of our friends took a trip to Lake Yohoa in Honduras. This lake, only recently opened to sport fishing, very quickly got a reputation as a "hawg" bass lake. Natives using handlines were catching largemouth in the 12- to 18-pound category regularly. Our friends were some of the first anglers to fish this lake with conventional tackle. They were so excited when they arrived that they skipped dinner in order to get out on the water and try their luck. Soon their joy turned to frustration. The lake was as clear as those wonderful springs in Florida where all the underwater movies are filmed. Not only was the water crystal clear, but the lake had weeds — weeds that grew to a depth of 25 feet and then sprawled on the surface, weeds that were almost impossible to fish in. Outside the weedline, the bottom structure dropped off to depths of 50-100 feet. That night, while deciding on their tactics, the final blow arrived in the form of a cold front. The wind kept our friends off the water for two days. When they finally got out, the sun was shining so brightly you could have fried eggs on the bow of the boat.

To make a long story short, their three-day "trip of a lifetime" netted them one two-pound bass.

Though clear water and heavy weeds don't usually go together, when they do, it pays to fish early in the morning or toward dusk. Start at the outside of the weeds and work your way toward shore. Consider vertical jigging with a Texas-rigged plastic worm, and be sure to check for open pockets and other irregularities in weedbeds. Lakes like Yohoa are not abundant in the United States, but there are enough of these spring-fed, weedy wonderlands that anglers should know how to cope with them. They present a special case study, similar to the analysis of strip mining pits that we will undertake in Appendix D. In that section, we will go into tactics in more detail.

Fish-holding Structure

Another important aspect of the aging process in lakes is the identification of fish-holding structure. Whether or not a piece of structure will attract gamefish is primarily a function of three factors:

1. access to cover
2. availability of food source
3. presence of other predator fish

Young lakes are typically very rocky with irregular contours. There are lots of rocky bars, rocky reefs, and rocky sunken islands. In one sense, these lakes are a structure fisherman's dream, and in another, they are a nightmare. With such an abundance of rocky structure to provide cover, the problem is how to identify those rocks that attract fish. During a recent trip to an oligotrophic lake in southern Manitoba, we discovered that both the contour of the rocky shelves and the actual shape of the rocks determined fish location. Rocks with sharp, angular sides always seemed to hold smallmouth bass, while rounded glacial boulders failed to produce. Apparently these angular rocks provide more cover for bass to use while waiting to ambush crayfish or minnows. The gently rounded glacial rocks apparently don't have enough nooks and crannies to satisfy the bass. When you are fishing a lake with a bottom content of 90% rock, it pays to discover the types of rocks the fish are using.

At the other end of the continuum are the weedy eutrophic lakes where few, if any, rock piles guide the angler. In this weedy wonderland it becomes important to identify different types of weeds, as some hold fish while others do not. To the unitiated angler, a weed-choked lake is tough to fish, because there seems to be such an abundance of cover. But just because there is cover does not mean that fish will use it. Bass desire not only cover, but a source of food and a convenient place from which to ambush their prey. Knowing this will help anglers eliminate unproductive weeds and identify those that hold fish. Because bass like to ambush their prey, the shape of a weedbed tells anglers where the bass might hide. Open pockets in thick mats of weeds, points at the edge of weedbeds, or channels that have been cut through the weeds — all are good places to begin prospecting for bass. If you fish the weeds with regularity you will soon identify

"Not all structure on a lake is a function of geological age. Here, Chet Meyers battles a largemouth bass on a resort lake where boat docks are important fishing structure."

some of these fish-holding patterns. Bobby Murray once amazed a friend by pointing to a small finger of lily pads and telling him there was a bass under it. The friend made a good cast and, sure enough, a three-pound bass came exploding out of the water. Magic? Certainly not. Bobby had pulled five bass off those same pads that summer, and he knew that one was likely to be there.

Sometimes not only the *shape* of the weed bed, but the *type* of weed, helps in fish location. Chet Meyers fished a lake last year where a variety of cabbage with a pink flower was a sure guide to the location of northern pike. Other types of cabbage grew in this lake, some with white flowers and some with green, but only the pink cabbage seemed to hold fish. You don't have to be a botanist and know all the scientific names of aquatic vegetation, but when you are fishing an old, weedy lake, you had better learn to recognize the weeds that fish like to use.

Another aspect of lake aging that determines the structure bass use has to do with the types of predator and prey present in the lake. As lakes age, their populations of gamefish, baitfish, and prey change. Smallmouth bass in an oligotrophic lake may feed on an open-water baitfish called the ciscoe or on crayfish, as both are often present in young lakes. If there is no other predator present, the smallies can change their diet from day to day. But if northern pike are present, the pike will feed on the ciscoes and will also try to feed on the bass. The presence of these toothy predators will force the smallmouth out of the open water zone to the cover of the rock piles, where the smallies will have to restrict their diet to crayfish.

In mesotrophic lakes, where smallmouth and largemouth coexist, competition often arises over various sources of food. Both smallmouth and largemouth love to feed on crayfish, but when competing for this food source, the aggressive smallmouth usually wins and ends up king of the rock piles. The largemouth must then move to another location and choose another prey, such as young perch or crappies.

Few anglers appreciate the importance of predator/prey dynamics and how this relationship determines the location of bass in a given lake. The easiest way to become informed on this subject is to contact your local department of natural resources. Most DNR's do regular test nettings and keep good records on the types and number of both gamefish and baitfish in specific lakes. Analysis of a lake's food chain will usually provide some clues to bass location.

SUMMARY

Being equally at home on a rocky Canadian smallmouth lake and in a weedy Louisiana largemouth bayou is the mark of a truly versatile angler. Understanding the different age classifications of natural lakes is an important part of determining the type of structure that bass relate to and the prey they feed upon. Of course there are no fixed rules. Each lake is a little different from every other lake. But there are some generalizations that can help anglers if they will take time to study a lake's personality. For example, bass location on reedy flats in mesotrophic lakes is fairly predictable, even though mesotrophic lakes vary greatly in size, shape, and water clarity. Similarly, once you have fished bass in a weed-choked bay on one eutrophic lake, you will have a pretty good idea where bass will locate in the "slop" on most eutrophic lakes.

Fish location ceases to be a mystery when you learn to treat each lake as a living organism and understand how its physical makeup, fish populations, water clarity, and structure determines fish location. Once you take the time to analyze one lake and understand how and where fish locate, not only will your fishing success improve, but the next body of water you fish will be much easier to "psych out."

CHAPTER 5-A
Case Study: Largemouth Bass in Small Natural Lakes

Though "old bucketmouth" is found across our country in just about every conceivable body of water, his natural home is in the many small eutrophic lakes common to the northeastern and north central United States. In this case study we will follow the seasonal movements of largemouth bass in one such lake.

To understand the many changes in attitude and location a fish can make during the calendar periods, we will study a small lake typical of central Wisconsin, southern Minnesota, central Michigan, areas just north of Toronto, Canada, or mid-state New York. We will see how a fish like the *adult* largemouth bass responds to the environment during *each* of the seasonal changes. It's important to stress that we are concerned with adult fish only, since small fish of all species respond to stimuli differently than the older, larger ones.

The body of water type we will use as an example is a 300-acre mid-eutrophic natural lake located near a populated region. Thirty homes dot the shoreline along the good hard bottom sections, and beaches are common. The lake has only one boat access and isn't heavily used. Since there is practically no tourist trade in the area, fishing pressure is mainly from residents or local panfishermen.

All in all, it's one of those little gems of a lake tucked away in an offbeat area where the bass population has been left to thrive untouched for many years. Since the population levels are high, it would be considered a *prime* largemouth bass lake. This means that the fish's movements would be "classic," even with the intrusion of man. Few locals have any conception of the bass available and fewer still would know how to go about catching them consistently.

The lake has a maximum depth of 25 feet. The water clarity is still pretty good and a fully-developed weedline ends at ten feet. There is a clean lip area that extends out to 12 feet (the point of the first drop-off), indicating that the weed growth at one time reached out this far. The weeds, when in full bloom, are dense, due to the steadily increasing fertility from the homes and runoff from the adjacent farms. The soft bottom begins at 18 feet.

In waters like these, the largemouth bass is the dominant gamefish. Bluegills are plentiful and the crappie population is fair. Perch exist but are not very common. The lake also contains fair numbers of suckers and spottail shiners. Rough fish like carp, although present, have not yet exploded into unmanageable numbers, nor have they severely depleted the vegetation. Northern pike are also present, but the population is low. Their average size, however, is big, ranging from six to eight pounds.

The Importance of Weed Growth

Before we actually study our hypothetical lake, it is important to understand the role that water weeds play in determining where largemouth will locate in this type of lake.

On most *natural* lakes, where there is sufficient weed growth, vegetation is the summer home of largemouth bass. This does not mean that they never move deeper. But it does mean that the vast majority of bass, most of the time, relate to the weeds. The bottom of a dense weed bed provides bass with most of the essentials of an easy existence: protection from bright sunlight, an acceptable water temperature, and easy access to food.

With few exceptions, summer movements of largemouth bass in eutrophic lakes are predictable, and weed growth is the key to that predictability.

Seasons of clear water can favor substantial growth of preferred weeds like cabbage, coontail, and cabomba. While this will attract fish, you'll have trouble working lures with exposed hooks through this dense vegetation. Presentation will be basically limited to the tops or edges of the weeds. On the other hand, years of fluctuating or dirty water, combined with prolonged high temperatures, will probably result in sparse or even a pronounced absence of preferred weeds. Under these conditions, junk weeds flourish. This condition will tend to scatter the fish and make selection of lures that cover a lot of territory necessary. Be aware that weed growth is not a constant and not always predictable from year to year. And changes in a lake's vegetation will affect fish location and your presentation accordingly.

If the weed growth is sparse in a natural lake, it's unlikely that the lake will host a decent population of bigmouth. Scattered groups, or even individual fish could possibly inhabit "available" weedcover, provided that it is the proper type of vegetation. The remaining fish might use rocks, or even go to deeper water, especially if they are forced there by the absence of adequate shallow cover. In some northern lakes, however, where northern pike patrol the outside edge of the weedline, the vast majority of bass will be forced out of these deep water areas.

The physical structure and bottom contour of most natural eutrophic lakes is rather simple when compared with the complexity found in younger or middle-aged lakes. The bottom contour usually demonstrates a gradual sloping, with few sudden drop-offs or fast breaks. There may be a few sunken islands with adequate weed growth, but most of the deeper open water zone is over a silt or muck bottom. Most natural eutrophic lakes contain weeds all the way from the drop-off to the shoreline. Though this vegetation can be composed of a variety of types of weeds, there will usually be a distinct outside edge to the weedline.

To better understand largemouth movements on eutrophic lakes, we will look at four different habitat zones.

53

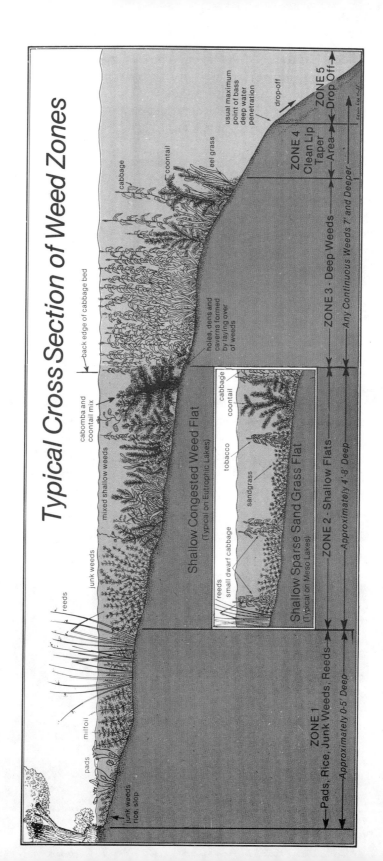

Typical Cross Section of Weed Zones

reeds

junk weeds

pads

milfoil

junk weeds
rice, slop

cabomba and
coontail mix

mixed shallow weeds

back edge of cabbage bed

cabbage

coontail

eel grass

holes, dens and
caverns formed
by laying over
of weeds

usual maximum
point of bass
deep water
penetration

drop-off

ZONE 5
Drop Off →

ZONE 4
Clean Lip
Taper
Area

ZONE 3 - Deep Weeds
Any Continuous Weeds 7' and Deeper

Shallow Congested Weed Flat
(Typical on Eutrophic Lakes)

reeds

small dwarf cabbage

tobacco

sandgrass

cabbage

coontail

Shallow Sparse Sand Grass Flat
(Typical on Meso Lakes)

ZONE 2 - Shallow Flats
Approximately 4'-8' Deep

ZONE 1
Pads, Rice, Junk Weeds, Reeds
Approximately 0-5' Deep

Zone #1 Shallow Water — On some eutrophic lakes, this zone can be quite extensive. Typically it runs from the shoreline to a depth of four feet. Given proper bottom conditions, this is where most of the largemouth spawning will occur. Though generally clean of weeds in the spring, in the summer this zone can host a mixture of wild rice, milfoil, lily pads, pickerelweed, and different varieties of sand grass.

Zone #2 Shallow Flats — This area functions as a link between the shallows and the deep weeds. The flats typically run from four to eight feet, but can run as deep as 12 feet, depending on bottom contour and water clarity. In very shallow lakes, the flats may run to a depth of only six feet. Weeds common to this zone include milfoil, the shallow water cabbages, coontail, sand grass, and shallow reeds. Locating bass on the flats can be frustrating, as they tend to scatter and their location changes from hour to hour.

Zone #3 Deep Weeds — This zone depends on the general water clarity. In clear lakes, deep weeds could grow to a depth of 15 or 20 feet. In most eutrophic lakes, however, eight to 12 feet is more common. At its furthest extent, this zone forms the outside "weedline" of the lake. Sometimes this weedline will correspond to the first major breakline into deeper water. On other lakes, there will simply be a gradual tapering of the bottom. Weeds common to this zone include deep water cabbage, coontail, and eel grass.

Zone #4 Drop-off and Open Water Zone — This zone is the open-water area found outside the lake's weedline. There are no weeds in this zone, except floating mats of coontail and other weeds that need not be rooted to survive. In most eutrophic lakes, the bottom content of this zone is silt and muck. With these four zones in mind, let's take a look at our hypothetical lake and see how bass respond to the seasonal changes during a typical year.

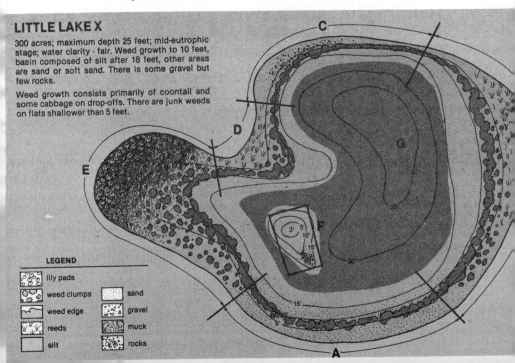

LITTLE LAKE X

300 acres; maximum depth 25 feet; mid-eutrophic stage; water clarity - fair. Weed growth to 10 feet, basin composed of silt after 18 feet, other areas are sand or soft sand. There is some gravel but few rocks.

Weed growth consists primarily of coontail and some cabbage on drop-offs. There are junk weeds on flats shallower than 5 feet.

LEGEND

lily pads	
weed clumps	sand
weed edge	gravel
reeds	muck
silt	rocks

Little Lake X

The structure of Little Lake X is relatively simple. It contains one spawning bay, one main shoreline point, one sunken island, one slow-tapering flat, one sharp-tapering flat, and two reed banks — and a soft bottom hole in the center.

We purposely used a small lake and arranged the conditions on the map so that there would be little overlapping. In this way the fish's options are well-defined and we can better visuallize the interplay of forces. Small lakes like this actually exist. In fact, this particular body of water is similar to a lake that the authors have fished.

Note that the lake is divided into seven sections: A, B, C, D, E, F, and G. Each is structurally and functionally different from the other, and, seasonally, each has something to offer the bass in terms of food, cover, comfort, or reproduction.

AREA A — A slow tapering, main-lake shoreline flat with a hard sand bottom.

AREA B — A very slow tapering, main-lake shoreline flat with reeds and soft sand bottom.

AREA C — A sharp-tapering, main-lake shoreline drop-off with a hard gravel bottom.

AREA D — A main-lake, slow-tapering, point adjacent to a soft-bottom bay. It has a soft sand bottom and contains reeds and weeds.

AREA E — A black bottom shallow bay.

AREA F — A weed-capped sunken island — medium hard bottom.

AREA G — The soft bottom, open, main-lake area which includes areas off the drop-offs where fish can suspend.

The ranges of temperature that are used in this case study are typical of those found in the north central and northeastern sections of our country. On southern lakes the temperature ranges would be a few degrees higher.

	Pre-Spawn	48° F - 58° F
Springtime Locational Patterns	Spawn	58° F - 65° F
	Post-Spawn	65° F - 68° F

While bass activity will fluctuate during these periods, the location of this activity focuses on the natural spawning grounds and the drop-off areas immediate to them. The actual number of spawning areas on a lake will vary with the size of the lake and its bottom conditions. On Little Lake X most of the bass will spawn in the western bay, marked Area A, and will also relate to Area D. On larger lakes with more complex structure, look for spawning to occur in bays at the northwest end of the lake, and be sure to check out any channels, cuts, or small protected sloughs.

During the pre-spawn period, fish activity can fluctuate dramatically. There will be a constant movement back and forth between spawning areas and the closest deep water area. This movement is in response to sharp changes in water temperature that result from typically unstable spring weather conditions. A warm sunny day can trigger an explosion of fish activity, while a cold rain or frost can give bass a bad case of lockjaw. When the fish are active, they tend to be schooled and fairly aggressive. On these occasions it is not uncommon to pull ten or 20 bass from a single school in less than an hour. As these fish begin moving in and establishing their beds they are in a less positive feeding mood.

There are no dramatic locational changes between the pre-spawn and spawn periods, except that most of the bass will be in the actual spawning bays and there will be less movement back to deep water. During this period, males are busy building nests and females are often moody and irritable. The fish are edgy. Contrary to widespread opinion, they are not that ready to grab a meal. In fact, they open their mouths to eat very reluctantly. But they will snap at or bump away intruders. While spawning activity may last a few weeks, the majority of it takes place when the correct water temperature coincides with either a full- or new-moon cycle.

It is important to remember that not all bass will spawn when the water temperature is optimal. Some will spawn earlier and a few will spawn later. This is Mother Nature's way of ensuring that a sudden drop in water temperature or water level does not wipe out an entire spawning season and that some fry will survive. IN SMALL NORTHERN EUTROPHIC LAKES, WE DO NOT ENCOURAGE FISHING FOR BASS WHEN THEY ARE BEDDING. Though some of these fish are catchable, they may be so weakened after being caught that they will not be able to protect their nests from other predators. Leaving bass alone during actual spawning is particularly crucial in northern tier states, where bass grow at a much slower rate and survival is more problematic. The spawning period should be viewed as a time when a species can replenish itself without man's intrusion.

The post-spawn period will see a general movement of bass away from Area E, though some fish may remain in this area throughout the summer months. After spawning is completed, the development of vegetation and location of prey becomes the key to locating bass on any lake. But before we move into the summer period, let's take a closer look at the key locations for springtime bass.

Area E — This is a black-bottom bay, the main spawning ground and the first place to warm on Little Lake X. During the pre-spawn, the lily pads will be just emerging in the one- to four-foot depths, and by the end of spawning they will be fully developed. Water temperature is very important, so be sure to carry a thermometer and note any upward or downward fluctuations. The weeds at the entrance to this bay will develop a little more slowly than the pads. By the time of actual spawning, weeds like coontail will be about half developed. During brief cold snaps, fish will likely be tightly schooled at the entrance to this area in eight to ten feet of water. As the water warms and fish actually establish their nests, action will be more scattered. After spawning is completed, there will be a slow movement out of this bay towards areas B, D, and F.

Area D — This area is the major point or bar and is directly adjacent to the main spawning bay. As lake waters warm, Area D will begin to pull fish from the spawning bay. During the spring, the area is composed of developing reeds, and, as the summer nears, it will have growths of milfoil, cabbage, and coontail. The reeds will be almost fully developed here by the end of spawning, and a number of spawned-out females may move to the edges of the reeds and deeper weed growth. As this particular point is located on the leeward side of prevailing winds, there may be some spawning, though the soft sandy bottom is generally not conducive to bass bedding. This section is a classic summertime area and will improve as a fish-holding area as the summer approaches. Bass may visit the reeds during the post-spawn, with time of day and wind direction and velocity the key factors.

Other Areas The only other area on Little Lake X that would see much fish activity during the spring might be Area B. During the pre-spawn period, this section might hold some cold-water bass. As waters begin to warm, there could be some fish movement up into the reeds and developing cabbage beds. There will also be some suspended fish in Area G as fish begin moving into their summer pattern, but these fish would be tough to catch.

Springtime Lure Selection — If we had to choose one lure to fish on springtime bass, it would undoubtedly be a single-spin spinnerbait. During the pre-spawn, some of the smaller ones, like the ¼-oz. size, work well, and as waters warm, the larger spinnerbaits become more effective. Remember: the cooler the water, the slower the retrieve. Water temperature should be checked each time out to determine the best retrieve. Other good springtime lures include topwater baits, like a Cordell Redfin Minnow. Usually the topwater baits work better toward the end of the springtime pattern. Plastic worms are a good choice during the post-spawn period, because they can be presented slowly.

Summertime Locational Patterns	Pre-summer	67° F - 70° F
	Summer-peak	about 70° F
	Summer	depends on region but over 72° F

The key to understanding these three calendar periods is the development of natural vegetation and the various food sources that bass will feed on all summer.

During the pre-summer, bass are in constant state of movement. Patterns are difficult to identify and will remain so until the summer pattern is established.

Small groups and even stray fish can be scattered from the four-foot shallows to the clean 15-foot drop-off. For the most part, they will be relating to cover and available food. This is a time when fish are here today, gone tomorrow. While good catches occur, they are usually not consistent. The best angling approach at this time of year is to cover a lot of ground and to not expect to find heavy concentrations of fish.

The summer peak provides some of the best fishing of the year. The reason is simple. Fish metabolism is now fairly high, but the lake's natural food production is not quite in high gear. Thus, fish are hungry and there is little to eat. In this period, also, rooted weed growth is mature. Patterns established at this time will last until turnover. As the weedline will now be fully developed, it becomes important in the determination of these patterns.

During the bulk of the summer, fishing can be tough unless you can identify regular feeding periods. Pattern fishing is the rule, and weather conditions will play an important role in identifying patterns. Fishing can be tough because there is so much natural food in the lake. Contrary to popular belief, fish activity does not slow down during those July and August "dog days." There is plenty of fish-feeding activity, but with all that natural food around, the bass are less eager to strike at a lure or unnatural-looking bait. While presentation can be pretty sloppy during the pre-spawn, a poorly hooked worm or improperly presented lure often spells failure for the angler during the summer.

Let's look at Little Lake X during these three periods and see where the fish can be found.

Area A — Though not a super spot, this are will host a number of bass throughout the summer. Thick beds of coontail will make fishing tough. You can expect to find the bass in this area relating primarily to the deep edge of the weedline. On overcast days they may move into the shallows.

Area B — This area will produce best in early summer, when bass will make periodic forays into the reeds to feed. Bass will also be caught on the deep weedline and on the flats. As the summer wears on and weed growth begins to thicken, the reeds will not produce as well as they did earlier this summer.

Area C — Due to sparse habitat, this area is not going to hold many bass. Weed growth is slow here due to the sharp drop-off.

Area D — The combination of a flat and a bar-like projection combining both reeds and cabbage will make this area a winner all summer long. Look for regular migrations of bass into the reeds, as well as schools of deep-water bass relating to the outside edge of the weedline. This is without a doubt the best place to concentrate your fishing efforts throughout the summer period.

Area E — During the summer periods, this former spawning bay will turn into a "slop" or "junk" area with thick, seemingly impenetrable weed growth. In Section 5-B we will discuss how to fish such areas successfully. The pads toward the back of the bay will be thick, and the entrance to this bay will have incredible weed growth of all kinds. Some bass will stay in this bay all summer long, but don't expect to find them in schools. In this area you are fishing pretty much for singles. Some of your largest bass will come out of this area.

Area F — Finally, this little sunken island comes into its own. It will reach its fullest potential during the summer period when weed growth is at its maximum. Then it will hold schools of fish along both the deep and shallow edges of the weed growth. Fish could also occasionally be in the clean lip areas tapering into deep water.

Area G — This open-water area is never a super fishing area. It will see some fish during transition periods but is not worth wasting much time on.

Summertime Lure Selection — A wide variety of lures and baits will work during summer periods, but selection naturally depends on the areas you are fishing. Both shallow and deep-diving crankbaits can be a super producer on the edge of weeds. Be sure to experiment with various speeds. On some hot days the fastest retrieve possible drives the bass crazy. In the reeds, a plastic worm or jig and eel can be very productive (more on that in Section 5-C). We like to use a Pow-RR head jig when fishing a jig and eel or jig and minnow, as the shape of its head makes it virtually weedless. Spinnerbaits, though not as productive as during the pre-spawn, will also produce fish now and can be fished in cabbage beds. In the "slop" bays, a special selection of lures and tackle is necessary and will be explained in Section 5-B. Early and late in the day, buzzbaits and chugger-type lures produce well when worked over the shallow weedy flats. Also, don't overlook the use of a plain minnow or crawler on a slip sinker. This approach would work best on the clean lip section of Area F and outside the weedline. Just let the conditions be your guide to presentation and don't become a one-lure angler. Versatility and successful bass fishing go hand in hand.

Post-summer and Cold-water Locational Patterns

Post-summer	72° F - 65° F
Turnover	65° F - 55° F
Cold-water	below 55° F

As the nights begin to cool and the angle of the sun allows less and less light to enter the underwater world, the food production of Little Lake X begins to slow down. This is a time of transition. Towards the end of the summer there will be another time of peak activity, but, sadly, many angler miss out on this. They have put away their fishing rods and are oiling their guns in anticipation of hunting season. This post-summer peak may last only a week or ten days, but it produces some of the biggest fish of the year. Once again, this activity is due to the high level of bass activity and the slowing down of natural food production — the old story of supply and demand.

Usually by the time the first hard frost hits Little Lake X, the cold top layers of water will sink, causing a general turnover in the lake's waters. While the actual turnover takes only a few days, its effects are longer lasting. This is a time of turmoil, and all species of fish are temporarily disoriented. As cooler water sinks, the lake "belches up" dead weed growth and other detritus from the bottom. Fishing during this period is tough, and it is usually best to switch to another lake until the effects wear off. Fish will tend to be scattered all over the lake and are generally in a negative feeding mood. As weedbeds die off, fish will abandon them and will relate to those few remaining green beds.

The cold-water period is a time of gradual slowing down of the entire ecosystem. It is a preparation for winter and even the rigors of spring that will follow. The big female's eggs will already be fairly well developed. They will be feeding quite heavily to put on layers of fat to sustain them through the coming

"Topwater lures are always a favorite way to take shallow-water bass."

shortage of food and the strenuous activity that will follow next spring. The bass groups will take up residence in their eventual winter locations and will set up predator/prey relationships different from those of summer. An exodus from the shallows will result in a tighter concentration of fish. Feeding activity, however, can vary, ranging from intense to almost non-existent.

During these calendar periods, anglers have to be on their toes. The stable patterns that existed all summer long are broken and water temperature will begin to fluctuate rapidly, as it did in the spring. The thermometer becomes an important part of post-summer and cold-water fishing. With all this in mind, let's take a final look at Little Lake X to see how the bass will respond to these changes in weather and water conditions.

Area A — During these three calendar periods, this section will attract fewer and fewer fish. By the cold-water period, fish will have abandoned it altogether.

Area B — The reeds will still hold a few fish, and activity can be good during the post-summer period. By the time the cold-water period settles in, this section will hold few fish.

Area C — Though not a good producer throughout the post-summer, this spot really turns on during the cold-water period. The sharp drop-off is the key to its fish-holding potential during this period. At times there will be heavy concentrations of fish in this area, but, remember, cold water means a slower presentation. A minnow on a slow-dropping jig can be extremely effective at this time.

Area D — The flats and shallow water weeds in this area (including the reeds) will hold considerable numbers of fish during the post-summer peak. And even as the lake moves into the cold-water period, this area will continue to hold bass. Look for them near the remaining green weedbeds and on the drop-offs.

Area E — This section goes from feast to famine during these three calendar periods. During the post-summer, this section is probably the best on the lake. The shallows receive renewed interest from bass that spent most of the summer on the flats or in deeper weeds. After the turnover, however, there will be an exodus of fish from these "slop" bays. There will still be some activity on warmer days, but as the water temperature gets below 50° F, this area will hold very few fish.

Area F — There is a general movement away from sunken islands toward shoreline structure during these three periods. Some bass will continue to relate to this section where deep green weeds still exist.

Area G — During the actual turnover, this section holds more fish than at any other time. Once again, however, most of these fish will be suspended and in a negative mood.

Lure Selection During a Time of Transition — The important thing to remember is that this time span is characterized by dropping water temperatures. During the post-summer period, many summertime lures will still produce, but as soon as the lake moves into the cold-water period, a change in tactics is necessary. The spinnerbait becomes a good choice, just as it was in the spring. Crankbaits and buzzbaits will work well in the post-summer, but when the water dips below 55° F, the jig and minnow or jig and pork rind become the most consistent producer. Most anglers think of the jig and minnow as a walleye presentation and fail to realize how effective it can be on cold-water bass. A slow-dropping jig with a fathead minnow or redtail chub can turn these cold-water bass on like no other combination. Towards the end of the cold-water period, just before freeze-up, live bait and a bobber presentation is probably the only guaranteed winner.

Lure size and speed of retrieve are two other considerations when fishing cold-water bass. For some reason, the smaller lures seem more productive than the normal size used in the summertime. In addition, slower fish metabolism means a slower retrieve. We continue to be amazed at the "one-speed" anglers whose retrieve never varies throughout the year. During the cold-water period, slow your presentation to a crawl if necessary.

The Frozen-Water Period

Though there are scattered reports of anglers taking largemouth through the ice, there simply is not sufficient information on this topic to make generalizations at this time. We do know that largemouth action is VERY, VERY SLOW and that smallmouth action is even slower. The few anglers we have talked with report that the little remaining green vegetation is important in attracting and holding frozen-water bass.

* * * * * * *

As you can see from our analysis of Little Lake X, largemouth activity and location on a natural lake are anything but static, Movement in response to the spawning urge, changes in water temperature, developing weed growth, and the location of prey is the rule rather than the exception. Of course our example was a hypothetical lake, and a rather simple one at that. Other lakes could have different structural elements. In that case the bass's response will be slightly different. It's up to you to study the examples and use the principles here to interpret situations which may be different.

This chapter should teach you that bass *do not* respond the same way to the same things day in and day out, month after month. The bass fisherman who ties on a spinnerbait and beats the lily pads from the beginning of the season until the end will obviously have some good days, but he will also experience many, many bad ones. By the same token, the plastic worm fancier who beats the edge of the weedline from spring until fall will also have his days, but he will also miss out on a lot of fantastic fishing.

The versatile angler who has mastered a number of different types of presentations is the only one who can follow bass throughout the year and catch fish consistently. What works in the summer may not work in the fall. And when nothing seems to work, the versatile angler will experiment and perhaps discover an approach never tried before. To aid you in developing your versatility, we will close this chapter with our best judgment as to lure selection for bass on natural lakes. If you rely pretty heavily on one or two approaches, we urge you to experiment the next time out and learn something new.

Summary of Calendar Periods for Largemouth Bass in Natural Lakes

Calendar Period	General Fish Location	Fish Attitude	Most Effective Lures	Retrieve
Pre-spawn	Movement from cooler water drop-offs into warmer shallow water areas	Extremely active	Spinnerbaits, Floating Diver Plugs, Small Plastic Worms	Slow to Medium
Spawn	Spawning bays, channels and cuts protected from the wind	Not very active	In small natural lakes, be a sportsman and don't fish at this time.	—
Post-spawn	Some bass still in the spawning areas, others will be on adjacent flats	Females are inactive Males are catchable	Spinnerbaits, Small Shallow-Running Crankbaits, Topwater Lures, Plastic Worms	Medium
Pre-summer	Newly developing weeds. Flats and shallows still good. Reeds can be super.	Moderately active	Spinnerbaits, Crankbaits, Topwater Plugs/Spoons, Plastic Worms	Medium Fast
Summer Peak	All weed zones	Very active	Crankbaits, Plastic Worms, Topwater Plugs/Spoons, Jig and Eel or Minnow, Buzzbaits	Quick
Summer	All weed zones - patterns well established. Daily weather conditions become very important.	Fairly active	same as summer peak	Fast Stop & Go
Post-summer	Same as summer period	Moderately active At times excellent	Spinnerbaits, Plastic Worms, Topwater Plugs, Jig and Eel/Minnow	Medium Fast
Turnover	Scattered and disoriented	Poor	Live Bait best choice	Very Slow
Cold Water	Shallow movements on warm days. Remaining green weeds are good. Some fish on flats but most on the drop-offs.	Early very active Later, action spotty	Spinnerbaits, Jig and Minnow/Pork Rind, Crankbaits, Live Bait on Bobber Rigs	Slow to Very Slow
Frozen Water	Green weeds	Poor	Live Bait, Slow Jigging	Very Slow to Stationary

CHAPTER 5-B
Largemouth Bass in Shallow Water Slop

Years ago, most bass anglers were confirmed shoreline fishermen. This was natural, for they had been taught to think of lily pads and bass as inseparable. Every year they beat the shallows to death, casting to every brushy overhang, tree stump, and lily pad in sight, just like their fathers and grandfathers had done. Then came the introduction of the depth finder and structure fishing. And it wasn't long until the shallows were abandoned and a new generation of anglers sought out deep-water bass on sunken islands and the deep-water breaks. Through extensive studies of fish location, we now know that bass tend to locate both in the shallows and on the breaks. Their location depends on the type of lake they inhabit and on the predator/ prey relationship in that body of water. But knowing where the bass are and catching them are two different things. In this section we want to explore the hows and whys of catching bass in really thick weedy cover, the type of weeds we affectionately refer to as "slop" or "junk."

The term "slop" refers to any thick, usually floating, vegetation located in shallow-water bays that is difficult to fish with traditional tackle. Some bass will spend most of the summer in these weedy jungles. Even the old-timers who loved to fish lily pads avoided these areas. The major problem the old-timers had was lack of proper equipment; it was just not designed to fish heavy cover. In addition, their knowledge of what type of "junk" to fish was limited. Let's face it; not all this water contains fish. And if you work these areas under the wrong light or wind conditions, it's going to be tough going. In order to better understand how, where, and when to fish these weedy nightmares, let's take a look at a typical slop bay and analyze it.

In many cases, slop bays offer protection from cool northerly winds. This is important because if the bays are shallow and wind-protected, they tend to warm faster and stay warmer in the early summer than most other parts of the lake. But as summer progresses, a change takes place. Gradually the weed growth thickens and prevents the sun's rays from warming the water underneath the plants. In a sense, these weedy mats serve as watery air-conditioners. Surprisingly, the water temperature underneath a four-foot-deep lily pad clump surrounded by thick weed growth can be as much as seven to ten degrees cooler than the surface water temperature. In fact, water temperatures under these thick mats may be cooler than temperatures on the more exposed flats. Don't be misled into thinking that these areas are too hot for summertime bass, for they can be well within the bass's preferred temperature range.

On most eutrophic lakes, the weed-choked bays are quite small. They range in size from only a few hundred square feet to as much as a couple of acres. In many

"A swirl like that is a sweet sight."

"These slop bass sure grow mean and sassy."

"A good battler like this deserves to swim another day."

cases, during the summer period, the weeds are so thick it looks as if you could walk across them. In fact, motoring your boat through this slop is usually next to impossible, even with a good weed guard and a strong electric trolling motor. In some cases, we've had to literally grab the weeds and pull ourselves in. That's what you call thick! Under these conditions a duck-billed push-pole can be indispensable.

Bass Location in the Slop

In such an abundance of weeds the inevitable question is, "Where do I begin to look for bass?" Well, experience is usually the best teacher. By just fishing with the old trial and error method you will soon discover patterns of location. Some pads will always hold bass while others never seem to attract fish. There are, however, a few clues we can offer to help you in your search.

To the uninitiated angler looking at the surface, these bays would appear to be completely weed-choked all the way to the bottom. Appearances, however, can be deceiving. In reality, the bass are living in an underwater forest with a thick canopy-like covering. Underneath, the weed stems resemble a maze of tiny tree trunks. In this labyrinth, you'll find openings similar to dark alleys, tunnels, and dens. It is these passageways that serve as a home base and feeding station for bass.

The key to finding these ambush points is to fish junk weeds as you would any structure. Look for something in this mass of weeds that is different from the surrounding area. Open pockets in a blanket of lily pads can be a good bet. Another winner is a long finger-like point of either pads or thick slop. This can provide a perfect feeding station for old bucketmouth. Open cuts that run between floating mats of weeds can be good, but make sure your lure is as close to the edge of the weeds as possible. When fishing in the slop it is important not to waste much time. Don't throw five or ten casts at the same pocket. Try one or two casts, then move on. Try to identify a pattern. On some days bass will be holding tight under open pockets. On other days weedy points will produce best. The diagrams on the next page illustrate good and bad pads. Look them over and then try using this information when fishing a slop area on your favorite lake.

When all other approaches fail, try laying your casts right across the middle of the weeds. Chet Meyers remembers his first experience working a slop bay in a lake near Peterborough, Ontario. After spending the morning fishing the edges of a thick blanket of duckweed and striking out completely, Chet and his dad hired a guide for the afternoon. There really weren't any open pockets to fish, so the edges seemed a logical choice, but their guide had another idea. He urged Chet to toss his weedless frog right next to the shore and to retrieve it over the top of the duckweed. There were no classic explosions, just a lot of slurping as bass after bass pulled those frogs down through the weeds. Sometimes the only thing they saw was a quick rise in the floating mat, and at no time did they actually see a bass. But Chet and his dad hooked eighteen bass that afternoon and learned a thing or two about slop fishing. One thing they learned was that you don't go

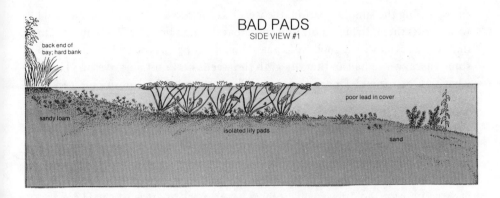

BAD PADS
SIDE VIEW #1

back end of
bay; hard bank

poor lead in cover

sandy loam

isolated lily pads

sand

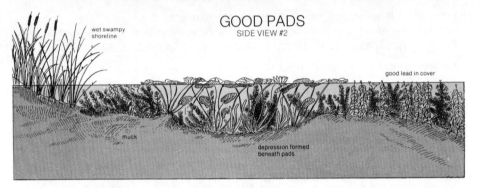

GOOD PADS
SIDE VIEW #2

wet swampy
shoreline

good lead in cover

muck

depression formed
beneath pads

Not all lily pads hold bass. These two diagrams show what to look for and what to avoid.

after junk bass with conventional spinning tackle. Of the eighteen bass they hooked, they landed only seven.

Choosing the Right Tackle

Make no mistake about it. Fishing junk is hard work. You must have proper equipment or the whole experience will end in frustration. To achieve the correct retrieves, fight fish, and handle the inevitable hang-ups, a stiff rod is indispensable. One slop-fishing fancier quipped, "If you could put rod guides on a pool cue and cast with it, you might have a rod that is about right for fishing junk." Although it isn't that bad, it does take a strong "stick" to horse even a three-pound bass out of the garbage. Yes, we said "horse him." The rule is to get the fish *out, up,* and *over* the weeds and *moving* toward you as fast as possible. To do this, keep your rod tip high and your reel drag screwed down tight. Once you lower your rod or give a fish some line, it's all over.

We recommend a heavy-action graphite rod combined with a quality baitcasting reel that has a five-to-one ratio. A reel with a three-to-one ratio will give you a bit more power, but a five-to-one will move the fish faster and keep him coming. The Ambassador 5500C, the Daiwa 5H Millionaire, or the Quick Champion will all do the job very nicely. Both open- and closed-faced spinning equipment and light line are out of place in the junk. While fine for other situations, they just don't belong here. The single most important factor under these conditions is to have the strength to move and control the fish. Most of the time the fish strike out of a reflex action or are definitely feeding, so they're not influenced much by line diameter. What size is best? The minimum would be 17-lb.-test and many times 20-lb. or more might be necessary. Because of the high abrasion factor, we recommend lines with little stretch like clear blue Stren or Berkley's Dura Tuff.

In shallow water it's important to move through the area as quietly as possible. If you make noise, the fish won't move far, but you can spook them out of casting range or drive them under cover where they can't see your lure. For this reason, additional equipment is absolutely essential. You must have a powerful electric trolling motor, preferably a 24-volt model, with a large weed guard basket. Finally, a duck-billed push-pole will get you out of situations where even a powerful electric motor will bog down. At times a push-pole is worth its weight in gold. The combination of electric motor, weed guard, and push-pole will help you land fish when they bury themselves in the thickest weeds. If you can't horse a bass out of the weeds, your next bet is to maintain constant pressure, get to the fish as fast as you can, and lift him straight out of the water.

A good pair of Polaroid sunglasses is also necessary for all types of shallow-water angling. You'll be surprised at how many times you can spot fish before you cast to them. More importantly, you'll be able to spot the underwater pockets and openings in the weed growth that are so important.

Lure Selection for Fishing the Slop

As you might imagine, the choice of proper lures is essential when fishing in

"A good selection of "slop" lures includes the Super Frog, Timber King Spoon, Johnson Silver Minnow, and floating plastic worm."

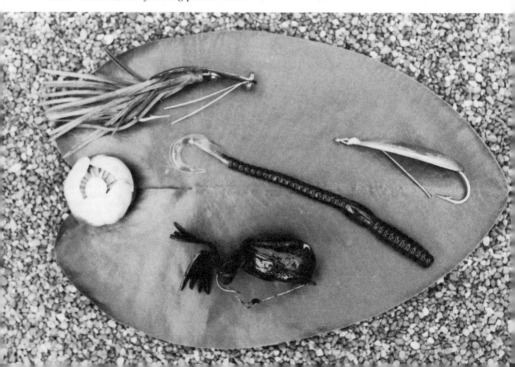

extremely heavy cover. This is definitely not crankbait territory. We've found three types of lures that have been particularly effective and workable. They are: (1) the weedless spoon, (2) the weedless rubber frog, and (3) the surface buzzer.

(1) *Weedless Spoons* — All spoons are not alike. Because of differences in design, each spoon has a unique action. In the slop, our favorites are the Timber King Spoon and the Johnson Silver Minnow. The ¼- to ½-oz. size of both examples are most effective for our purposes; the heavier models tend to sink too fast and foul too easily in the junk.

The two spoons mentioned above are *not* interchangeable. They have different shapes and, consequently, distinctive actions. The Timber King Spoon has a flat bottom and wide base so it can be fished very slow. Instead of just sinking, it flutters beautifully when falling and still maintains a slithering action when it is slowly snaked across the grass. And it rattles in the process. A disadvantage, however, is that it loses action when pulled too fast. On the other hand, a Johnson Silver Minnow swivels its hips like a rock and roll star when retrieved quickly, but sinks rapidly into the slop and doesn't dance when crawled along slowly. It's best to use a Johnson spoon when fishing the edges of the pads or through open cuts. The Timber King spoon works best for fluttering down through small openings or pockets.

To flutter a spoon effectively, cast beyond your target and skitter the spoon across the surface until you reach an opening or a pocket. At that point, allow the spoon to fall or flutter down into the opening. If nothing happens, simply continue your retrieve to the next pocket and repeat the process. When you're faced with a larger opening, twitch your rod tip to make the spoon dance back and forth and flutter up and down. Once you establish the proper ryhthm, the spoon will almost stay in place while fluttering. Finally, remember to keep a tight line so that you're ready to set the hook.

To fish a thick growth of weeds with no openings or pockets in the center, make your cast to the top of the weeds beyond the edge of the growth and skitter the spoon across the top of the weeds. When the spoon reaches the edge, let it flutter downward, and begin to twitch the lure up and down for two or three feet beyond the weeds. Sometimes a fish will grab the lure at the edge of the weeds at the last moment before it gets away. If you don't get a strike within a few feet of the weed's edge, retrieve your lure quickly and cast to a different area.

The fluttering action is what makes the bass strike when a spoon drops in the pockets and openings of the weeds. Therefore, it's important to attach an "O" ring or plain snap (not a snap swivel) to the spoon rather than tying your line directly to the lure. It will help give the spoon added life.

(2) *Buzzbaits* — The "buzzers" resemble single-spin spinnerbaits in many ways. The difference is that the blade is shaped like a propeller and is constructed of lightweight aluminum so that it rides up quickly. The name *buzzer* tells the whole story: this group of lures actually buzzes across the

surface of the water. "Hack" Jackson, who introduced buzzbaits back in 1967, believes the commotion will call fish from 20 feet away. There is no question that a buzzer gets a fish's attention. Buzzing is an effective way to cover a lot of water fast. It is best used where the weeds are slightly under the surface and less effective where thick vegetation grows to the surface. Buzzers can be run along the front face of a patch of lily pads and the edge of a choked weedbed that grows to the surface. Although buzzers work in shallow bays, they really shine in mid-depth ranges on shallow flats.

(3) *The Rubber Frog* — This is not something your mother buys you for Christmas or a kid's toy. New designs have made the rubber frog dynamite on slop bass. Bill Plummer's original frog was a soft rubber version with paper-thin folded legs. A few years ago, Cecil Hoge (Harrison-Hoge Industries) remodeled this deadly bass weapon with a more durable rubber that is practically indestructible. He calls his version the Super Frog. It is your best option in the junk, not only because of its life-like qualities, but because it is virtually weedless. This imitation lies perfectly on the water, head up and legs down, just like a real croaker. It can be left motionless next to a pad or pocket, hopped with a series of jerks, or simply twitched in place. This "slowpoke" approach is sometimes just the ticket for bass that only swirl at your spoon or buzzer.

One of the best ways to fish Mr. Froggy (Ron Lindner's kids call it Kermit) is to cast the frog directly on top of the pads near an edge or opening or on top of a clump of slop and begin to hop and crawl the frog over the tops of the vegetation. This action gets a lot of attention but few hits until you reach an opening, where you should let the frog rest and hope it will trigger a strike. Sometimes you'll experience "passes" from directly underneath the pads. In this case the fish probably didn't see the lure very clearly and only perceived movement. He made an instinctive snatch at the intruder and created only a boil. But there will be times when bass with a positive feeding attitude will actually burst through and part the pads or heavy weeds and grab the lure (and a mouthful of salad, too).

Many times you'll see a "V" or a bulge of water moving toward your bait. It would only be human nature to want to set the hook immediately, as soon as you hear a slurp. Most novice "froggers" tend to do this and miss the fish. The right time to set the hook is a split second *after* the sound of a "slurp." That moment is crucial! Try to force yourself to pause momentarily before you set the hook. Your percentage of hooked fish will more than double. However, even this advice is not sure-fire. Sometimes the bass will make no sound at all — one moment the frog is there and then it disappears without a ripple. When this happens, set the hook!

When to Fish the Slop

A good thick growth of junk weeds does not usually develop until three or four weeks after the spawning season. Thus, these bays come into their own during the

"When you reach down to grab a "slop" lunker like this you often come up with a few pounds of vegetation."

bulk of the summer calendar period. While many bass move out of the shallows, some bass maintain residence in the slop all summer long. A mass exodus from the slop will occur only after the water temperature drops below 55° F. From that point on, the weeds quickly die off and there will be only brief feeding forays into the shallows on warm sunny days. During the summer, however, the slop can produce excellent fishing once feeding patterns are established.

As with fish in other zones, slop bass can be in different feeding moods, depending largely on local weather conditions. Bass on the breaks with a neutral attitude can be taken at midday under a bright sun. Slop bass, in contrast, usually have a negative attitude when the sun is high in the sky. Their most active periods are the morning and evening. Under a hot bright sun, during strong winds, or after a cold front, slop bass can be tough.

The amount of sunlight has a definite effect on the feeding mood of junk bass. On overcast days, bass in the slop may move about freely, and the fishing action, though not fast, can continue for extended periods of time. On these days it pays to spend a little more time fishing open water areas that lead out of the slop to deeper water. On sunny days, however, a fish will hold close to cover and accurate casts become important. Don't expect a bass to move more than a foot or two when he is lying under a nice shady clump of weeds. Feeding periods on sunny days will usually be in the early morning and at dusk. The action will be fast and furious, and a good eye can help detect the telltale swirl of a feeding bass. Open water areas will be less productive on these sunny mornings.

Adapting Slop Tactics to Other Bodies of Water

The tactics described in this section were developed by anglers fishing natural lakes but are readily applicable to other situations. Many southern reservoirs have small pockets of slop that can be fished with the methods we have outlined.

Similarly, small backwater areas of older rivers or tidal rivers often teem with largemouth bass that haven't been fished in years because no one knows how to present a lure in this heavy weedy cover.

If you have never attempted this type of fishing, we suggest you try to find a buddy who has and let him give you some pointers. You will find it a most exciting form of bass fishing. It just won't seem possible to fish in some of the slop you will locate, but once you overcome the natural hesitancy to cast your lure into a jungle of weeds, you will be pleasantly rewarded with some of the biggest bass of your life.

CHAPTER 5-C
Largemouth Bass in the Reeds

After mastering the techniques for fishing bass in the "slop," learning how to fish bass in the reeds is a breeze. Not only is lure presentation much easier in the reeds, the feeding attitude of the fish is usually very positive. For some strange reason, the bass, typically a cautious fish, becomes aggressive and almost fearless when prowling the reeds. While we don't fully understand the change in attitude, we have observed it on countless occasions.

Once, when Al Lindner was shooting photographs for a magazine article, he hooked a nice three-pound bass right next to a big clump of reeds. Al's photographer, Jeff Zernov, quickly jumped over the side of the boat and crouched down in the shallow water to get some good action shots of a jumping bass. After shooting about ten photos and making enough noise to scare every bass for a radius of half a mile, Jeff climbed back into the boat. Al immediately made another cast to the same reed clump and this time a two-pound bass nailed his spinnerbait. All this took place in the span of about five minutes. We can only assume that, rather than being frightened, the second bass was actually attracted by all that commotion.

This naturally aggressive mood of bass in the reeds contrasts with the fish's normal attitude on deep water drop-offs where it is often in a neutral or negative mood. And it even contrasts with the positive but cautious feeding attitude that bass normally exhibit on shallow water feeding forays into other weedy shallows. About the only place where bass and reeds are not a sure-fire combination is in the shallow natural lakes of Florida. Here bass spend most of their time in the reeds and quite obviously can't be actively feeding every waking hour. In northern natural lakes, however, bass move into the reeds from deep water or heavy weed-holding areas, and when they move to the reeds, they feed.

Of course bass activity in the reeds is not an ironclad rule, but anglers can usually tell the mood of bass in the reeds by observing their action firsthand, with the help of Polaroid glasses. If bass dart away from an approaching boat or if they zip out of sight at the mere motion of a cast, then the fish are skittish and fishing could be tough. Most often, however, bass in the reeds will slowly swim off, stopping a short distance from the boat. On other occasions they will trail a lure or another hooked fish to the boat. When this occurs, bass are vulnerable and can be caught, even though they are aware of the angler's presence.

Bass movement *into* the reeds is also a departure from typical largemouth behavior. Usually the key to shallow water bass movements is a function of minimal light penetration. In the reeds, however, the *wind* is the controlling factor. A boiling hot, calm, cloudless day could bring the heaviest concentration

"Largemouth in the reeds are aggressive critters."

"Now there's a pretty picture."

"Just a little closer."

of bass to the reeds, while an overcast day with a strong wind will keep bass out of the weeds.

Through interviews with experienced biologists, we have concluded that when a strong wind blows into the reeds, adult bass will not remain or feed there. There is no question — they just up and leave. There may be several reasons why bass will not stay in windswept reeds, but we have been able to pin-point only a few.

In the opinion of top fishermen and scientific authorities, the main reason bass will not stay in wind-swept reeds is that *they do not like turbulent water!* Bass are a calm-water fish and, apparently, the rolling of the waves and stirring of the bottom bothers them. Some conservation officials have observed that bass are difficult to transport in "sloshing" tanker trucks, where they often get sick and weak. It is interesting to note that walleyes and northern pike do not show the same type of reaction.

Another reason bass vacate the reeds may be that heavy winds retard insect hatches, and the chain of events necessary for a shallow-water feeding movement is disturbed. Now that we know a little about bass behavior in the reeds, let's take some time to understand the different types of reeds and the locations that bass prefer.

Bass Location in the Reeds

Plants of the sedge family — commonly called bulrushes, rushes, or reeds — can be found virtually all over the North American continent and in many parts of Europe and Asia. In the United States, some of the most common are the bulrushes *Scirpus acutus, S. validus,* and *S. americanus.*

By reeds, we mean any hollow-stem, shallow-water plant found in natural lakes with the right bottom content. We do, however, divide them into three types: soft-stem reeds, hard-stem reeds, and a short variety we call "spike rushes."

Reed lakes that are important to the angler are mainly found in the northern continental United States, along the southern portion of Canada, and, of course, in Florida.

The bulrush, or reed, is nature's purifier. This amazing plant is able to absorb and break down polluting chemicals such as ammonia and phosphate, both of which help to quickly age and, ultimately, destroy a lake. Reeds are among the most desirable type of weeds to man, fish, and wildlife, not only because of their cleansing abilities, but also because of the ideal habitat they provide for spawning, rearing, and feeding of the sunfish species, including bass. Reeds also break the force of waves and help prevent erosion of shoreline. And they provide excellent shelter and food sources for waterfowl.

Aquatic life associated with reeds and providing food for bass includes the crayfish, a scavenger. The crayfish, also an important part in the ecosystem, converts waste material into a vital protein food source for bass.

Hard-stem reeds *(S. acutus)* tend to grow in hardwater lakes. Soft-stem reeds *(S. valipus)* are more common in medium- to soft-water lakes. Both, however, can be found in the same body of water. Hard-stem reeds tend to grow in thicker clumps, stand up straighter, grow taller, and not bend over as much in the wind. They are also less likely to be uprooted by anglers, wave action, boat traffic, or water skiers than the soft-stem variety of plant. The ability of the hard-stem reed and spike rush to stand more upright makes them much easier for anglers to fish, since "avenues" can be found for casts, and baits do not have to climb up and down a stem every few feet. The hard-stem reed can grow to a total length of about ten feet, with six feet of the reed submerged. Obviously, this can vary with water levels. When the water level drops, a reed can become top-heavy and droop. Or the entire bank may tend to migrate toward shallower water.

The soft-stem reeds are less hardy and do better in a sheltered environment. Usually, they do not grow over large areas. The soft- and hard-stem reeds thrive best in about two to four feet of water with two or three feet of the plants above water. It is at the two- or three-foot level that the thickest clumps exist.

The spike rush *(Eleocharis)* is a shallow-water reed with a maximum length of four feet. These reeds grow in one to two feet of water and extend one to two feet above water. Spike rushes are thin-bodied reeds. They grow very evenly and do not usually form clumps, as do the other reeds. Because spike rushes grow closer to shorelines, they can be found among water lily pads, cane, wild rice, and cattails.

Naturally, bass location in the reeds is not unlike bass location in any other part of the lake. Structural considerations are of prime importance. Some reeds tend to hold fish and may produce bass throughout much of the spring and summer pattern. Other reeds never hold fish. But before we take a look at specific configurations of reeds, a few generalization about bass location will be useful.

Usually the shallowest reeds, those which abut the shoreline, provide good fishing during the pre-spawn and spawn periods. However, after this brief flurry of activity, the shallow shoreline reeds are seldom used by big bass. The key location for summer bass is where reeds exist on a slight ledge or drop-off. This drop may be only one or two feet in an overall depth of three feet, but slight drop-offs and ledges are prime fish attractors. Another safe generalization is that thick reed patches seem to be the key to fish location. And, finally, we can say with good assurance that the deepest reeds, those in five or six feet of water and mixed with other types of vegetation, do not hold large concentrations of bass. In fact, strange as it may seem, the back side of thick reed banks produce many more fish than the front, or deep-water, side.

As we move to consider specific configurations of reeds that have good or bad fishing potential, we discover that the patterns are pretty consistent. The following areas never seem to hold many bass:

1. Sparse reeds on a slow-tapering flat
2. Small isolated patches of sparse reeds
3. Projecting "fingers" of sparse reeds
4. Front faces of reed banks (even thick reeds)

5. Long narrow banks of reeds

Some good places to begin prospecting for bass in the reeds include:
1. Thick banks of reeds near slight drop-offs
2. Fingers or projections on the back side of reed banks close to shore
3. Saddles, or areas where two reed patches are joined by a small strip of reeds
4. Rear pockets on the back side of reed banks
5. Cuts or alleys through thick reeds — sometimes man-made

These descriptions are brief, but should help in the location of potential hotspots. Only time on the water will help anglers learn how to identify productive patterns of reeds, but these few pointers should get the novice reed angler started. If we had to describe the prototype perfect reed bank for largemouth bass, it would be a large reed bank in two to three feet of water with a yellow sand bottom sprinkled with clam shells. It would also have clumps of thick reeds mixed in with sparse weeds. That way we could easily locate the fish. Finally, it would have nice thick reed fences along the back side, with a few fingers and indentations just big enough to hold some four- and five-pound bass. The nice thing about writing a book is that we can describe the perfect conditions . . . now you can do the hard part. Try to find that perfect reed bank on your lake.

Choosing the Right Tackle

The balance between rod, reel, and line is especially critical in reed conditions. Although the stems of reeds are spongy and soft, the fibers are strong. Hooks will penetrate the stalks easily, but the fibers will bind on the barbs of hooks, making it very difficult to unsnag your lure. Since we use either spoons and spinners or plastic worms, our choice of rod and reel varies, but in either case we like rods that are short and have stiff butts and medium action tips. This is not the place for "buggy whip" rods that shake back and forth like a wet noodle. When using a casting reel, we like to have one with a fast retrieve. A high gear ratio reel helps not only when you are buzzing a spinnerbait through the reeds, but also when a fish takes off and you have to keep up with its jumping, rolling, and cutting through the reeds.

There are a few other tips on equipment that will be useful in fishing the reeds. One is to use a tough, abrasion-resistant line when casting spinners and spoons. Reeds are tough and will wear out your line quicker than almost any other type of fishing. When you use a plastic worm, a high visibility line is crucial. In either case, don't use less than 12-lb.-test. You'll need all the muscle you can muster once old "linesides" wraps you around a few reeds.

Other equipment helpful in fishing the reeds is a good pair of Polaroid sunglasses. As we mentioned earlier, bass in the reeds are aggressive and, if you can spot them, you can usually catch them. Polaroids cut down on glare and will help you locate both holding and moving fish. A high quality weed guard for your electric motor is essential in the reeds, for reeds are often mixed with junk

"Spinnerbaits and buzzbaits are good approaches to fishing the reeds."

weeds that can easily clog your motor. And for the diehards, a duck-billed push-pole, like the kind duck hunters use to get into thick sloughs, is helpful in trying to reach those shallow, out-of-the-way places that no one else has ever fished. Don't think that these areas do not hold fish. There have been occasions when we had to use the reeds to pull our way into areas with only a foot of water, and the fishing was unbelievable.

Lure Selection in the Reeds

Only a narrow range of lure types can be used effectively in the reeds. You could cast a Big O or a Rapala to the face of a reed bank, but this is not true reed fishing. With the exception of spinnerbaits, any lure with exposed hooks is ineffective in the reeds. It is very difficult to pull such lures out of the bases of even soft-stemmed reeds. So you can rule out the use of most plugs, jigs, spoons, and spinners with exposed treble hooks.

When fishing the reeds for largemouth bass in the summer period, we recommend three basic types of lures:

1. Slip-rigged plastic-bodied baits
2. Weedless spoons
3. Single-hook spinnerbaits

In our experience, these three lure types will handle about 90 per cent of the situations you will encounter.

Slip-Rigged Plastic-Bodied Baits: We prefer the six- or four-inch plastic worms, in Florida as well as in the North. This length is easier to handle than the seven and a quarter, nine, or 12-inch worms, and experience has shown us that a hawg bass will hit the shorter worms just as readily as, and in some cases faster than, one of the longer varieties.

Use harder worms than you might normally select. Soft worms, which work well at other times, will be bitten in half by bluegills, and they will hang up or tear when dragged through the reeds. Harder worms will drop through the reeds when cast and will not tend to cling or wrap around the reeds, as the softer worms often do. With harder worms, however, you first have to "channel" a hole through the bait a few times so that when you do set the hook it will penetrate the fish's jaw.

Under most conditions, we use a ¼-oz. bullet- or cone-shaped slip sinker. In very thick reeds, we will switch to a ⅜-oz. or even a ½-oz. sinker to get the worm to the bottom of the reeds. Even with "rocket" casts, it is often difficult to get the bait to the bottom.

Although we said that color is not of major significance under reed conditions, we usually start fishing with a solid black, grape, or blue worm. Or we might try a black worm with a chartreuse or "hot pink" tail. A 1/0 barbed sprout hook in bronze or blue is best in most parts of the country. In Florida, however, we go to a 2/0 or 3/0 hook. In either case, stay away from gold- or nickle-finish hooks.

Spoons: Spoons can often be used when a spinnerbait *cannot* be snaked through the reeds or where too many bent, broken, or floating reeds make normal retrieves very difficult. There are also times when the fish will prefer a slower, wobbling surface or sub-surface presentation rather than the hard-driving vibration of a spinnerbait. Under these conditions, we recommend the ⅜-oz. Johnson Silver Minnow (the real one, not a copycat version) dressed with either a reversed rubber skirt, a small single or double twister tail, a piece of Uncle Josh pork rind in the three-tailed variety, or a small six-inch worm.

The Johnson Silver Minnow is a heavy spoon but should be retrieved at a steady, not rapid, rate. If this approach brings up fish but results in short strikes and missed fish, we suggest changing to a ¼-oz. Barney Spoon. This is a light thin version of the Silver Minnow. Because it is so light, it can be retrieved very slowly and occasionally fluttered down in open pockets.

Spinnerbaits: Today, spinnerbaits come in hundreds of colors, sizes, blade types, and skirt materials. There are, however, specific qualities a spinnerbait must have to work well in reeds.

We found that ¼-oz. or ⅜-oz. spinners with medium-size Colorado blades are the best. If you want to cast to open pockets in the reeds and let your bait flutter down, use a single-blade spinner. If you want to "gurgle" the bait just under the surface, use the tandem-blade spinner.

We do not feel that body, skirt, or blade color is of great importance, although we personally like white baits with white blades or yellow ones with copper blades.

You can dress the rear of spinnerbaits with pork rind, short plastic curly tails, or even minnows. We feel that this is somewhat like "gilding the lily," but it probably doesn't do any harm. Dressing a spinner might just keep that bass hanging on a bit longer than otherwise.

When you select a spinnerbait, make certain that the hook or blades are not too big or the spinner shaft too long or short. We use a great many spinnerbaits but one well-functioning spinner for the reeds would be the Blakemore ⅜-oz. Baby Buzz-Spin. This bait holds its balance and does not ride to either side on a retrieve.

Above all, do not use the free-swinging jig-type spinners. Make certain that the spinner shaft is molded directly to the head and not connected by a "safety-pin" arrangement. The spinner jigs are prone to ride to the side, to have their blades catch on the hook, and to snag on reed stems. Remember, spinners must be guided through some pretty narrow pathways, so weed-lessness is very important.

Presentation in the Reeds

Though fishing bass in the reeds is not as problematical as fishing in heavy "slop," there are a few important considerations. Some of the casting techniques anglers use when fishing shallow water structure will simply not work. "Lob-casting" in tall, bent-over or tangled reeds is asking for trouble. The bait is out of the water and forced to "climb" up and down over reeds during much of the retrieve. For the angler faced with this situation, the "rocket" cast is one of the best solutions. Rocket casts are never long, generally, never more than 25 feet. Hold the rod at the 12 o'clock position and, with a "hammer-the-nail" motion, whip the bait as hard as you can toward a clump of reeds or other target. The cast will put the bait into the base of the reeds. Then point your rod tip toward the water and shake the line from side to side to clear it of any stems. Retrieve the bait with the rod tip down until the bait is off the bottom or near the boat. This retrieve takes practice when fishing a plastic worm, since most anglers are used to holding the rod tip at the ten or 11 o'clock position while waiting for that telltale rap of a bass.

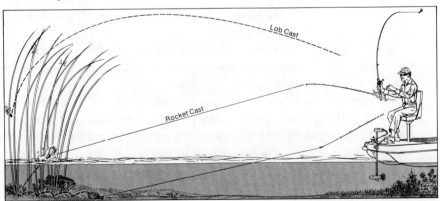

"Lob" casting over reeds is just asking for trouble. The lure is then forced to climb up and over the reeds and is often out of the water. The "rocket" cast is a much better method of presentation.

Another method, called the "flutter" presentation, can be used in open pockets or along the face of any thick reed bank. You begin with the rocket cast, but only penetrate into the reeds up to two or three feet. If you use a spinnerbait, crank it in as soon as it flutters halfway to the bottom. Single spins work better than tandems. If a fish does not strike, crank the bait in as quickly as possible and cast again. If you use a worm, cast and let the worm lie on the bottom. Twitch it a few times in place before retrieving. With a spoon, cast and quickly retrieve to the edge of the reeds. Then shake the rod tip from side to side, allowing the spoon to flutter down about one third of the way to the bottom. The main thing to remember is that once the lure is a foot or two outside the reeds it is probably in "dead" water. A slow retrieve from that point on is usually a waste of time.

You may invent some new techniques or even some variations on the lures and casts we have described. Use whatever works. You may find, as we have, that when you fish a new situation you begin to experiment and often discover a method of presentation that you can apply to other situations. As one sage remarked, "Necessity is the mother of invention." We hope that these tips will get you started on reed fishing and that you will come up with some new and better techniques that will produce fish. Whatever techniques you decide to use, we know that once you start catching bass in the reeds you are going to like it. This is fast, shallow-water action at its best. The fish are aggressive and waiting to be caught. Just don't get addicted and forget about the bass in other parts of the lake.

CHAPTER 6
Reservoir Classifications

More than 4,000 years ago, the civilizations that developed along river valleys in Egypt, Mesopotamia, China, and India constructed impoundments. Man began building earth, rock-filled, and stone dams to store water for irrigating thirsty crops and controlling floodwaters. About 2700 B.C., the Sadd el Kafara Dam was built in Egypt. This dam, now in ruins, is the world's oldest known masonry dam.

It was quite some time before the first reservoir graced the landscape of the new world. In fact, the first recorded impoundment in the United States was built by nature, not man. In 1811-1812, a winter earthquake near Union City, Tennessee, diverted part of the Mississippi River. As a large part of the earth sank, the Mississippi actually ran backwards for a time, filling the depressed area and creating Reelfoot Lake.

The first man-made reservoirs in this country were constructed for purposes of water storage, flood control, and irrigation. There was little thought of their recreational potential, and their potential as a bass fishery was never a consideration. Naturally, the first reservoirs were constructed in the eastern United States. By the turn of the century, there were only about 100 in existence. During the depression, however, with the institution of public works projects and aid from the Army Corps of Engineers, reservoirs began to grow in size and in number. By the 1940's, there were nearly 700 of them. By 1960, the total had increased to 1,006. And now, according to the National Reservoir Research Program, there are 1,480 reservoirs (over 500 acres) — twice the number of 30 years ago.

Though most modern reservoirs were constructed for purposes of flood control, irrigation, or hydroelectric power, it wasn't long until their recreational potential became evident. Many reservoirs were stocked with largemouth bass, and where smallmouth and spotted bass existed in the original river system, these species flourished also. In recent years, walleyes, northern pike, and striped bass have been introduced, so that reservoir angling provides a real smorgasbord for anglers in certain parts of the country.

Today, reservoirs in the United States total a whopping ten million acres — all potential fishing water. That's practically the equivalent of all the fresh water lakes (save the Great Lakes) in the nation. In effect, the construction of these reservoirs has doubled the available angling opportunities of a decade or two ago.

Texas leads the nation in both number and total surface of reservoirs. The Lone Star State boasts 193 impoundments, covering 1,547,000 acres. Texas always does things in a big way. Incidentally, with this much water, the state naturally leads the country in the number of bass clubs and total membership.

California ranks second in reservoirs (143), but many are water storage facilities and are relatively small. So, despite the number of artificial impoundments, the state ranks eighth in reservoir acreage.

Oklahoma, on the other hand, has only 57 reservoirs, yet nationally ranks second with 590,000 acres. And some of these Okie waters are big!

Many fishermen feel that reservoir fishing is mostly a southern or western phenomenon. Among the top 20 states, however, there are a number of northern states. North Dakota, for instance, ranks a lofty third; South Dakota is fifth; Montana is seventh; and the state of Washington is tenth.

Many reservoirs are still under construction and others are being planned. Future development, however, has spawned some heated controversies among conservationists, politicians, and builders (usually the Corps of Engineers). The feasibility, cost, and long-term impact of these reservoirs on the ecology and economy is often questioned. The famous Garrison Diversion Project is only one example of a reservoir project that has become a "hotbed" of dispute among farmers, environmentalists, and sportsmen. The days of facile reservoir construction are at an end. The coming years will be a time of reassessment, and future reservoirs will be studied long and hard before the Army Corps of Engineers dams another river.

UNITED STATES RESERVOIRS*

RANK	STATE	NUMBER OF RESERVOIRS	TOTAL AREA IN ACRES	RANK	STATE	NUMBER OF RESERVOIRS	TOTAL AREA IN ACRES
1	Texas	193	1,547,000	31	Ohio	41	92,000
2	Oklahoma	57	590,000	32	Michigan	42	84,000
3	Tennessee	31	475,000	33	Nebraska	19	82,000
4	N. Dakota	11	469,000	34	Pennsylvania	31	77,000
5	S. Dakota	15	454,000	35	New Mexico	16	66,000
6	Alabama	35	432,000	36	Iowa	8	51,000
7	Montana	44	424,000	37	Minnesota	11	49,000
8	California	143	370,000	38	Indiana	20	43,000
9	S. Carolina	16	356,000	39	Florida	8	43,000
10	Washington	43	351,000	40	Massachusetts	5	32,000
11	Arkansas	58	338,000	41	New Hampshire	18	30,000
12	Georgia	27	262,000	42	Connecticut	12	16,000
13	Idaho	42	248,000	43	Maryland	8	16,000
14	Louisiana	34	245,000	44	New Jersey	11	14,000
15	Utah	19	222,000	45	West Virginia	7	11,000
16	Kentucky	19	202,000	46	Vermont	9	8,000
17	Oregon	51	196,000	47	Alaska	2	4,000
18	Wisconsin	71	182,000	48	Rhode Island	2	4,000
19	Maine	21	180,000	49	Delaware	0	0
20	Missouri	25	178,000	50	Hawaii	0	0
21	N. Carolina	37	169,000		Interstate	1,520	9,693,000
22	Kansas	29	148,000		Duplications	-40	
23	New York	51	131,000			1,480	
24	Mississippi	15	131,000				
25	Wyoming	25	128,000				
26	Illinois	38	121,000				
27	Arizona	22	116,000				
28	Nevada	10	108,000				
29	Colorado	52	101,000				
30	Virginia	16	97,000				

*Reservoirs greater than 500 acres at average pool levels, ranked by total area at mean annual pool levels. Interstate reservoir areas are apportioned to the respective states. (As of January 1, 1976.) Source: National Reservoir Research

"Some reservoirs cover 100,000 acres with hundreds of miles of shoreline — overwhelming at first, but relatively easy to fish, if you know what to look for."

How Reservoirs Differ From Natural Lakes

Despite the incredible number of natural lakes, their classification is rather simple when compared to reservoirs. Most natural lakes are remnants of the glaciers and are located in the northern reaches of our country. Reservoirs, on the other hand, are man-made and their character depends on the original river system in which they are constructed and on the general makeup of the surrounding land.

River systems are water courses. A dam placed to impede this flow of water is fighting nature, and nature responds by doing its best to move that obstruction out of the way. From time to time, nature succeeds. A reservoir is contrary to the normal scheme of things and, consequently, there is a constant struggle between the forces of nature and man-made obstructions. Erosion, infilling, siltation, salinity buildup, and a host of other negative environmental factors are the result.

Infilling and erosion often are more pronounced in reservoirs than in natural bodies of water, due to the carrying capacity of the impoundment's waterways. Reservoirs, therefore, tend to age faster than natural lakes.

As reservoirs age, their fishing potential changes dramatically. Peak fishing years for largemouth bass are usually anywhere from the fourth to the eighth year. As a reservoir matures, the cover begins to diminish and natural populations of fish become less and less scattered and begin concentrating in more predictable patterns. The fishing quality of some reservoir types then levels out, while in others it declines rapidly. Introduction of species that use open water areas, such as stripers (rockfish), rainbow trout, and walleye, is gaining more and more popularity in older reservoirs to supplement the declining bass population.

In natural lakes, movement patterns of fish are fairly predictable, and, seasonally, quite stable. In almost all natural lakes, largemouth bass relate directly to weeds. Go to any natural lake; if it has weeds and largemouth bass, you'll find them together. Weeds, as we have seen in Chapter 5-C are the pivotal point of bass location. In reservoirs, on the other hand, weed growth is a minor factor. The main points of fish location in impoundments are the channel beds and banks of the flooded river.

Weed lines are a product of nature and, consequently, have rhyme and reason. But in certain reservoir types, "good looking structure" may be totally devoid of fish. For example, in the canyon or plateau classifications, an old riverbed meeting an "active" creek bed may be covered by 150 feet or more of water, making it unsuitable structure for bass. In natural lakes, bass seldom go deeper than 25 or 30 feet, regardless of the structural elements available to them. In canyon reservoirs, however, bass have been caught in 60 feet of water and deeper. Yes, for those used to fishing natural lakes, reservoirs are a different world altogether.

There are, of course, some similarities in fishing reservoirs and natural lakes. Points, sunken bars, and sunken islands can be good fishing structure in both types of water, but, as always, consideration must be given to available prey and to water depth and clarity. There are, however, certain structural considerations in reservoirs that lake anglers seldom encounter. For the reservoir angler, flooded river channels, channel bends, and tributaries play a big role in bass location. Flooded man-made structure is also a big consideration when fishing a reservoir. On occasion, entire towns were flooded, and, if the depth is right, that old graveyard might just be a bass hot spot. In the remainder of this chapter, we will look at five different classifications of reservoirs and focus on the identification of fish-holding structure. But before we do that, let's take a look at some structural features typical of almost any reservoir or impoundment. The diagram that follows is self-explanatory.

Factors Influencing Reservoir Personality

Each reservoir has its own personality, and, though many factors combine to produce this uniqueness, there are four of prime consideration:

1. Water Level Fluctuation — While natural lakes experience noticeable changes in water level only during periods of drought or intense rain, reservoirs may experience such changes weekly or monthly. The amount of water level fluctuation depends on how a reservoir's water supply is used and its water source.

Lewis and Clark Lake, a flatland reservoir in South Dakota-Nebraska,

TYPICAL RESERVOIR FEATURES

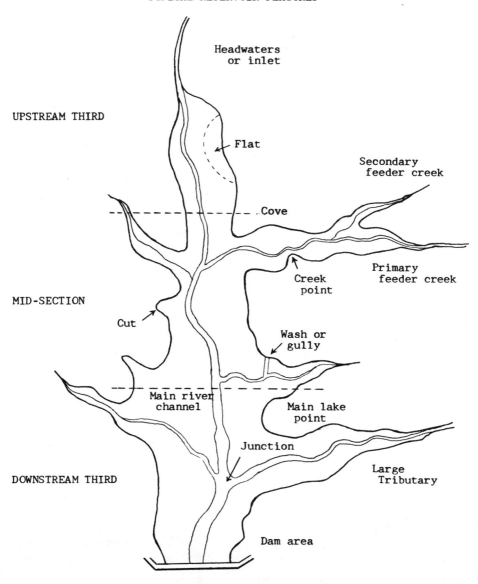

discharges an amount of water equal to its total volume (it's 21 miles long, two miles wide, and has a 16-foot average depth) every five to eight days from March through November. This means that in about a week the entire reservoir has had a complete transfusion. This kind of fluctuation plays havoc with a fishery.

The rate of water exchange and fluctuation also depends on the type and size of the feeder creeks. Pool level depends a great deal on how wet or dry the total drainage area is seasonally. Water level in a small reservoir can fluctuate from about three to five feet in a season, while in a large, deep impoundment it could vary from 20 to 200 feet. Lake Powell in Utah (a canyon reservoir) has dropped as much as ten feet or more in a single day! A full season can see 100-foot drops and rises.

In general, high water conditions tend to be a plus for a reservoir, while low water tends to kill fishing. During rising- or high-water periods, green vegetation is flooded, and this provides an additional influx of food to the biological chain. The 1973-74 period provided high water to many reservoirs in the Midwest, while 1976 was a seriously low-water year.

Bull Shoals and Table Rock reservoirs literally came back to life, due to excellent spawns and additions to the food chain introduced by flooded vegetation.

2. Water Color — Water color depends on the condition of the drainage area above and along the length of the reservoir. If black soil, red soil, or clay deposits are characteristics of the landscape, chances are that heavy rain will profoundly affect the water color and the fishing as well. If the main river and creeks drain through rock, gravel, or sandy areas, most likely the water will remain relatively clear.

The composition of the banks and the effects of wind on them also help determine overall color. Black earth or red clay banks slapped by waves can turn a shoreline very turbid for considerable distances, while waves beating rocks or sand may only affect the water for several feet.

In very large reservoirs, the main body of the impoundment is usually affected much less by runoff than the headwaters and creek arms. Headwaters and creeks may be murky, but the main body of water can remain quite clear throughout the entire "flow-through cycle."

If you are planning a trip to a reservoir, it pays to call ahead and find out what the water conditions are. A cold, rainy spring in one of those Georgia red clay reservoirs can mean water the color and consistency of tomato soup. Cold turbid water like that always make for tough bass fishing.

3. Fertility — Fertility is the result of a complex interaction between a reservoir's water source, the mineral makeup of the surrounding terrain, and man-made contributions from fertilizers and septic tanks.

A small, shallow reservoir with a slow flow-through rate and many homes around its shoreline could be very fertile due to surface runoff and leaching from septic tanks. Often, however, the reservoir's water source plays the most important role in determining overall fertility.

Lake Sidney Lanier, a 20-year-old highland reservoir in Georgia, has considerable development around it, but, as a whole, the lake is not extremely fertile. In fact, the water is quite clear and clean, since the source is the runoff from the highlands and foothills of the Appalachian Mountains. Lake Eufaula (Walter F. George), on the other hand, is a 14-year-old flatland reservoir in Alabama-Georgia. It drains the soft bottomlands of the Chatahoochee River. Consequently, it is highly fertile, supporting tons of shad and rough fish. The water also is usually "off-color."

4. Water Temperature — As with natural lakes, water temperature in the reservoirs is determined by a variety of factors. Shallow flatland reservoirs can get so warm that cool water species, like the smallmouth bass, will not survive. On the other hand, deep highland reservoirs often support both smallmouth and walleye. Some reservoirs develop thermoclines, while others do not. On a plateau reservoir, wind can effect not only water temperature, but the location of the entire food chain, from insects to top-line predators.

Depending on their geographical location, some reservoirs will develop ice cover; others never cool below 50° F. Even in the northern climes, there may be open water all year round in sections of a reservoir near a warm water discharge. Discharges from nuclear or fossil fuel power plants can keep fair-sized sections of water free of ice and often will attract schools of gamefish.

Sangchris, in central Illinois, ices over during a hard winter; that is, two of its three fingers ice over. The center one, due to warm water discharge from a power plant, permits a year-round fishery. Some years ago, the discharge finger was closed to angling. The reason given was that too many fish were bunching up in one place and becoming much too easy to catch.

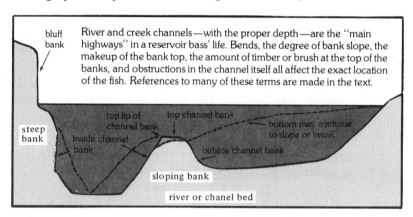

bluff bank

River and creek channels—with the proper depth—are the "main highways" in a reservoir bass' life. Bends, the degree of bank slope, the makeup of the bank top, the amount of timber or brush at the top of the banks, and obstructions in the channel itself all affect the exact location of the fish. References to many of these terms are made in the text.

steep bank

top lip of channel bank

top channel bank

bottom may continue to slope or break

inside channel bank

outside channel bank

sloping bank

river or chanel bed

The Reservoir Classification System

To attempt a classification system of all the reservoirs in this country is an immense task. Luckily, such a system depends on the geological "lay of the land." If you were to drive cross-country from New York City to Los Angeles, you would immediately become aware of how the land changes.

Taking a number of cross sections of the United States, you would see that the terrain is either low, sort of swampy or marshy, or rather flat in the old flood plain regions of the large river systems. In other places, the terrain is hilly — not high ridges but simply a series of rolling hills.

In other areas, mountains and highland ridges jut up from the earth's surface. In the plains of the Midwest, west of the Mississippi, are the high plains. Just west of them is an immense plateau that lifts step-like across the mid-section of the country. This plateau is adjacent to the rugged Rocky Mountains.

All these changes in terrain provide a clear-cut basis by which to classify water impounded within each of these landforms. We have labeled our classification system as follows:

1. Flatland
2. Highland
3. Hill-land
4. Plateau
5. Canyon

In the five sections that follow, we hope to give you an idea of what it is like to fish these different classifications of reservoirs. Such a brief summary cannot answer all your fishing questions, but it will provide the begining point for further analysis. We have substituted pictures and charts for narrative to simplify matters. In each case, we have also given an important fishing tip from Bobby Murray, a man who knows reservoirs and their fishing potential better than anyone.

Flatland Impoundments

These impoundments are easily identified by taking note of their overall shape and the makeup of their shorelines. Flatland reservoirs were constructed in river flood plains and, consequently, the surrounding land probably was utilized as some sort of crop land. In general, these reservoirs are very shallow, covering huge flats with some gentle rises or depressions. High, sharp shorelines are rare. Instead, the submerged basin tapers to the shoreline.

The main body of the lake covers vast areas of formerly cultivated land — the old flood plain. The central section of this type of reservoir tends to be the widest portion, but may only have a maximum depth of about 25 feet, and that's in the river channel itself.

Some examples of flatland impoundments are Walter F. George (Eufaula), Ala.-Ga.; Dardanell, Ark.; Millwood, Ark.; Lake Seminole, Fla-Ga.; Carlyle, Ill.; Rend, Ill.; Monroe, Ind.; Cheney, Kan.; Barkley, Ky.-Tenn.; Falcon, Mex.-Tex.; Ross Barnett, Miss.; Greenwood, N.J.-N.Y.; Pymatuning, Ohio-Pa.; Eufaula, Okla.; Robert S. Kerr, Okla.; Santee-Cooper, S.C.,; and Tawakoni, Tex.

Bobby Murray's Flatland Reservoir Tip

"In the early summer of 1974, I got a call from an old fishing buddy of mine who lived near Santee-Cooper (Marion-Moultrie), a very famous flatland reservoir. Tommy Salesberry of Summerville, S.C., phoned and said that the BIG fish were really moving on the creek channel banks. I immediately packed my bag, loaded my boat, and headed for Charleston.

"After hours of hard driving, I arrived late at night, but Tommy and I still had time to form a game plan for the next morning's fishing trip.

"Now the fish he had found previously were lying in 12 to 18 feet of water along a winding creek merged with the main channel of the Cooper River. Adjacent to the creek channel were the flats so typical on this type of reservoir. The water was 'off-color' from the spring rains and the consequent runoff from this flat terrain.

"We started off by using black slip-rigged plastic worms on 20-lb. test line. Fairly stiff-action casting rods and level-wind reels naturally had to be used with this heavy line.

"We positioned our boat along the banks of a small ditch that tied into the creek near the spot where the creek finally fed into the main channel of the Cooper River. We had previously marked off the channel with buoys so we could actually see all the bends and turns in the small, deep ditch and creek.

"We were working "down creek" (toward the main river channel) with our trolling motor. That morning we immediately caught several fish in the three- to five-pound class on the plastic worm. But later, as the sun got higher, the action slowed, so we moved off the creek channel and started following the shallower connector ditches and found some small cypress trees.

"Here, Tommy and I switched to black and yellow spinnerbaits. We pitched our lures underneath the trees' overhanging limbs, getting them as close to the trunk as possible, and we found the super kind of action we all dream about. In about 45 minutes, Tommy and I had three fish that weighed in the ten-pound class as well as several others in the seven- to eight-pound bracket.

"These lunkers were lying very tight against the trunks of these small cypress trees. If we could successfully cast under the low limbs and hit the tree trunks themselves, we could then momentarily stop and let the lure flutter back to the boat. Most fish struck just as the lure righted itself and the blades began to spin.

"That day we caught and released many five- and six-pound fish. At the boat dock, later that day, we weighed in a ten-fish limit that totaled 75 pounds!"

FLATLAND IMPOUNDMENT

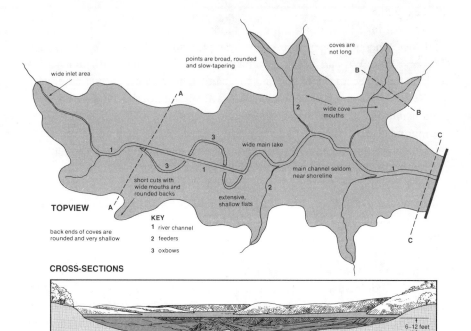

coves are
not long

points are broad, rounded
and slow-tapering

B

wide inlet area

A

2

wide cove
mouths

B

C

3

wide main lake

1

1

main channel seldom
near shoreline

1

3

3

1

short cuts with
wide mouths and
rounded backs

2

TOPVIEW A

extensive,
shallow flats

C

back ends of coves are
rounded and very shallow

KEY

1 river channel

2 feeders

3 oxbows

CROSS-SECTIONS

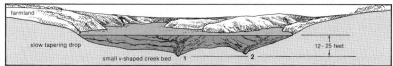

3   1   levee

6-12 feet

Cross-section A

farmland

slow tapering drop

small v-shaped creek bed   1   2

12 - 25 feet

Cross-section B

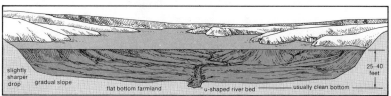

slightly
sharper
drop   gradual slope

flat bottom farmland   u-shaped river bed   usually clean bottom

25-40
feet

Cross-section C

Edwin Lee Hoff

Flatland Reservoir Characteristics

Water Clarity	Off-color
Bottom Content	Black soil, mud flats and some hard clay.
Average Big Bass	15 lbs.
Predator Forage	Shad, bluegill, frogs, and fresh water eels.
Water Level Fluctuation	2 to 8 feet
Depth	6-12 feet upstream 25-40 feet at dam
Main River Channel Characteristics	Seldom near shoreline, meanders, altered by dredging, and straightened with dikes and levees. Trees and brush along banks. Oxbows present, where channel has been straightened.
Feeder Stream	Creeks or ditches, usually less than 20 feet wide. 1-6 feet deep with V-shaped bed.
Cuts and Coves	Short and shallow with small feeder creeks running through wide mouths. Short cuts and wide mouths, with rounded backs. May contain weeds, brush, and timber.
Points	Broad, rounded, and slow-tapering. Some with brush, but usually lacking in timber.
Shoreline	Mainly long, slow tapers. Steeper bluff banks on rare occasions.
Brush, Timber and Vegetation	Standing timber common in main lake. Primarily cypress and willow. Brush in backs of coves. Moss is primary vegetation.
Common Man-made Features	Dams, roadbeds, causeways, ponds, levees, building foundations, rip-rap and cemeteries.
Main Fish Attractors	Deep pools created by oxbows; ditches, especially those with lip-like mounds where oxbows connect to main river channel; outside portion of willows; cypress trees; moss beds; man-made features.
Type of Dam and Purpose	Earth; some with small concrete spillways. Flood control and irrigation.

Highland Impoundments

The term 'highland' is somewhat ambiguous. These reservoirs are usually dammed in foothills where some narrow ravine provides an easy closing point. The water is backed up in areas that border on the highlands of low mountain ranges. In fact, we almost called them "foothill" impoundments, but we thought that this term could be misleading. So, if the impoundments that fill the bottomlands of a slow, rolling terrain are a hill-land type, then the next category would logically be highland.

These low mountains are mostly confined to the eastern half of the country, primarily the Appalachian, Boston, Ouachita, Ozark, and Cumberland ranges. Here, clear water, rock outcroppings, and steep-banked, timber-covered hills, and bluffs mingle to produce impoundments of outstanding beauty. The waters of such impoundments harbor multiple species and are home to the Kentucky bass, as well as largemouth, smallmouth, walleye, sauger, and, in some places, trout, and more recently, stripers.

Some examples include Lewis Smith, Ala.; Ouachita, Ark.; Bull Shoals, Ark.-Mo.; Shasta, Calif.; Pine Flat, Calif.; Oroville, Calif.; Don Pedro, Calif.; Sidney Lanier, Ga.; Cumberland, Ky.; Stockton, Mo.; Table Rock, Mo.-Ark.; Hopatcong, N.J.; Broken Bow, Okla.; Center Hill, Tenn.; Norris, Tenn.; and Amistad, Tex.-Mex.

Bobby Murray's Highland Reservoir Tip

"In the spring of 1973, I was fishing with sales rep Dave Hughes, then with the Daisy-Heddon company. We were looking for bass on 18,220-acre Center Hill in central Tennessee.

"It was during the spawning period. The lake already had experienced a majority of its seasonal springtime rainfall, and the lake was at a high level and still 'on the rise.' Dave and I were looking for largemouth or smallmouth. It was early April and the water was very clear in the main body of the reservoir, but it had just a slight bit of stain in the arms of the feeder creeks.

"Spring in the high country brings out a lot of blossoms. There was quite a bit of pollen on the water, indicating that the water was sufficiently warm and would continue to stay so.

"We were headquartering out of the Cove Hollow resort area down near the dam. At first we tried several of the shallower main river channel banks that crossed open water, but had only limited success. Dave and I then started looking for fish in the creek coves. In the Indian Creek area, which is a very long arm down near the downstream third, we found a spot that was protected from the cool, prevailing northwest winds that whip up occasionally at this time of the year and drive the bass down or out.

"The water had risen out of its normal winter pool about three feet, so we found some green brush and the bases of cedar trees in three to four feet of water in the back ends of these small protected coves. Wherever we found small flooded brush, we also found fish. Protected coves tend to have the warmest water at that time of the year and consequently will 'call up" spawning fish faster than other sites. These sites afford adequate spawning areas and holding places for both largemouth and smallmouth bass. Spinnerbaits and slip-rigged plastic worms are standard bass lures. We used them and they were effective.

"We caught most of the largemouth on the plastic worm and most smallmouth on the spinner baits. The plastic worms were used on light-action rods with $\frac{1}{8}$-oz. jigheads or slip sinkers, dressed with a 3- to $5\frac{1}{2}$-inch purple or green worm. We fished these slowly across the bottom with very small hops.

"The spinners were $\frac{3}{8}$-oz. tandems. They combined a #3 Colorado blade with a #6 Indiana blade to give the bait enough torque to vibrate well. Chartreuse or green-chartreuse combinations seemed to work best.

"Dave and I ended up catching 40 to 60 bass a day, both smallmouth and largemouth. They ranged in size from $2\frac{1}{2}$ to $5\frac{1}{2}$ pounds. The smallmouths, however, were larger. The largemouths ranged only from $1\frac{1}{2}$ to $3\frac{1}{2}$ pounds."

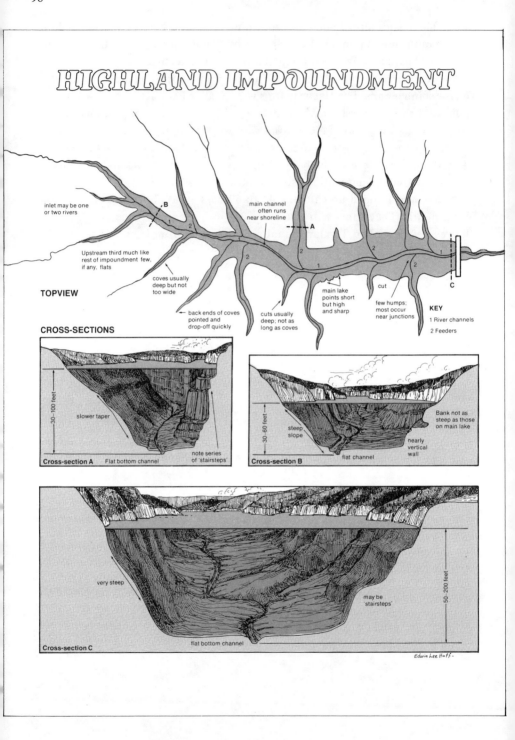

HIGHLAND IMPOUNDMENT

inlet may be one
or two rivers

.B

main channel
often runs
near shoreline

--- **A**

Upstream third much like
rest of impoundment few,
if any, flats

TOPVIEW

coves usually
deep but not
too wide

back ends of coves
pointed and
drop-off quickly

cuts usually
deep; not as
long as coves

main lake
points short
but high
and sharp

few humps;
most occur
near junctions

cut

C

KEY

1 River channels

2 Feeders

CROSS-SECTIONS

30-100 feet

slower taper

note series
of 'stairsteps'

Cross-section A   Flat bottom channel

30-60 feet

steep
slope

Bank not as
steep as those
on main lake

nearly
vertical
wall

flat channel

Cross-section B

very steep

may be
'stairsteps'

50-200 feet

flat bottom channel

Cross-section C

Edwin Lee Huff -

Highland Reservoir Characteristics

Water Clarity	Typically clear
Bottom Content	Sand, clay, and rock (usually shale or limestone)
Average Big Bass	12 lbs.
Predator Forage	Shad, crayfish, freshwater eel, and salamanders
Water Level Fluctuation	12 to 20 feet
Depth	60-200 feet, depending on size
Main River Channel Characteristics	Often runs near the shoreline. Flat channel with steep walls. Not dredged. Many creek and river junctions, but often too deep for bass use.
Feeder Stream	Rock bottoms. Some are intermittent (i.e., carry water only after heavy rains).
Cuts and Coves	Coves are often deep and long, but not very wide. Brush and timber common. Sharp rocky points. Deep cuts not as long as coves. Some steep-walled, some rather flat.
Points	Short, but very sharp and steep. Mostly rocky, but some with trees or brush.
Shoreline	Varies from heavily timbered with moderate slope to cliffs. In some cases "stair step" ledges.
Brush, Timber and Vegetation	Timber composed mainly of hardwoods, pine, or cedar. Brush varies regionally. Moss or weeds not common.
Common Man-made Features	Same as hill-land reservoir, except causeways, bridges, and rip-rap not as common.
Main Fish Attractors	"Stair step" shorelines, man-made features, timber and brush, shallower river channel banks, some points.
Type of Dam and Purpose	Earth or concrete, multi-purpose; power and irrigation and flood control.

Hill-land Impoundments

The hill-land reservoir is the most structurally varied impoundment of all our classifications, both in terms of bottom configuration and content. In these reservoirs there is plenty of shallow water and a great deal of relatively deeper water. Bottom content can include hard clay, sandy clay, loam, and even some patches of rock and sand. Vegetation runs the spectrum from large to small trees and bushes of all sizes and varieties. Humps, hills, flats, sharp drops, winding riverbeds, large and small creeks, and creek arms all call for the greatest flexibility in any angler's approach.

The earth's crust is subject to the movement of the plates, faults, rifts that lift or settle portions of the crust. Wind, water, and warming and cooling of the surface also alter the landscape. In certain regions of the country, hillocks are formed. In other places, rivers course through valleys that formerly held much wider and deeper waterways.

The result of impoundment construction under these conditions is variety. A hill-land reservoir is deeper than the flatland type, but since it's bounded by hills, it is not as wide. The original terrain of these valley impoundments was not farmed to the extent that the land under the flatland type was. Consequently, vegetation is much more abundant.

While difficult to regionalize, this class of impoundment is rather easy to identify. Some examples include Felsenthal, Ark.; Shelbyville, Ill.; D'Arbonne, La.; Toledo Bend, La.-Tex.; Sam Rayburn, Tex.; Livingston, Tex.; Palestine, Tex.; and Lake of the Pines, Tex.

Bobby Murray's Hill-land Reservoir Tip

"Early in 1976, Bobby Harter, a fellow promotion man for Cordell Tackle Co., and I were fishing Toledo Bend on the Louisiana-Texas border, trying to establish a winter pattern for largemouth bass. We were going to entertain some tackle buyers and wanted to be 'on fish' when they arrived.

"At first we found the fishing tough. The spots we thought would surely produce were dead. It was late January, historically a tough fishing time on this type of impoundment. We had anticipated a pre-spawn situation where the fish would be moving up the 15- to 18-feet-deep flats. We figured to catch our fish on spinnerbaits and Big Os, cranking them slowly along and over the tree tops and channel edges. However, this didn't pay off.

"After a day and a half of beating the water, we had to change our game plan. By working down the channels, we discovered that the fish had not migrated into their shallower pre-spawn sites. Most fish were still holding a deep, cold-water period pattern. However, some fish had started moving out into the deep river channel.

"Toledo Bend has a slow slope from the shore. The deep water is in the channel itself so the channel might be a very long way from the actual shoreline. Now this part of the river channel was lined with one particular type of vegetation, old ironwood trees. These are small trees about 18 to 20 feet high with very gnarled limbs. At times they are perfect bass cover. These types of trees mainly grew in the old pre-flooded high points or along bluffs on the river channel.

"Bobby and I found that by casting a jig and eel or grub to the top of the bank and letting the lure free-fall off the ledge and into the channel, we would get most of our strikes. For several days we worked this pattern and discovered we could more than triple or quadruple our catch if we let a spinnerbait free-fall from the top of the bank into the channel. Our strikes were coming in the 25- to 30-foot-drop range while the top of the bank was from 12 to 18 feet deep. The fish were lying from four to ten feet down from the top of the bank along the inside channel banks. Because hill-land reservoirs have such an abundance of usable structure, a good fisherman must be well versed in more than one presentation method."

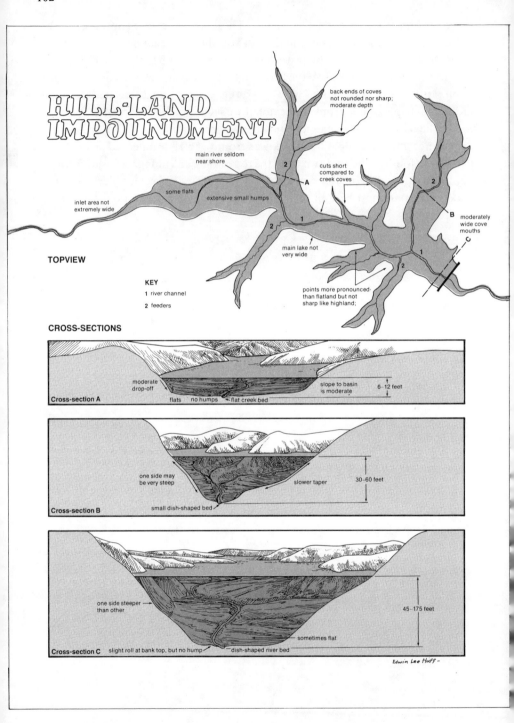

HILL·LAND IMPOUNDMENT

TOPVIEW

back ends of coves
not rounded nor sharp;
moderate depth

main river seldom
near shore

cuts short
compared to
creek coves

A

some flats

extensive small humps

inlet area not
extremely wide

2

2

B

moderately
wide cove
mouths

C

1

main lake not
very wide

2

1

2

points more pronounced
than flatland but not
sharp like highland;

KEY

1 river channel

2 feeders

CROSS-SECTIONS

moderate
drop-off

slope to basin
is moderate

6–12 feet

Cross-section A   flats   no humps   flat creek bed

one side may
be very steep

slower taper

30–60 feet

Cross-section B   small dish-shaped bed

one side steeper
than other

45–175 feet

sometimes flat

Cross-section C   slight roll at bank top, but no hump   dish-shaped river bed

Edwin Lee Huff –

Hill-land Reservoir Characteristics

Water Clarity	Slightly off-color
Bottom Content	Sand, clay, loam, some mud flats, and extensive small humps.
Average Big Bass	10 lbs.
Predator Forage	Shad, crayfish, bluegill, freshwater shrimp.
Water Level Fluctuation	2 to 10 feet
Depth	45-175 feet, depending on region
Main River Channel Characteristics	Near center of reservoir. Riverbed is usually rounded, not dredged. Runs fairly straight.
Feeder Stream	Most have a distinct channel with sloping banks. Often brush or tree-lined.
Cuts and Coves	Coves are deep towards the dam and may have large timber stands. Upstream they are much like flatland coves. Cuts typically short.
Points	Rounded, usually with standing or cut timber. In a few instances large boulders.
Shoreline	Fast-sloping to 7-12 feet of water, then gradual slope to main river channel.
Brush, Timber and Vegetation	Brush and timber in coves. Moss on shallow flats in main reservoir. Weed growth greater than any other reservoir type in the southland.
Common Man-made Features	Dam, rip-rap, high lines and pipe lines, fence rows, rock piles, road beds, cemeteries, drainage ditches, railroad beds, building foundations, and marinas.
Main Fish Attractors	Shoreline points, humps, brush, timber, and man-made features.
Type of Dam and Purpose	Earth, some with small concrete spillways. Flood control

Plateau Impoundments

In the high plains and low plateau regions that run along the Rockies and in the lower plateau valleys that lie within the Rocky Mountain range, we find a class of impoundments that differ dramatically from preceding types. Even within this class, bottom makeup can vary greatly; only basic shape is alike.

While the flatland, hill-land, and highland impoundments are favorable bass habitat, most plateau impoundments are just not that hospitable. They are primarily constructed for irrigation, so the water exchange rate is fantastic. These large waters can experience a complete transfusion in a matter of a week, so there are tremendous fluctuations in water levels. These conditions make it tough for fish to survive. In addition, the regions where such impoundments are found are lacking in cover. In the high plains (but not on the rocky plateaus), erosion and siltation is considerable. In some areas, forage such as shad cannot survive in some of the seasonally low-water temperatures. All these factors combine to produce tough going for a nest-builder like the largemouth bass.

As a rule, a pleateau reservoir is big. Some of the nation's largest reservoirs fall within this class. However, there are some small impoundments exhibiting plateau characteristics. These are mainly found in states like Colorado, Idaho, and Washington.

Typical plateau reservoirs include Roosevelt, Ariz.; Clear, Calif.; John Martin, Colo.; Ft. Peck, Mont.; McConuaghy, Neb.; Garrison, N.D.; Oahe, S.D., Meredith, Tex.; Nasworthy, Tex.; and Banks, Wash.

Bobby Murray's Plateau Reservoir Tip

"In 1975, I got together with Don Lee, a tackle rep from Sam Ramon, Calif., on 24,900-acre Banks Lake. It is located on the high plateau desert region of central Washington. Banks is a unique reservoir. Its water is actually pumped up into the lake from the Colorado River rather than just flowing naturally into it. The water then flows down some 120 miles more and is diverted back into the Columbia River. The lake itself gradually slopes to a shallow end as the water leaves the reservoir, unlike most reservoirs which operate just the reverse. But Banks' purpose is irrigation for the entire valley below the reservoir.

"It was June and the snow was starting to melt in the high mountain peaks surrounding this plateau region. After checking with some local people, we found that the bass fishing was supposed to be very slow. But Don and I went out anyway.

"On our way to the lake, the road passed close to perhaps 15 or 20 miles of shoreline. I spotted a number of good steep banks that I thought might hold some fish. As soon as we launched our boat, I headed immediately to this area, but we didn't do very well. We caught some scattered fish in the two- to three-pound class, but by noon, we had only six fish in our live well.

"Moving back up the lake, I saw there were some small flats that had been built up where the water was being pumped into the reservoir. There were little humplike walls built around these flat areas to break the force of the water flow and reduce erosion. Here the flats and walls combined to create eddies, not unlike those typical of river fishing. The flow of water behind these short walls created a slack water pocket. I felt this would be a fish magnet if any were around. And here is where Don and I found the concentration of fish we were seeking.

"They were lying in six to ten feet of water, holding tight against the walls that produced the eddies. Most of the fish were caught at the time the water was being pumped into the reservoir at the maximum rate. When the water *was not flowing,* we had minimal action. The more water was coming in, the more fish seemed to move up to these sites to feed and the better they fed. I'm sure that they were just like a fish that migrates up a river to a dam during high water. These fish were seeking the flow, but in strange circumstances.

"We were using ultralight tackle with six-pound-test line since the water was extremely clear at this time of year. We tied on a ¼-oz. jig-head with Cordell's small olive-green grub. And it worked like a charm! We also caught some bass on a medium-running Big-O in the perch pattern. However, we took more fish on the grub.

"This particular reservoir has no shad. It's just too cold and the fish mainly feed on yellow perch. I think this is the main reason they hit the green grubs and the perch-scaled Big-O better than other colors or patterns we tried."

106

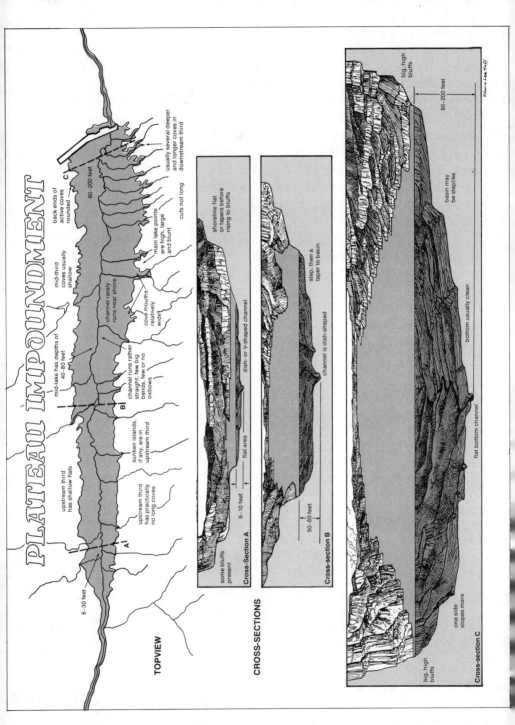

PLATEAU IMPOUNDMENT

TOPVIEW

6-30 feet

upstream third has shallow flats

upstream third has practically no long coves

mid-lake has depths of 40-80 feet

sunken islands, if any, are in upstream third

channel runs rather straight; few big bends, few or no oxbows

channel rarely runs near shore

cove mouths relatively wide

mid-third coves usually shallow

main lake points are high, large and blunt

cuts not long

80-200 feet

back ends of active coves rounded

usually several deeper and longer coves in downstream third

CROSS-SECTIONS

Cross-Section A

some bluffs present

flat area

6-10 feet

dish- or V-shaped channel

shoreline flat or tapers before rising to bluffs

Cross-section B

50-60 feet

channel is dish-shaped

step, then a taper to basin

Cross-section C

big, high bluffs

one side slopes more

flat bottom channel

bottom usually clean

basin may be steplike

big, high bluffs

80-200 feet

Edwin J. Keppe

Plateau Reservoir Characteristics

Water Clarity	Clear to off-color
Bottom Content	Varies from rock to sand or silt, depending on region. Bottom usually clean with upper 1/3 composed of shallow flats.
Average Big Bass	5 lbs.
Predator Forage	Shad and salamanders
Water Level Fluctuation	5 to 25 feet
Depth	50-200 feet, depending on location
Main River Channel Characteristics	Center of reservoir, quite straight, usually not deep, with flat bed. Banks generally clean, but some with brush present. Downstream third is generally too deep for bass.
Feeder Stream	Little gullies or washouts from flash floods. Main feeders have high walls and most prevalent on downstream third. Short and wide at mouth.
Cuts and Coves	Coves have flat basins; short and usually wide in relation to length. Some brush present. Short cuts with high steep walls in downstream third. Not as prevalent upstream.
Points	Vary from very sharp to well rounded
Shoreline	Gradually sloping upstream. Steep bluffs downstream.
Brush, Timber and Vegetation	Quite limited. Some present in backs of coves. Vegetation in upstream third.
Common Man-made Features	Dams, roadbeds, marinas, spillways. Usually limited due to low population density where plateau reservoirs are constructed.
Main Fish Attractors	Points, wherever they are found. Brush, timber, vegetation and man-made features.
Type of Dam and Purpose	Earth, with small concrete spillways. Mainly irrigation.

Canyon Impoundments

All canyon impoundments are impounded by huge concrete dams, since earthen dams would not be adequate to hold back the massive pounds-per-square-inch of pressure exerted on the dams' faces. In the west, some of these dams are monuments, both in the engineering and national park sense. Hoover Dam, which backs up 115,000-acre Lake Mead, is a national recreation area.

Canyon impoundments are unique in many ways. It's true they are the deepest of all our impoundment classifications, but that's only the beginning. Water clarity, structural configuration, and bottom content combine to place these reservoirs in a distinctive category. They are sparsely vegetated and encased in rock. Despite the clear water and lack of vegetation, carp and other rough fish species thrive. Species such as trout counterbalance a bass fishery, making for an extensive two-story fishery. All in all, canyon impoundments are quite interesting bodies of water offering a distinct challenge to any angler.

Some canyon reservoirs are Lake Havasu, Ariz.-Calif.; Mohave, Ariz.-Nev.; Lake Mead, Nev.-Ariz.; Lake Powell, Utah-Ariz.; and Flaming Gorge, Wyo.-Utah.

Bobby Murray's Canyon Reservoir Tip

"In early April, 1976, I was fishing with Elliott Wolfe, a sporting goods dealer from Salt Lake City, Utah, on Lake Powell. We headquartered at the Bull Frog Marina near the middle of Lake Powell so we could travel up or down the reservoir, depending on conditions.

"Elliott was helping me try to establish some type of pattern. The previous day we had found a few scattered fish suspended against some of the sheer cliffs, but we couldn't find any decent concentration of fish. The next morning we got into our boat and started up the reservoir. We were trying to find some broken rock lips. Elliott told me there was a spot called Knowles Canyon 15 or 20 miles away that had this type of fractured rock. Once we got back into this feeder cove, we found that we had not only some broken rock but also underwater vegetation in the form of old cedar and cottonwood trees.

"Previously, we had caught a few bass on spinnerbaits, so we tried them here. But we were not getting the depth out of them that we thought we needed. It was early spring and the fish were just about pre-spawn. I began using a ¼-oz. black jig with a three-inch black trailer — sort of black on black. Immediately, I began catching fish, not only more fish but larger ones than we had caught on the spinners. By using six-lb.-test line and allowing the jig to slowly free fall down the sides of the rock, I was coaxing some lunkers out from the deeper rocks.

"Elliott also started using the same type of lure combination and began picking off a few fish. It wasn't long, however, before we realized that the number of strikes we got was determined not only by the presence of the rocks. We noticed that the sunny side of a large broken rock was almost barren of fish, but the shady side was something else. To coax a strike we had to cast the lures to the back or off to the side of the rock — in the shade. There was no doubt: the shady side of the rocks held the fish. We might catch four or five off one large boulder.

"Most of these rocks were the size of an automobile or even larger and were 15 to 18 feet off the bottom. By letting the jig free fall along the sides of these rocks, we would get just a small 'peck.' This was the signal to set the hook immediately and try to move the fish away from the rock. We caught very few fish we could actually see. Most bass were good size — in the three- to six-pound bracket. If they got into the crevices, POW! They'd break the line.

"Water color was extremely clear. The bottom was visible to 50 feet. When we set the hook, we could immediately see the fish in the water and were able to watch all its movements. Six- or eight-lb.-test is the maximum for this type of situation. In this clear water, we kept the boat positioned with the sun directly behind us so we could cast into the shadow areas. The sun and reflection of the sun tends to blind the fish to the angler's presence. We always try to attack from the sun to the shadow areas. This is a good trick to remember on gin-clear waters.

"Anyway, on this particular day, we caught fish all day long, early or late — it made no difference. The larger fish tended to hole up in the eight- to 12-foot range. We worked the 20-foot depth but this didn't give us any bigger fish — or any more.

"In Lake Powell, a big bass is a six- to seven and a half-pounder. The lake record is in the ten-pound class, but an eight- or nine-pounder is a rarity. Most of the fish, however, are very healthy and short — they look like footballs. And they provide a good battle."

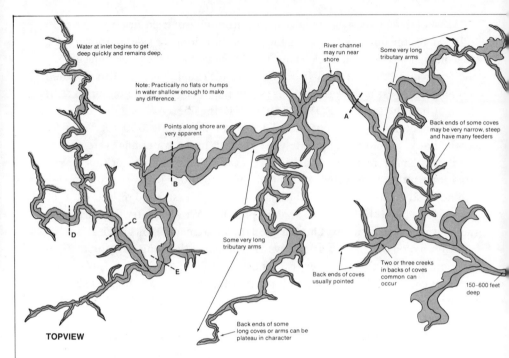

Water at inlet begins to get deep quickly and remains deep.

River channel may run near shore

Some very long tributary arms

Note: Practically no flats or humps in water shallow enough to make any difference.

Back ends of some coves may be very narrow, steep and have many feeders

Points along shore are very apparent

A

B

Some very long tributary arms

Back ends of coves usually pointed

Two or three creeks in backs of coves common can occur

150–600 feet deep

C

D

E

Back ends of some long coves or arms can be plateau in character

TOPVIEW

CANYON IMPOUNDMENT

CROSS-SECTIONS

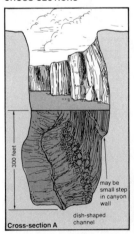

300 feet

may be small step in canyon wall

dish-shaped channel

Cross-section A

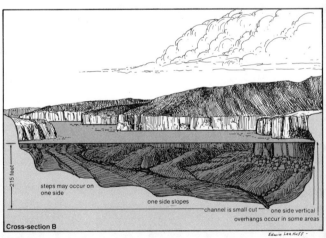

215 feet

steps may occur on one side

one side slopes

channel is small cut

one side vertical overhangs occur in some areas

Cross-section B

Edwin Lee Huff

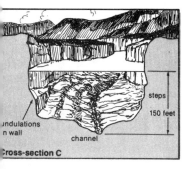

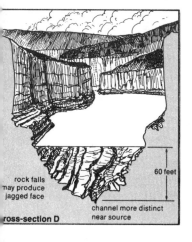

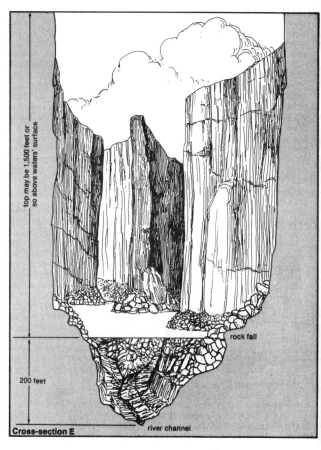

In canyon impoundments, parts of a solid rock wall may break away and fall toward the basin. On such waters, this is the "spot of spots" for bass because it provides cover in the clear water. Such sites attract baitfish and spawning fish. Although suspension is sometimes necessary for bass, they will, when possible, select sites as this one in canyon reservoirs.

Canyon Reservoir Characteristics

Water Clarity	Very clear
Bottom Content	Mainly rock, some sand and gravel in back coves.
Average Big Bass	10 lbs.
Predator Forage	Shad, crayfish (some canyon reservoirs have no shad)
Water Level Fluctuation	10 to 150 feet
Depth	500-600 feet downstream; a few feet to 40 feet near inlet.
Main River Channel Characteristics	May run near shore. Very distinct, dish-shaped gorge upstream. Less distinct downstream. Generally too deep to be used by bass.
Feeder Stream	Very long creeks and small rivers. Up to 40-60 miles long and shaped like main channel.
Cuts and Coves	Almost all coves are fed by creek or river. Some have two or three creeks. Some "dry-wet" with wide mouths can be very long.
Points	Very distinct along sheer walls of reservoir and downstream portions of coves. Most composed of jagged rock, can rise 1200 feet above water and drop 300 feet below water.
Shoreline	Mainly sheer cliff with some broken rock slopes and solid rock faces or mesas.
Brush, Timber and Vegetation	Some sage brush or other scrub vegetation. Cottonwood trees and some highland cedars at extreme backs of coves.
Common Man-made Features	Very few; some marinas and dams.
Main Fish Attractors	Points, broken rocks on shoreline, shadows or points or cliffs, cedar trees, man-made features, schools of suspended shad.
Type of Dam and Purpose	Concrete. Mostly hydroelectric power, some irrigation and flood control.

CHAPTER 7-A
Case Study: Largemouth Bass in Hill-land Reservoirs

Flooded forests, rivers where water seldom flows, and roads that are traveled by fish instead of cars — sounds fantastic, but all are common features in the depths of a hill-land reservoir. The hill-land reservoir offers the greatest variety of structure, both natural and man-made, of any impoundment in our classification system. In its upper reaches, a hill-land reservoir has features not unlike flatland and lowland impoundments. In some of the main body and lower areas, hill-lands often resemble highland reservoirs. Because the hill-land impoundment usually covers fertile farm land, there are rolling open areas, areas of thick timber with distinct timberlines, roadbeds, culverts, secondary creek channels, old farm buildings, cemeteries, and a wide variety of other man-made structure. By learning to recognize fish-holding structure on a hill-land reservoir, anglers can easily adapt fishing tactics to other bodies of water. It is for this reason that we have selected a typical hill-land impoundment for our reservoir case study on largemouth bass.

Timber, Timber . . . Everywhere

If there is one trait that typifies a hill-land reservoir, it is flooded brush and timber. Though fish will frequently relate to creek and river channels and to varieties of man-made structure, to effectively fish a hill-land reservoir, anglers must learn to fish in timber. For those unfamiliar with sunken trees, timberlines, and log jams, this can be a frustrating experience. But with a little practice and lots of patience, tactics can be mastered that will pay dividends well worth the investment. One of the presentation sections of this chapter will assist novices in the development of skills that will help in "tackling the timber."

Though some anglers view flooded timber with disdain, the wise angler realizes not only that fish use this structure in their daily migrations and feeding patterns, but that different types of trees are an excellent clue to the original lay of the land. Because of the different ecological niches that different trees filled before the land was flooded, it is possible to read some bottom contours just by recognizing different trees. Cypress trees grow on low swampy ground, so cypress treetops are a sure sign of lowland depressions and old sloughs. Willows usually indicate old creek and river channels, with the smaller trees outlining the secondary channels and the larger ones defining the main river channel. Hardwoods like oak and maple grow on the flat plain just off the channels. Pines, which after a few years resemble pole timber, originally grew on hills and higher ground. And ironwood trees typically grew on the highest land adjacent to the river and creek channels. Because of its incredible density, ironwood does not decay as quickly as other woods and its branches provide excellent cover for bass year after year. It may sound from the foregoing like one needs to be a botanist to recognize these "clues" to bottom topography, but a few trips on a reservoir are all that is needed to distinguish the different types of fish-holding timber.

Lunker Haven Hill-land Reservoir

The average natural lake is small enough that most anglers can quickly learn the entire body of water and the seasonal locations of gamefish. Most reservoirs, on the other hand, are so immense that they tend to boggle the imagination. In this case study we will look at one section of a hill-land reservoir, a small section of the main reservoir, and one creek arm. Here we will be looking at the *general movements* of bass, that is, how most of the fish in this section of water respond to changes in the calendar periods. It's important to remember that, because of the tremendous size of many reservoirs, fish may be in different calendar periods at the same time. Bass in the warmer upper reaches may be through spawning before fish near the dam have begun. Another important consideration is that different schools of bass behave quite differently. One school of largemouth may cover a lot of ground in a year, while another group may spend the entire season in one area of one creek arm. In the case study that follows we will try to focus on how the majority of bass respond and will leave small isolated schools to their own idiosyncracies.

In this case study we will also limit the number and types of structures used to illustrate seasonal movements. An investigation of all the varieties of structure in hill-land reservoirs would take a separate book. The general locations listed

Brush like this is a common occurrence in shallow creeks and coves, particularly during the first few years of a reservoir's formation.

below provide an excellent starting place for locating masses of fish. From there, anglers can go exploring the more isolated schools of bass and discover their private "Hawg Heaven."

Area A A timbered point that intersects with a secondary creek channel. Usually these points have well defined timber lines.

Area B Isolated sunken islands that "top out" between 20 and 30 feet.

Area C A secondary creek channel that leads from the main river channel to a creek arm or cove

    C-1 A sharp "U" bend in a creek channel, where the creek doubles back on itself and forms a "saddle."

    C-2 A sharp turn in an otherwise gently meandering channel.

    C-3 The intersection of a creek channel with the main river.

Area D A sunken roadbed that runs from the shoreline to a depth of 40 feet.

    D-1 A culvert, where a roadbed crosses an old stream bed.

    D-2 A roadbed intersecting a secondary creek channel.

    D-3 A bridge over the old river channel.

Area E The main river channel.

Pre-Spawn	50° F - 59° F
Spawn	60° F - 66° F
Post-Spawn	67° F - 72° F

Springtime Locational Patterns

Largemouth bass on hill-land reservoirs follow a seasonal pattern typical of largemouth behavior on most reservoirs. In the spring, fish begin to move from the river channels in the main reservoir to the secondary channels and into the coves and creek arms. This movement begins when water temperatures move into the high 40's and low 50's. Initially, location will focus on the main creek mouths, but as water temperature reaches the upper 50's the bass will move up the secondary channels toward their spawning grounds. Pre-spawn bass are school fish, and during the early pre-spawn these schools will be tightly packed. The first stages of the pre-spawn migration occur in 20 to 30 feet of water; at the end of this period the fish will be in the 10- to 15-foot depths.

As the fish move to their actual spawning grounds, not all schools will follow the same migration pattern. One school may move up a secondary channel until it reaches a timbered point. Here the fish may swing away from the creek channel and follow the edge of the timberline toward the spawning flats (see area A). Another school may follow a creek channel until it intersects with a sunken roadbed. It may then follow the roadbed toward the shallows (see Area D). How shallow the fish will move depends on weather conditions and water clarity. On a warm overcast day a school may move up on the flats and begin to scatter in 10 to 15 feet of water. But the passing of a cold front and plummeting water temperatures could quickly drive these fish back down into secondary channels and 20- to 30-foot depths. Because of erratic weather and water conditions, the

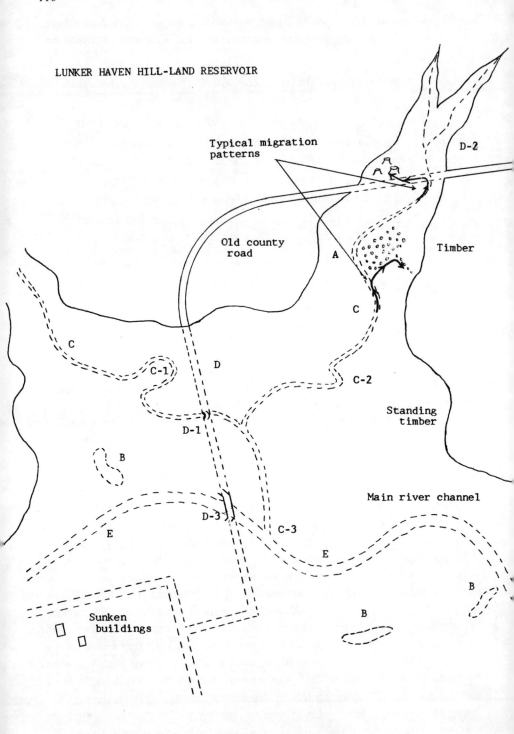

LUNKER HAVEN HILL-LAND RESERVOIR

Typical migration patterns

Old county road

D-2

Timber

A

C

C

C-1

D

C-2

Standing timber

D-1

B

Main river channel

D-3

C-3

E

E

B

Sunken buildings

B

B

early spring can frustrate anglers, with fish "here today, gone tomorrow."

During most of the pre-spawn, fish will hold close to cover. This means that lure presentation has to be "right on the money." With water temperatures in the 50's, a bass's metabolic rate is slow and it will seldom chase a lure more than a few feet. The reason many anglers fail to catch bass during this period is that they ignore the overall activity level of the fish and use the same speed of retrieve as during the bulk of the summer. For slow-moving pre-spawn bass, a slow dropping jig and eel combination or a single-spin spinnerbait is the best choice. And remember, during the pre-spawn, stick to water in the 10- to 30-foot range. Many anglers make the mistake of fishing too shallow and miss out on the fine action of this period altogether.

As water temperatures move into the low 60's, schools of bass will begin to scatter and move into the shallows. The males will move into three to five feet of water and begin building their nests, while the females usually hold in the eight- to ten-foot range awaiting a courting male. Nesting takes place on a mud or mud/gravel bottom, and the nest is invariably located up against some type of cover. The bass instinctively seek some type of object in order to cut down on the amount of territory they have to defend from marauding bluegills and crappies. If a bass can build its nest against a stump or under a log, it can face out toward these pesky predators and will not have to worry about attacks from behind.

While actual spawning may take place over a period of three to four weeks, the spawning peak will occur when the water temperature is about 64° F, and if this temperature coincides with a full moon we can look forward to a "bumper crop" of baby bass. During the spawn, water clarity can vary quite a bit, depending on whether it is a dry or wet spring. Fishing tackle can vary between spinning and baitcasting, and line size can vary between six- and 12-lb. -test, depending on water clarity.

After the spawning rites are complete, bass are very difficult to catch for three to six days. It seems that they use this time to clean out their systems and to recuperate from the rigors of mating. At this time bass move into a little deeper water and once again hold close to cover. But when this resting period is over, the mood changes dramatically from one of lethargy to aggressive feeding. At this time the bass form into small schools of eight to ten fish. You can expect to find these "wolf packs" in eight to 15 feet of water with long points, humps, ditches leading to secondary channels, and roadbeds the key locations. Fish location during the post-spawn is not easy, for small schools of bass are constantly moving and cover a lot of ground. It takes hard work to locate post-spawn bass, but once you do, you're in for the time of your life.

During the post-spawn, lure selection is the widest of any time of year. Topwater baits and deep-diving crankbaits can both produce fish, depending on bass location and mood. Topwater lures may seem a strange choice because most fish are not located in the shallows, but they feed so aggressively during the post-spawn that a noisy surface plug will actually "call them up" from the 10- to 12-foot depths.

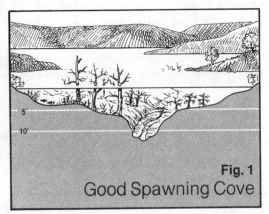
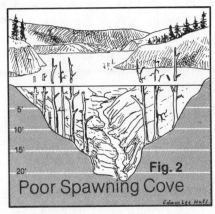

Good spawning coves have an abundance of shallow water and cover, while poor coves may have cover, but lack the necessary shallow flats that attract pre-spawn bass.

Summertime Locational Patterns   Summer   73° F - 85° F

Unlike natural lakes, hill-land reservoirs do not experience distinctive pre- and post-summer peaks in fish activity. This is due to the extended length of the calendar periods. The summer period for many reservoirs may last four to six months, while on a natural lake the entire summer period may be over in less than two months. Because reservoirs in the south have such an expanded time frame, changes in locational patterns are more gradual and peak activity periods more difficult to pinpoint.

Typically the summer period is characterized by a movement of fish out of the creek arms and back to open water. The structure on hill-land reservoirs is quite varied, but some of the best locations include sunken islands (Area B), secondary creek channels near the main river (Area C-3), roadbeds (Areas D-1 & D-3), and the main river channel (Area E). The best locations will be where there is a combination of good structure, for example where a roadbed crosses an old creek channel, or where an isolated sunken island touches the main river channel.

During the summer, patterns of fish location are sometimes difficult to establish and at other times amazingly simple. It is important to remember that, throughout the summer, bass will school by size and that different schools exhibit different migration patterns. Billy Murray remembers when he and Bobby located a school of bass that were using the intersection of two creek channels as a home base. They always seemed to catch fish here toward sunset. One day, however, they tried hitting this "honey hole" in the middle of the afternoon. Nobody was home. Using their depth finder, Billy and Bobby headed up one of the creek channels and soon located a school of bass. They stopped their boat and noticed that with each cast the fish moved closer to the boat. Soon the fish actually passed under the boat and the two men had to turn around and cast in the opposite direction. Using their trolling motor, they followed the bass until they came to the original creek intersection. Here the bass stopped and the fishing continued, though not as fast and furious as before.

The point of the story is that, though some fish may stake out a home base area, when bass are feeding in the summer, they are actually moving. It can be tough to stay on moving fish, so once you locate them, make as many casts as you can and don't stop to take pictures of the fish. When the action slows, try to determine what structure the fish are migrating along and follow it until you reestablish contact. Summertime bass may move slowly or rapidly, depending on the cover available. If the fish are following an old creek channel devoid of timber, they will move quickly. If, on the other hand, the creek channel has lots of timber and brush, the fish will linger as they move up the creek bed. It's difficult to say how far feeding fish will move, for behavior varies from school to school. But if a school has a definite summertime home, it probably won't move more than a quarter of a mile from sunrise to midday. And during the cold-water period, the school may move less than 100 yards in a day.

The depth of summertime bass depends on water clarity, light penetration, and water temperature. In the early summer, fish are often found in 15 to 20 feet of water. But even if the temperature gets over 75° F, largemouth will not move as deep as their cousin, the spotted bass. It is unusual in a hill-land reservoir to find largemouth in over 30 feet of water. Hill-land reservoirs are usually more stained than highland reservoirs. Thus, the lack of light penetration and extensive amounts of cover enable largemouth to live comfortably in water 20 to 30 feet deep during the height of the summer season.

Time of day is an important determinant in locating summer bass. Early morning and late evening will find good shallow water movements of bass on shallow tapering points and around vegetation such as coontail, moss, pads, and various grasses. Topwater plugs are a good choice when fishing the shallows. Sunken islands are also a good bet for early morning and late evening fishing and can be worked effectively with a plastic worm or a jig and eel. A classic early morning hotspot is the shallow tapering flat of an old sunken roadbed. As the sun gets high in the sky, the bass will simply move down the roadbed until it intersects a creek channel. Then the fish will meander down the creek, stopping at about the 20-foot level. Transportation routes are the least of a hill-land bass's worries.

A variety of lures work during the summer period, but the plastic worm is without a doubt the best choice. In Chapter 7-C we will investigage how to use a plastic worm when fishing sunken creek beds. Other good choices for the summer are vibrating lures and crankbaits. Surprisingly, live bait is seldom used for summer largemouth on hill-land reservoirs. Of course, there are a few old-timers who use nothing but live bait, but the vast majority of anglers stick with artificials throughout the calendar periods.

	Fall	
	Dropping from 85° F - 55° F	
Cold Water Locational Patterns	Winter	54° F - 40° F

The two cold-water periods of fall and winter slowly blend into each other, without any drastic changes in fish attitude. As water temperatures begin to cool, bass form into schools that are much larger and tighter than summertime schools. While a large school of summertime bass may contain 30 or 40 fish, a school of late fall bass may number over 200. A summer school of bass tends to spread out horizontally and is loosely grouped. In contrast, a cold-water school is tightly packed, with fish stacking vertically 12 to 15 fish deep. Thus, a large school of bass in the fall will occupy less space than a smaller summertime grouping. Another cold-water behavioral pattern than differs from the summer is that fish hold close to cover. All these factors combine to make fish location during the cold-water periods more difficult than at any other time of year. Billy Murray says that often during the late fall he will spend three or four hours patiently working different structure until he finally gets his first fish. But once the first fish is located, a limit can be taken on consecutive casts.

Of course tightly packed schools of bass do not develop overnight. As the summer ends and the first crisp nights of fall cause a slight fog on the water, bass continue to relate to classic summer structure; they simply begin a slow migration into deeper water. They begin seeking out the deeper roadbeds, the deeper timberlines, and the deeper creek and river channels. The general preference, however, is the channels. When water temperature reaches 50° F, it is not uncommon to find largemouth in 30 to 40 feet of water. The best fall location is where two creeks join on a timbered point. Another classic fall location is where a creek doubles back on itself forming a "saddle" (Area C-1).

The main difficulty with fishing cold-water bass is that it requires patience and a methodical approach. This means fishing an area slowly and thoroughly before moving on. The cold-water period is not the time to quickly fancast an area and move on. The best approach is to select an area that looks as if it holds a concentration of fish and then work it slowly. Vertical jigging is a popular fall and winter technique. With fish reticent to move more than a foot to inhale a lure, it is a good idea to slowly drop the jig, bounce it in place for a few minutes, and then move only four or five feet and repeat the process. A lure must be presented right in front of a bass's nose. We have seen occasions when a man in the bow of a boat catches a limit of fish, while his buddy in the stern, using the same lure, strikes out. When fishing in the timber, move from tree to tree, one angler working one side of the tree, and the other the other side. Relax, and resign yourself to not covering much ground. There is simply no way to fish deep *and* rapidly. The bass are definitely catchable, but finding them can take plenty of time.

A few years ago, many anglers assumed that bass quit biting when water temperature reached 50° F, so many of them quit fishing until the next spring. The problem, however, was not that the fish were inactive, but that the anglers were too active. During the cold-water periods it is almost like fishing a different species than the aggressive lure-chasing bass of the summer period. While it's still the same fish, the cooler water, decreased metabolism, and tighter schools make this a different ball game altogether — and the cold-water ball game takes patience.

Though most of the bass move to deeper water when the water is in the low 50's and mid 40's, there are days when the fish will be two or three feet below the surface. They will not, however, be in the shallow coves, but rather suspended in the tops of sunken timber, over 40 or 50 feet of water. A warm sunny day in December or January can pull fish to the surface like a magnet. This is a vertical migration, however, and the bass will quickly drop back into deep water when weather conditions change.

The key to fishing cold-water largemouth is locating steep drop-offs or timber near deep water channels. Once a cold-water school of fish is located, it will stay in that same vicinity most of the winter. There may be some minor migrations, but the fish will not move the great distances they often do during the summer. If

"Bobby Murray works a small creek arm, a good place for springtime bass, but not usually a good choice for late fall fishing."

you know an area holds fish, simply work it over slowly. If you are "on fish," it's only a matter of making the right presentation and that means selecting from a few proven cold-water methods.

The standard repertoire of cold-water lures includes tailspins, twinspins, jig and eel, and jigging spoons. We will look at vertical jigging in Chapter 7-C. One lure that often works during the early cold-water period, and is usually overlooked, is the deep-diving crankbait. The reason many anglers fail to use a crankbait during the cold-water period is that they have trouble keeping the lure down and at the same time moving it slowly. The fall is one time when it is crucial to use plastic-bodied or sinking crankbaits. The balsa lures work fine in the summer when bass are aggressive and can chase a lure some distance, but when the water is cold, bass move more slowly and it is impossible to keep a balsa lure deep unless you add a sinker or two. If you try to fish a balsa crankbait without additional weight it will simply bounce to the surface. We recommend a good neutral bouyancy or sinking crankbait that can be cranked down to the proper depth and then slowly crawled across the bottom.

We will close this chapter with one final hint for fishing cold-water bass on hill-land reservoirs. Observations by skin divers and our own experience have taught us that cold-water bass almost always take a lure as it is dropping. When casting to locations that you think hold fish, position your boat so that the cast is made from deep to shallow water. Then, when you retrieve your jig or spoon, it will be working downhill. This allows you to slowly drop the lure down a ridge and into a creek channel, where the bass often hold during the fall and winter. In the summer, simply reverse your position so you are casting from shallow to deep. Then you can work your lure uphill and over the lip of the creek where summertime bass often hold. Of course under both circumstances line watching is very important. At the slightest sign of movement in your line, set the hook and quickly make a mental note of the depth at which the fish struck. If you get one strike there are probably a hundred more bass down there just waiting to fill your limit.

It's difficult for most anglers to believe that they catch 40 or 50 bass out of one school, but it can happen in the fall and winter. So long as water temperature stays above 41°F and the water is not muddy, cold-water fishing can be exceptional. However, once the water temperature drops below 41°F, or if a cold winter rain muddies the water, it's all over. The combination of cold, turbid water is the death of bass fishing. In one tournament held a few years ago on a southern reservoir, the contestants faced these conditions and set a record that still stands. The winning angler came in with a whopping two-day total of one 14-inch bass. He took big fish, most fish, and total weight — no one else saw a fish. So while the winter can offer good fishing, there are times when it's best to stay home. Besides, when the winter rains are over, it's only a few weeks until pre-spawn bass are moving to the creek mouths and another season is underway.

Summary of Calendar Periods for Largemouth Bass in Hill-land Reservoirs

Calendar Period	General Fish Location	Fish Attitude	Most Effective Lures	Retrieve
Pre-spawn	Movement from the main reservoir to main creek mouths. Timbered points and roadbeds leading to spawning flats.	Very Active	Spinnerbaits (single-spin), Grubs, Jig and Eel, Deep-diving Crankbaits	Slow to Medium
Spawn	Mud or gravel bottom flats in secondary creek channels and coves. Nests will be close to cover.	Not Very Active	Spinnerbaits (single or tandem), Plastic Worms, Topwater, Jig and Worm, Jig and Frog	Medium
Post-spawn	Movement back to main reservoir areas. Roadbeds, humps and secondary channels.	Females - Males + to neutral	Plastic Worms, Topwater, Crankbaits, Grubs	Medium to Fast
Summer	Patterns established. Sunken islands, creek channel intersections with main river, roadbeds and timber.	Very Active	Plastic Worms, Crankbaits, Vibrating Lures, Topwater (early and late in the day)	Varied Stop & Go to Fast
Fall Cold Water	Deep roadbeds, creek channels and creek saddles. Deep timber and some main reservoir shallows.	Very Active in Deep Water	Tail Spins, Jig and Eel, Grubs, Single Spins, Medium-Deep Crankbaits, Spoons	Medium to Slow
Winter Cold Water	Main reservoir areas, deep timber, steep rocky channel banks, bluffs.	Not Very Active	Jigging Spoons, Tail Spins, Jig and Eel, Twin Spins, Grubs, Spinnerbaits w/ pork rind	Slow

CHAPTER 7-B
Vertical Jigging the Timber

One of the most enjoyable aspects of bass fishing is the variety of angling styles if offers the fishing fraternity. Anglers can spend a lazy afternoon fishing with a cane pole and bobber from an old wooden johnboat, or can race a modern bass boat around a reservoir, tempting bass with sophisticated lures and using the latest Boron rods and freespool reels. During most of the fishing season, in the summer period, a variety of tactics work, for bass are on the move and actively feeding. And anyone who sticks with a tactic long enough is eventually going to catch a few fish. In the late fall and winter months, however, the pace of underwater life slows, with bass feeding less aggressively, small schools joining together, and larger, loose schools tightening up. Locating cold-water bass can be like finding the proverbial needle in a haystack, and neither the "sit and wait" nor the "hit and run" tactics that many summer anglers rely on are going to pay off.

Many summer anglers like to cover a lot of ground when fishing reservoirs. They will hit one spot, work the area quickly with a variety of lures, and then zip to another creek arm, underwater hump, or roadbed and give it a try. In half a day's fishing, a "reservoir runner" may cover 25 to 50 miles of water and work an equal number of spots. But as water temperatures drop and the fall season rolls around, cold-water bassers need to take a hint from Mother Nature and slow their pace accordingly. When water temperatures reach the low 50's, a fisherman might spend the entire day slowly and methodically working a few hundred yards of one creek channel — and if he's lucky he will locate one school of bass — but what a school!

Locating Cold Water Bass in the Timber

In hill-land reservoirs during the late fall, bass location is primarily determined by the migration patterns of shad. The seasonal changes on southern reservoirs are not as dramatic as they are on northern natural lakes, but they are present nonetheless. Beginning in the late fall, there is a slow, yet perceptible, movement of shad and bass toward the shallower waters of the reservoir. At the beginning of this period, water temperatures are in the low 60's, and the fish are typically found in 35 to 40 feet of water. As the temperatures continue to cool, both predator and prey begin to follow the creek and river channels, with some penetration deep into the secondary creek arms. The migration will continue until the water temperature reaches the mid 40's, at which point the bass are usually in 18 to 20 feet of water. This is about as shallow as bass move into coves and creek arms in the late fall.

Such a pattern of movement might take between six and seven weeks, and during all this time, both bass and shad are relating to creek and river channels. When water temperatures drop into the low 40's, however, there is a sudden dissipation of shad and a reverse movement out to the mid-depth ranges. The bass quickly follow and for the remainder of the winter will locate in 25 to 35 feet of water. While depth varies throughout the late fall and early winter, location remains fairly constant. The home of most cold-water bass is the lips or channel drops of sunken creeks and rivers, and, if timber is present, all the better for the bass.

What is good for the bass, however, often strikes terror in the hearts of most fishermen. Fishing in the timber brings with it visions of snagged lures, broken lines, and lunker bass hopelessly twisted around a branch just out of reach, but not out of sight. While some of these visions are based in reality, if anglers have selected the proper equipment, know where fish are located, and can effectively present the proper lure, fishing the timber can be one of the most productive types of angling.

Presentation in the Timber

It was 11:00 a.m. and Billy Murray peered up the creek arm. There was still a light fog on the water, and he could just barely see his first marker buoy, where he had begun fishing three hours ago — three hours without a fish, or even a strike. Still, he watched his line as intently as when jigging that first willow tree early that morning. Man! Sometimes fall fishing really takes patience. Billy paused to take a can of pop from the cooler and then slowly lowered his jigging spoon over the side of the boat. After momentarily snagging between two limbs, the spoon came free, and suddenly the line gave a short twitch off to one side. Billy immediately set the hook. He felt solid resistance as he leaned into the fish and tried to keep its head coming through the tangle of branches. Then, for a brief instant, the line stopped coming as the bass wedged in between two branches. Billy quickly dropped his rod tip, and when he felt the fish move, horsed it up through the branches and into the boat. Three pounds of almost bleached largemouth glistened on the bass boat floor. This was a good omen, for Billy knew that a light-colored fish was the sign of a school fish and there were probably a hundred or more fish right under his boat. Had the fish been a darker color, it would surely have been a loner. In the next 20 drops, Billy hauled in 17 beautiful bass, all between two and three-and-a-half pounds. He then noted the spot in his log book, picked up his marker buoys, and was back to the dock in plenty of time for lunch.

The story is typical of cold-water bass fishing and illustrates the patience needed to finally make contact with fish. Of course, the most crucial part of late fall to early winter bass fishing is adapting to the slower metabolism of the fish. For some reason, the slower winter metabolism causes bass to group together much more tightly than they do during the summer. A cold-water school of bass can be packed as tightly as a can of sardines, and this makes them tough to

"Standing timber can be a good place to begin prospecting for cold-water bass in highland reservoirs."

locate. In the summer, with schools more scattered, and with a lot more single fish, an angler can work his way quickly through an area and contact a few actively feeding fish. During the late fall, a slower, more methodical approach is necessary, and even then there is no guarantee that fish will be located.

The best starting point is to accept the fact that you are not going to cover a lot of ground and then to get a good overview of the limited area to be fished. For example, let's say you choose a typical creek arm in a hill-land reservoir when the water temperature is about 52° F. The first step is to motor to the end of the creek arm and locate the creek channel. In many hill-land reservoirs, the back end of creek arms is heavily timbered and you can clearly see the outline of the channel by the way the creek cuts through the old standing timber. If, however, the reservoir has no obvious above-water clues, then a depth finder will be essential. If this is the case, you may have to lay out a dozen or more marker buoys to get some idea of where the channel runs. Then, with either standing timber or marker buoys to guide you, you are ready to begin prospecting for bass. Since the fish will seldom be shallower than 15 feet, it is best to begin in that range and slowly work your way toward deeper water.

With a constant eye to the depth finder, work both sides of the channel lip, using a silver jigging spoon or a jig and eel. A classic location for cold water bass is in the timber immediately adjacent to the channel drop. If there is standing timber near the channel lip and some distance between trees, it is important to not skip from tree to tree. Very often there will be invisible sunken timber or brush. We suggest working down a channel in 10- or 15-foot intervals, making sure to jig both sides of the timber.

It takes not only patience, but also courage, the first time you drop a jigging spoon down through the timber. Most of us can't conceive fishing a lure with a treble hook through treetops and heavy brush, but it is possible. Of course, jigging the timber necessitates medium to heavy baitcasting tackle and line in the 17- to 20-lb.-test category. The spoon itself, however, is the real secret to successful jigging. Vertical jigging spoons, like a Hopkins model or a C-C spoon, are not your normal everyday casting spoon. They are narrow and thin at the top and heavy at the bottom and weigh from ¾ to 1 oz. This shape and weight assures that the spoon drops straight to the bottom and does not drift off to one side as most other spoons do. The favorite color is silver, in either a gloss or hammered chrome finish.

To present the spoon properly, make a short "pitch cast" of ten feet or less, or drop the spoon over the side and free-spool it to the bottom. Long casts will simply not work in the timber, as the line will inevitably hang over branches and make retrieves impossible. By dropping the lure straight down, you can work it through the branches all the way to the bottom. The fish could be anywhere in

"Jigging Spoons and tailspins are often good approaches for deepwater reservoir bass."

between. As you drop the lure, keep the rod tip low and feather the spoon to the bottom. One mistake that novice anglers make is to jig the spoon up and then drop the rod tip quickly as the spoon falls. In so doing, they lose touch with the spoon and often miss the telltale bump of a bass. Since bass almost always hit a spoon as it is dropping, the best approach is to jig the spoon up and then feather it down, trying to remain just an inch or two behind the lure as you lower your rod. If the spoon fails to fall, set the hook. Sometimes bass will strike just as the spoon begins its descent. If the spoon should hang up, lower your rod tip, let out a little slack line, and gently shake the rod tip. The weight of the spoon is such that the lure becomes its own "bait knocker" and usually works itself free.

As you work your way down the channel, crossing from side to side, be sure to work both sides of the trees. We have often jigged one side of a tree with no results, and then moved three feet to the other side and taken a limit of bass on consecutive drops. Work the lure through the branches to the bottom, jig it up

"Billy Murray works some sunken timber for early fall bass."

and down eight to ten times, and then move on. Keep your eyes on the line, and when you do get a hit, set the hook immediately and keep the bass's head up, working him quickly to the boat. Then get down to the same depth as quickly as possible. If the activity stops, take a break, but don't move. Once late fall or winter bass are located, they can be caught all day long. After giving the school a brief rest, go at it again. They'll probably be receptive.

Under stable conditions, cold-water bass will not move great distances from day to day. If you locate a school one day, you can be pretty sure it is nearby the next. Most movements that do take place are vertical. One day the fish may be suspended at 20 feet and the next day at 28 feet.

When you are working over a given channel, be sure to watch the depth finder as you move back and forth across the channel. While cold-water bass often hold close to the timber or creek channel, there will be some days when they will suspend just off the lip of the channel. It's tough to pick out fish from the brush when you are directly over timber, but when you move across the channel, a school of suspended bass stands out clearly on the old flasher dial.

If you do locate suspended fish off the channel lip, you can switch tactics from a jigging spoon to a flutter spoon or a tailspin. In this open-water situation, you can also use lighter spinning tackle and have a little more fun playing the fish. Long casts can be made parallel to the channel edge, and, once the lure is counted down to the proper depth, a pumping and sweeping motion will trigger strikes. If, for example, the fish show up on the depth finder at 20 feet, count the lure down to about 25 feet, then raise your rod quickly, pulling the lure to 15 feet, and "tight line" it back down to 25. By continuously dropping the lure through the school, you are bound to get some action.

While suspended bass provide a nice break from the tedious work of jigging in timber, more often than not the fish will be snug up against the trees. If you're the patient type and can develop a slow systematic method of fishing, then cold-water bassing can result in some of the largest catches of the year. If you don't find fish in the upper end of the creeks, just work your way to deeper water. We have found some schools of bass in 50 feet of water, though usually they aren't that deep. As winter progresses, you can expect to find them in the mid-depth ranges of 25 to 35 feet.

Adapting Reservoir Timber Tactics to Other Bodies of Water

Jigging the timber originated as a technique in the newly formed reservoirs of the highland reservoir belt but, obviously, is applicable anywhere there is flooded timber. One of the more natural adaptations is on flooded strip mining pits or iron ore pits. Many of these excavations are small but have extremely deep water. Some flooded pits in northern Minnesota, for example, may be only 30 acres and yet have water over 200 feet deep. Most pits have steep sides and get progressively deeper toward the middle. This makes fish location rather simple. Usually 95% of the bass will be within a hundred yards of the shoreline. Flooded timber is a natural part of strip pits, so northern anglers can get in practice for a southern reservoir trip by jigging the timber on these mini-reservoirs.

Another place where jigging can be practiced is on natural lakes that have had a disruption of the normal water table. For a variety of reasons, natural lakes often experience rising water levels, and as the water spreads out and inundates timber, reservoir-like conditions are created. In both pits and rising natural lakes, we prefer using a Texas-rigged plastic worm for vertical jigging. The bass seem to have a definite preference for worms over spoons, probably due to the lack of shad as natural forage. We urge you to try adapting vertical jigging to the pits or natural lakes of your area. Because most northern anglers are not familiar with tactics for thick timber, you may find yourself tapping a virgin fishery. If you do, give Billy Murray a call and invite him up. He'd love to fish a Yankee reservoir.

CHAPTER 7-C
Fishing the Creek Channels with Plastic Worms

About 20 years ago, a southern legislator introduced a bill to outlaw the plastic worm in his state. The plastic worm had been around for a few years before the state senator took action, but it was proving to be so deadly on bass that one man, at least, feared for the continued existence of the largemouth. Luckily for anglers, the bill failed to pass, and, not surprisingly, largemouth bass still abound in southern waters. The very attempt to have a lure *outlawed* is the strongest statement that can be made for its effectiveness. Probably more bass have been caught on plastic worms than on any other lure man has created. Numerous books have been written on worm fishing. In what follows we will not attempt to cover all the intricacies of line weight, knots, hooks, types of rigging, and ways to set a hook. Rather, we will investigate one important locational pattern in hill-land reservoirs and explain why the plastic worm is hard to beat under these conditions.

Summer Locational Patterns in Creek and River Channels

Of all the structural considerations on hill-land reservoirs, creek and river channels are the most important in the location of summertime bass. After spawning is completed, the majority of largemouth bass begin to move back toward the main creek and river channels, using the secondary channels as migration routes. Some fish will migrate all the way back to the main body of the reservoir and throughout the summer relate to humps, roadbeds, and the main river channel. Other bass move out of the shallow end of the secondary creek arms and set up summer housekeeping in the main creek arms and primary creek channels. In either case, the channel systems and, particularly, the brushy and timbered lips of the channels, are the most consistent producers for summertime bass.

Once located, there is no great secret to fishing creek and river channels. Indeed, for many novice reservoir anglers, the very location of the channels can be the biggest problem. The vast expanse of water in large reservoirs overwhelms most newcomers and often sends them scurrying back to the smaller, more manageable creek arms. Here, in psychologically reassuring confines, anglers can cast the shoreline and easily identify sunken creek channels that wind their way through visible stands of timber and brush. The only problem with this approach is that during most of the summer months there aren't large concentrations of bass in the smaller creek arms. The majority of bass are in the larger creek arms and in the main body of the reservoir. Here, locating creek and river channels is more problematical and almost impossible without the aid of a good topographic map, depth finder, and set of marker buoys. If you have never fished a reservoir before, it pays to use the services of a guide the first few times out. Be sure to take along a log book and make some mental notes on how to locate channels in open water.

Channel width and depth will vary. Toward the back end of creek arms, channels may be less than ten feet wide and only a foot or two deep, while out in the main reservoir a river channel can be hundreds of feet wide and 40 to 200 feet deep. Locating the lip of a channel can be fairly easy on the steep-dropping side, which usually occurs on the outside bend, but location is more difficult on gently sloping sides. Time on the water and a few surveying sessions with marker buoys are all that is necessary until you begin to feel at home finding the summer hideouts of bass.

Once sunken channels are located, they should be treated like any other type of structure. Though fish will congregate in old creek and river systems, they are not evenly scattered throughout. The natural holding stations for largemouth are those areas that provide food and cover and are distinct from the surrounding area. Typical summer locations include sharp bends in otherwise gently meandering streams, old bridges or culverts, timbered points that drop off into a channel, creek "saddles," the outside bends of rivers and creeks, and, best of all, the intersection of a creek and a river near a brushy or timbered point.

These classic structures may serve as a home base for a school of bass or as a temporary stopover for nomadic schools. Actual fish location depends on a number of factors, including food source, water clarity, depth, and amount of cover. Given this variety of considerations, it is impossible to offer a guaranteed prescription for bass location, but a few generalizations are possible.

One of the most important factors determining how and when bass will feed has to do with water clarity and the amount of light penetration. Hill-land reservoirs are usually dingy in early summer and clear as the season progresses. Naturally, a heavy mid-summer rain will muddy the water in the creek arms, but the entire water system will not be as murky as it is during the spring rains. If the water is in typical, semi-clear, summer condition, the most predictable feeding times will be early morning and toward dusk. Usually the early morning "bite" is the best one. On sunny days the morning "bite" lasts from a half-hour before sunrise 'til an hour and a half after sunrise. On overcast days, fish activity ranges over a longer period. The summer period also has a late-day "bite" which usually occurs immediately before or after sunset. Scientists speculate that the rapid change in light intensity triggers this feeding response in many gamefish.

Another behavior pattern typical of summer largemouth is visible surface schooling activity during the early morning hours. On most reservoirs, the local anglers can tell you where to find schooling bass. The furious action of bass breaking the surface as they slash into schools of shad typically occurs over immense flats. Many anglers pull into areas where bass school and simply wait 'til the action begins. Then they swing into action with vibrating plugs and topwater baits and abandon the area as soon as this flurry of activity is over.

TYPICAL CREEK OR RIVER BED FEATURES

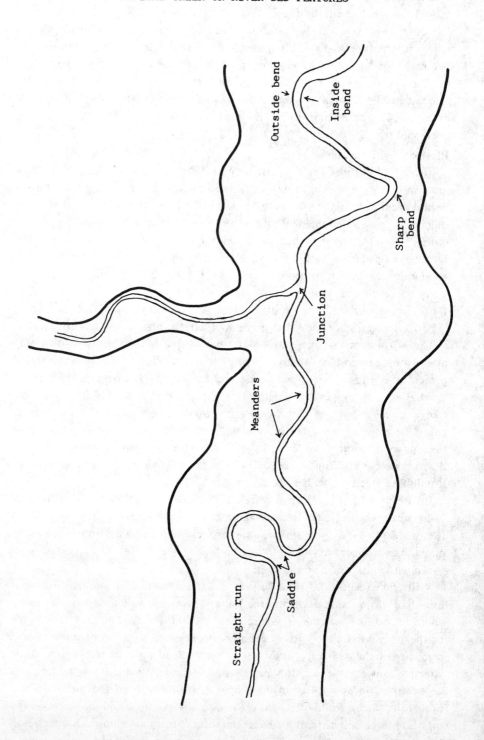

Knowledgeable anglers, however, learn to work areas adjacent to where bass school early and late in the day. Bass that school over flats seldom remain on the flat after they have finished feeding. They naturally gravitate to the closest adjacent structure, and this often means the closest creek or river channel. The fish may have to move a hundred or more yards to find such a channel, but they do. Our experience has been that, as the bass drop down off the flats, they usually relocate in 15 to 25 feet of water. And, because the most attractive channel lips are rimmed with brush or timber, the plastic worm becomes the best method of presentation.

Plastic Worm Tackle

Fishing schooling bass offers an incredible high to any angler. But the actual amount of time the largemouth are churning the surface during the summer period is minimal. When fish are up and active, you throw artificial plugs as quickly as you can get them into the water. You don't even stop to put fish on the stringer or in the live well, because the action is only going to last a short time. During the remainder of the day, when the fish are deeper, a slower, more meticulous method of presentation is called for. Enter the plastic worm.

As we mentioned in Chapter 7-A, the best creek and river channels to fish are those whose channel lips are lined with sunken brush and timber. And to effectively fish timber and brush in the summer, the plastic worm is unbeatable.

The worm is primarily a warm-water bait. It really comes into its own only after water temperatures are over 60° F. The worm's effectiveness as a method of presentation is due to its weedless nature. A Texas-style worm can be worked through brushy tangles that would cause old Brer Rabbit to shake his head. We like to use a six- to eight-inch worm and favor purple, blue, black, and green as colors. In recent years, the fluorescent "firetails" in any of these colors have become very popular. While color preference is pretty much a personal matter, it does make sense to fish darker colors when the water is off-color or murky. We usually use green only when the water is fairly clear.

Bullet-type slip sinkers are preferred, and weight depends on the conditions. A ¼-oz. sinker works well in shallow water, but when channel depths reach 15 or 20 feet, we like to use a ⅜-oz. sinker so we can feel when we hit bottom. In a wind, it might even be necessary to go to ½ oz. of lead. The important thing is to be in touch with your worm at all times.

With the exception of brief periods of surface schooling, summer fishing is usually bottom fishing. During the fall and winter, suspended bass are fairly common, but in the summer, fish relate to the bottom. And anglers don't agree on the best approach to bottom fishing. There is some argument among bassers regarding the slip sinker. Many insist that the lead must be free-sliding to be effective, but others, like Bob Underwood, disagree. While doing underwater observation on how different lures operated, Bob noticed that in brush and timber the worm would often end up on one side of a limb and the sinker on the other. This made it difficult to detect the soft tap of a bass inhaling a worm. Bob also observed that often the worm would snag in the crotch of a branch when a retrieve was made. From that day on, Bob Underwood carried a supply of toothpicks in his tackle box. He used them to secure the slip sinker snug against the worm, inserting the toothpick in the sinker hole and breaking off all but the tip.

Another reason it makes sense to "fix" the slip sinker is that when you are fishing heavy brush the slip sinker does not function as intended. The purpose of a slip sinker is to allow a bass to pick up the worm without feeling any weight. This works well on a clean bottom, but anyone who lets a bass run with a worm in heavy brush might as well kiss the fish goodbye. When fishing in timber, set the hook as soon as you feel the "tap." Then get the fish headed toward the boat as quickly as possible. Don't play with your food.

"Everyone has his or her own favorite rigging. Here are a few of ours: (r. to l.) a slither worm on a keeper hook, a plastic lizard, a reaper worm on a Pow-RR head jig, a ring worm, a Texas-rigged sinking worm, a floating worm, and a twister tail."

Working bass in brushy creek and river channels necessitates a rod with some backbone. While we don't advocate the old cue-stick-type rods, a rod must have fairly stiff action. The best worming outfit is a 5½-foot medium action graphite casting rod, teamed with a free-spool baitcasting reel and 14- to 20-lb.-test line. There are plenty of good rods and reels on the market to choose from.

One final clue to worming success is to purchase an abrasion-resistant, high visibility line. Line-watching is the only effective way to fish plastic worms, and the constant rubbing of line against and through brush wears out a line quickly. Don't skimp and buy cheap line. It's the only thing between you and the lunker of a lifetime.

We won't even get into the argument about when and how to set the hook after a bass takes a plastic worm. Bobby Murray says you should only let a bass move with a worm a distance as long as the worm is — and that ain't much, unless you're fishing really huge worms.

How to Fish a Creek or River Channel

Now, assuming you have the proper equipment and have located a likely bass hangout, what is the best way to proceed? There are a number of different ways to work a worm, from a hopping motion to an almost motionless dragging action. Experiment, and you'll soon discover that the mood of the bass can demand different presentations on different days. No matter how you work a plastic worm, it is important, particularly during the summer, to keep the worm on or near the bottom. This sounds easy but can be a real problem when you are fishing an extremely brushy creek channel.

In newly-formed reservoirs, the brush or timber on a channel lip can be so thick that it forms a canopy over the bass. When you encounter this, the best approach is to use short casts of six to ten feet. We like to anchor on *the shallow side* of the channel lip, toss the worm over the lip, and work it back toward the boat in an uphill manner. Working at about a 45 degree angle to the channel seems best. This allows you to cover some territory and still work down to the bottom.

Worming creek channels is slow, meticulous work. Crawling the worm up over one limb, dropping it to the bottom, and then working it over another limb takes time and patience. Many anglers cast the length of the channel lip with long casts and work the worm through the treetops. By failing to work the worm up and down across the bottom, they are missing 95% of the fish. Sometimes even short casts won't work, and the timber will be so thick that vertical jigging is the only workable approach. Choose whichever approach is called for, but remember to keep your worm in contact with the bottom.

If you should encounter a creek or main river channel that has sparse timber — and this may be the case when fishing older reservoirs — then you can make longer casts and work through an area more quickly. In older reservoirs, bass move quickly along channels devoid of timber and will often hold in other types of structure, such as old bridge abutments and culverts where roadbeds crossed old streams. The plastic worm works in these situations as well as in brush and timber. Plastic worms can also be fished where stream channels swing against a rocky bluff. It's difficult to think of places where a plastic worm won't catch fish, but the worm does its best work on brush and timbered channels. Don't go reservoir fishing without a few dozen in your tackle box.

CHAPTER 8-A
Case Study: Spotted Bass in Highland Reservoirs

Before investigating the specific seasonal movements of spotted bass on highland reservoirs, a few general comments are in order. Fishing reservoirs can be frustrating to anglers who are used to the narrow confines of their favorite river or the manageable boundaries of a small natural lake. On first appearance, a highland reservoir can seem almost boundless with "water, water, everywhere." These impoundments can have hundreds of miles of shoreline and can be 75 or 80 miles long from their source to the dam site. Another peculiarity of reservoirs is that water temperature can vary greatly from the headwaters to the damsite, especially in the spring of the year.

The best tactic for novice reservoir anglers is to break a reservoir down into manageable sections and learn one section well. This makes more sense than speeding up and down the water course looking for active fish. When fishing spotted bass, anglers should concentrate their efforts on the lower half of the reservoir, from about midpoint to the dam. Because this area provides the deeper rockier habitat, it will attract the biggest population of spotted bass. By taking a map of a highland reservoir and blocking off a section of the lower reservoir that has two healthy creek arms, anglers will quickly be able to establish the seasonal movements of spotted bass.

In this case study, we will focus on such a section of reservoir. We will look at the *generalized seasonal movements* of bass between the main and secondary creek arms and the main reservoir. While there may be small localized populations of spots that spend the entire calendar year relating to one rocky bluff, most spotted bass will be following these generalized movements.

How Calendar Periods on Reservoirs Differ From Natural Lakes

The calendar periods for natural lakes that we outlined earlier in the book do not always apply to reservoirs, though they are pretty close. One difference, due to the geographical location of highland reservoirs, is that the individual calendar periods are much longer than on northern natural lakes. Another difference, also due to the narrow geographical band of highland reservoirs, is that we can more easily assign specific months and weeks to the calendar periods.

In this case study we will analyze a hypothetical reservoir in the mid-range of the highland belt, perhaps near central Arkansas. When our case study departs from the "classic" natural lake calendar periods, we have discussed the departure. The main differences have to do with the lack of a brief pre- and post-summer feeding binge and with the fact that most reservoirs do not experience the dramatic fall turnover that natural lakes do.

One final difference between lakes and reservoirs has to do with water clarity. In natural lakes that are not part of a flowage system, water clarity changes little during the year and is primarily a function of algae growth. The water clarity of most highland reservoirs is generally excellent, but heavy spring and winter rains can wash large amounts of soil into creek arms and bring a drastic change in water clarity. During the spring rains, even the main reservoir body can become quite muddy, but after the spring deluge, the water begins to clear. By the time fall rolls around, the water is usually at its clearest.

Water clarity is an important consideration when fishing spotted bass, for this fish is very light sensitive. Thus, during the fall, anglers who have never fished for spots may be surprised to find them in 70 or 80 feet of water, a depth almost unheard of on most natural lakes. During the pre-spawn, however, when creek arms can be very muddy, it is not uncommon to find the spot lying in three or four feet of water. The depth of these fish will often depend on water clarity, and the perceptive angler will take this into consideration when locating fish.

Murray Hill Highland Reservoir

It would be impossible to cover all the possible fish locations on a highland reservoir, so, as in our previous case studies, we have chosen to focus on the typical structures that are key to seasonal movements. Because highland reservoirs are so immense, bass movements tend to be very nomadic. Typically, bass will move into the creek arms and secondary arms to spawn, but this could mean traveling a distance of six or seven miles from the main body of the reservoir. With all this movement, it is natural that often the bass will be *in between* the locational points we are going to outline. For anglers to make sense of these "in between" times, they must recognize that the primary source of prey for spotted bass is either threadfin or young gizzard shad, or crayfish. Even while migrating, bass have to feed, so prey location should help establish where the bass are. Crayfish will relate primarily to rocky areas, and a good depth finder will help in the location of open water shad.

Area A   A steep-dropping rocky bluff that intersects with the original river channel or with a creek channel.

Area B   A rounded and protected bay or cove with a broken rock or gravel bottom. Typical spawning structure for the spotted bass. Usually located on the secondary creek channels.

Area C   A long tapering point that comes quite a way from the shore before dropping into the main river or creek channel. These points can either be bare or have scattered timber.

Area D   A long underwater point that slowly drops until it intersects with the main river channel or deep water. These can be confusing, as there may be no clue to their existence when looking at the shoreline.

MURRAY HILL HIGHLAND RESERVOIR

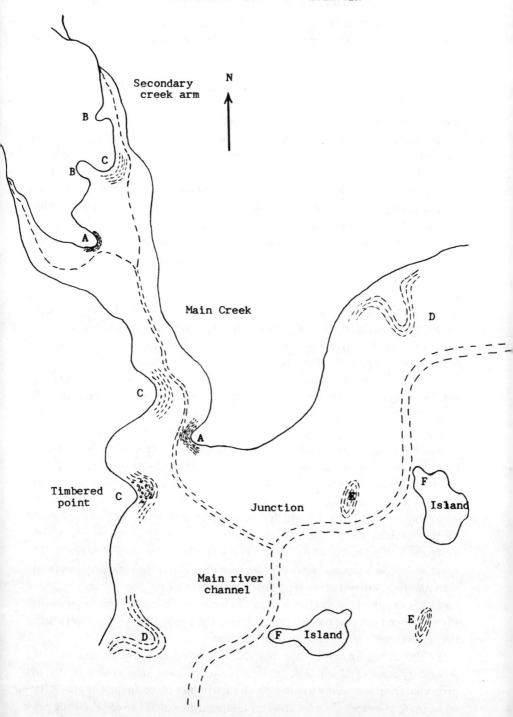

Area E An underwater rocky reef or island with depths of at least 25 to 30 feet. Isolated reefs tend to produce better than groups of reefs.

Area F A main reservoir island that has a steep bluff. Ideally the bluff should intersect with the main river channel and the channel should be 70 to 80 feet deep.

Pre-spawn	50° F - 57° F
Spawn	58° F - 65° F
Post-spawn	66° F - 72° F

Springtime Locational Patterns

The pre-spawn locational pattern for spotted bass focuses on the main creek arms of the reservoir. As water temperature gets into the low 50's, the fish will locate at the mouths of the main creeks, and then will begin to slowly move up the creek to where it divides into the secondary channels. When the spot first moves in from open water areas of the reservoir, it will locate adjacent to the steep bluff points at the entrance to the main creek mouth. High bluffs with slate rock, or broken rock in combination with clay, are the best places to begin prospecting during the pre-spawn. The fish will be tightly schooled on points such as area A, but, as the water warms, they will begin migrating up the creek channel, sometimes a distance of three to four miles, to where the secondary channels begin. As they move up the main creek channel, spots will relate to the steeper banks, particularly to areas of broken rock with a red clay base.

Because of the narrow geographical band of highland reservoirs, the pre-spawn period typically takes place between mid-February and mid-March. During this period, the fish can be in water anywhere from four to 40 feet deep. Water clarity and sunlight determine the depth. It's important to remember that the spotted bass is very photosensitive, and, except during the actual spawn, will seek to avoid sunlight. In the spring, highland reservoirs often experience heavy rains, and creek channels are the first to show the effects. When the water is highly colored, spots may lie in shallow water, four to five feet deep, right up against steep bluffs. A good presentation under these circumstances is to slowly crawl a small crankbait parallel to the bluff face. If it is a very dry spring and the water remains clear, the fish will drop down into deep water, and anglers would do best working a small jig/grub combination or a small plastic worm straight down the bluff. The key to presentation is small lures and slow movement. The spots will be in a generally positive feeding mood, but their metabolism is still slow and they will not move long distances to take a lure. Usually they will hit a jig as it is dropping, so anglers who fail to watch their line will miss a lot of fish. Live bait need not be a consideration during the pre-spawn, as these fish are not finicky and will readily take an artificial lure.

As the actual spawning approaches, the fish will move further into the secondary creeks and will seek out small rounded bays, such as area B, that are protected from prevailing winds. Spawning will take place on rock or gravel flats adjacent to the creek channel at water temperatures of 58° to 65° F. While peak spawning will occur at about 60° F, some spotted bass will still be around after

"Bluffs and spotted bass go together like ham and grits."

the largemouth has completed spawning. The actual spawning behavior of spots is different from that of largemouth in one important respect. Largemouth like to fan out a distinctive nest and will often seek some type of cover, like an old stump or log, when building the nest. The spot, on the other hand, will spawn over bare rock, much like the smallmouth, and its nest will not be visible to most anglers.

Spawning spotted bass are also much more jittery than spawning largemouth. When this spooky nature is combined with increasing water clarity, it can make for tough fishing. Knowledgeable anglers learn to look for the fish and not the nest. Because of their distinctive black horizontal bar, the spot often appears to be a narrow black pencil lying in the water. The best approach is to look 30 or 40 feet ahead of the boat and, once a fish is located, cast well beyond it so the lure swims over the fish from behind. Because these fish are so nervous, they will usually swim off the nest if they see a lure approaching from a distance. But if the lure approaches from behind, they will often strike out of instinct, as if nailing a pesky bluegill that has gotten too close to the nest.

Billy Murray prefers a small four- to six-inch green plastic worm during the spawn. Small jigs between 1/8 and 3/16 oz. or jigs in combination with plastic worms are also deadly on spawning spots. These fish are not easy to catch, but a cautious approach, a good pair of Polaroid glasses, long accurate casts, and light line will often turn the trick.

After spawning is completed and water temperatures reach the upper 60's and lower 70's, the spotted bass immediately heads for deeper water. While the largemouth will often follow the shoreline out towards the main reservoir, the spot follows the creek channels. Because of the spot's constant movement, depth, and negative feeding mood, this is the toughest time of year for anglers. Fish can be caught, particularly off the long tapering points such as area C, but generally fishing is slow. Usually, where tapering points intersect the main creek channel is the best location for post-spawn spotted bass. Here fish may suspend in 10 to 15 feet over a 25-to-35-foot bottom, and swimming a grub at the proper depth is a good tactic, as is a big topwater splash-bait like a Boy Howdy or Zara Spook. Some fish can also be taken on a jig and worm combination, but during this period many anglers simply stay off the water. Fish may be hard to find, but the persistent angler will be rewarded.

	Early Summer	72° F - 78° F
Summertime Locational Patterns	Mid-Summer	78° F - 85° F

As we mentioned in our earlier comments, the calendar periods for highland reservoirs are a little different from those of northern natural lakes. During the summer there are really only two distinct patterns: early summer and mid-summer.

The early summer period typically occurs from about the middle of May until the middle of June. This can be one of the best fishing times and actually is not unlike the pre-summer peak in terms of fish feeding attitude. Location, however, becomes a problem for many anglers. While some spotted bass will remain in the deeper parts of the creek channels or even off the main bluff points all year long, most of the fish will move back into the main reservoir. As the spots move out of the creek channels and into open water, they will mix with post-spawn largemouth, and anglers will often catch mixed strings of fish — if they find any fish at all. The reason that location is so difficult during the early summer is that

"Chet Meyers lips a spotted bass near a bluff on a highland reservoir creek arm."

fish are suspended, usually in relation to long, slow-tapering underwater points. The longer the point, and the further from shore before it drops into deep water, the better. A good early summer point is one that slowly tapers out two or three hundred yards before falling into deep water. Spotted bass school off the tip or parallel to the sides of these points in about 12 to 15 feet of water, *over a bottom 50 or 60 feet deep*. Points such as area D, illustrate this typical early summer location.

Many anglers fail to locate these underwater points or, when they do, insist on dragging lures across the bottom. The best presentation for early summer spots is to position the boat out from such a point in 60 to 70 feet of water and to cast toward the tip or parallel to the sides. Strange as it may seem, surface lures work best. Even though the fish are suspended in 12 to 15 feet of water, they will move up to hit a surface plug, like a Zara Spook or Boy Howdy. Because these are school fish, they will move up to the surface and toward the boat if one of them is caught. But once they get within sight of the boat, they will drop back down to about 12 feet. When this occurs, a small jig/grub can be drifted down to them, and anglers will continue to catch fish. Fishing surface lures over 60 to 70 feet of water is a strange pattern, so many anglers fail to score on early summer spots. But once this method is mastered, it can produce some of the fastest fishing of the entire year.

As we move into the mid-summer period, between the middle of June and the end of September, the spotted bass begin to drop back into deep water. During the mid-summer period, surface temperatures can be between 75° and 85° F, and the water in the main reservoir becomes very clear. This means that most of the fishing is done early in the morning or after sunset. Billy Murray estimates that almost 90% of the spotted bass caught in mid-summer are taken after dusk. This does not mean that spotted bass cannot be caught during the day, but with calm, hot days and air temperatures hovering in the mid- to upper 90's, not many anglers are willing to "fry their brains" for a few fish.

Throughout mid-summer, spots will continue to school with largemouth, but rather than suspending, both species will be either on the surface or near the bottom. The choice of prey determines the location, and in highland reservoirs bass are either feeding on shad or crayfish. During the early morning hours and toward dusk, anglers will actually see schools of bass "busting shad" on the surface. The best approach under these conditions is to use light line and throw a small clear or chrome-colored lure like a Skip Jack, a Near Nothin', or a small white marabou Bass Buster jig. Though shad are an open water baitfish and move about freely, some of the best locations for this schooling bass action are where the mouths of creek and tributaries intersect the main reservoir, and large flat open areas near the end of certain creek arms.

The other locational pattern that typifies the mid-summer period focuses on crayfish as a prey. The crayfish is a nocturnal creature, so night fishing for spots means fishing close to the bottom. Rocky underwater reefs or islands (such as Area E) that are close to deep water or the main river channel are prime locations for spots feeding on crawdads. Other good locations are the same long tapering points that held suspended fish in the early summer. Now, however, the bass will move up on the point and will feed on the bottom in 15 to 20 feet of water. When fishing these rock piles or points in the evening, the best choice of lures is either a single-spin spinnerbait, a plastic worm with a ¼- or ⅜-oz. slip sinker, or a jig-worm combination. One tip on fishing rocky reefs is that an isolated reef will usually hold better concentrations of fish than a series of reefs. Also, the rockier the reef is, the better. A hard mud reef or hump may hold fish, but they will probably be largemouth and not spots.

Cold Water Locational Patterns

Fall   85° F - 60° F (dropping)
Winter 60° F - 40° F

Due to their extreme depth and the fact that water is constantly moving through them, highland reservoirs do not experience the trauma of a fall turnover. Rather, the onset of the cold-water period is signaled by slowly dropping water temperatures and by a temporary dissipation of the thermocline. Because the arrival of the cold-water period is so gradual and calendar periods in highland reservoirs are longer than those in northern natural lakes, there is also no post-summer feeding binge. There is, however, excellent fishing during the fall and winter periods, if anglers can learn not only the locational patterns of the spot, but also appropriate methods of presentation. During the cold-water periods presentation must be exact, as only a limited range of lures and baits will produce fish.

The fall location of spotted bass is determined by the movement of shad from the main reservoir back to the main creek mouths. In these wide creek mouths, the spots will relate to points — both the steep-dropping bluff points, like area A, and the long-tapering points, like area C. Spots will also be found on timbered points where creeks intersect the main reservoir. During the fall period, which extends from the middle of September to the beginning of November, fish located on these points will exhibit two different feeding patterns, surface and deep-water.

During the early morning and late evening, spotted bass will often be found herding shad on the surface. By using your eyes and ears, you can locate this frenzied activity. Obviously, visual contact is easiest on calm days. Most of this activity will take place in a fairly wide area of a creek mouth. It will not extend into the creek narrows. As soon as the sun gets up, the surface activity ceases and both the shad and bass drop into deeper water. On overcast days, however, there can be extended periods of excellent topwater fishing. After locating surface feeding spots, you will notice the bass moving the shad around. One moment they will be breaking water out in the middle, and a few minutes later, the bass will be pushing the shad toward a timbered point. Since these fish move up and down so quickly, fast accurate casts are essential. Small, clear, or chrome lures, like those used during the midsummer period, are very effective when the fish are up. After the bass have crashed into shad on the surface, they will swing around and hit the dead or injured ones as they drop to the bottom. At this time, a slow-dropping

"Jig/grubs are a particularly effective way to take spotted bass when they are feeding on shad."

crappie jig or small tail-spin is most effective. It's a good idea to have two rods, one rigged with a surface plug and the other with a small jig, in order to capitalize on this fact action.

Once the sun comes up and the topwater action ceases, the bass move into deep water. Because the thermocline has dissipated and the water is at its clearest in the fall, it is not uncommon to find midday spots in 40 to 70 feet of water. When this occurs, anglers are faced with a strictly live bait situation. The fish will be on the bottom, on both the bluff and tapering points. The type of point doesn't matter, but water in the 40- to 50-foot range is crucial. The best presentation is a live crayfish, 1½ to 2 inches in length, rigged with a large split shot and dropped straight to the bottom. We will investigate the specifics of this presentation in Chapter 8-C, but for now it is important to note that artificial lures like jigs and grubs simply do not produce effectively during the fall period at midday. Live bait is the only answer.

These two patterns of early and late surface feeding and midday bottom feeding will hold until the water temperature reaches about 50°F. At this temperature, the winter cold-water period begins, and there is a minor shad kill. The remainder of the shad migrate up the creek channels, and, though a few spots will follow, most of the bass turn around and begin a migration back to open water. The spotted bass is overwhelmingly an *open-water wintering fish*. The classic location during this final calendar period is where the main river channel intersects a main reservoir bluff or the bluff of an island, such as area F. Highland reservoirs often have a number of islands, and these island bluffs are the stronghold of the wintering spot.

Fish location is fairly easy to establish. After the fall dissipation of the thermocline, the water begins to restratify and bass will be found in close relation to the new thermocline. This can be anywhere from 25 to 70 feet deep, but a normal winter depth is about 45 feet. Presentation must be slow and accurate, with a small 1/4- to 1/16-oz. jig or forked twin spin of from 3/8 to 5/8 oz. being the best choice. Jigs can be fished on light line; grey and brown seem to be the best colors. The twin spins can be fished on heavier line; white or a white/green combination are the best colors.

Presentation on these bluffs is difficult because the bass will lie right next to the bluff face and will not move more than a foot or two to take a lure. Spots can usually be caught at any time of day during the winter period, but a windy day makes presentation and line watching next to impossible. We will take a close look at this method of presentation in the next chapter. The switch from a fall live bait to a winter artificial presentation is very important and may confuse northern anglers who rely on live bait throughout the cold-water period. In highland reservoirs during the winter, live bait simply does not seem to work. At this time of year, crayfish burrow in the bottom, and shad are not available. Still, you can't help but wonder if some innovative angler might not stumble on some type of live bait to tempt the wintering spotted bass.

Summary of Calendar Periods for Spotted Bass in Highland Reservoirs

Calendar Period	General Fish Location	Fish Attitude	Most Effective Lures	Retrieve
Pre-spawn	Steep bluff points near entrance to main creek channels. Some movement into the secondary channels.	Very Positive	Jig/grub combination and small, deep-diving crankbaits	Slow
Spawn	Move into secondary channels, rock/gravel flats and small coves.	Positive but in clear water spooky	Small jigs (1/8-3/16 oz.), topwater, small spinnerbaits, 4 to 6 inch plastic worms.	Slow steady swimming motion
Post-spawn	Main and secondary channels. Water 25 to 35 feet deep. Long tapering rocky points.	Positive	Jig/grub or jig/worm combinations. Topwater and buzzbaits.	Faster
Early Summer	Slow tapering main reservoir points. Some fish relate to main channel. Often suspended.	Positive	Surface lures on points and jig/grub combinations. Plastic worms.	Erratic hopping action
Mid-summer	Intersections of creek channels and main river. Underwater reefs near main river channel. Long tapering points.	Positive	Plastic worms or jig/worm combination. Clear or chrome topwater lures.	Varied
Fall	Creek mouths, bluff points and tapering points. Early and late on surface. Midday fish are deep. Some migration up creek channels.	Very positive	Surface lures early & late. Small jigs and live bait during midday.	Erratic
Winter	Main reservoir areas where main river channel intersects with bluff point. Deep water 15 to 35 feet. Light penetration a key factor	Positive	Smaller lures. Jigging spoons, forked twin spins, jig/grubs.	Very Slow

CHAPTER 8-B
Spotted Bass Off the Bluffs

Rocky bluffs and spotted bass go together like ham and eggs (or ham and grits). In the preceding section we have seen the important role that bluffs play in both pre-spawn and winter cold-water location of spots, and how small, isolated populations of spots hang around these cliffs all year round. In this section we are going to look at one method of presentation that is extremely effective when fishing rocky bluffs during the *winter cold-water period*. This is a technique that few anglers have mastered. It is a slow method of presentation that requires a lot of patience and pinpoint accuracy. Anglers that like to shotgun a lot of casts and cover a lot of ground may not be attracted to this method at first glance; but once this method is mastered, it becomes the single most effective way to catch cold-water spots.

Bass Location on the Bluffs

As water temperature drops into the upper to mid-50's, many spotted bass move from their primary concentrations near the main creek mouths back into open water and steep island bluffs. Some bass will also remain off the bluffs at the entrance to the creek mouths, and a few bass will even locate in the deeper water of the creek arms near the bluffs. In the early winter, with the surface temperature in the high to mid-50's, the bass often suspend in 20 to 30 feet of water and a distance of 20 to 30 feet from the bluff face. As the temperature cools to the upper and mid-40's the bass simply move closer and closer to the bluff face. Location is fairly easy during the earlier period because fish clearly show up on the depth finder. Presentation is also fairly easy, as anglers can cast to and work a jig through these fish with little difficulty. In the colder period, however, when fish are "nosing" the bluff face, they don't show up on a flasher unit, and presentation can be most difficult. When bass are this close to the bluffs, vertical jigging and normal jig casting simply does not work. A new technique is demanded, one that we will investigate as soon as we identify the best winter fishing bluffs.

The obvious place to find Kentuckies is along the bluff face itself. In the last ten years many anglers have become quite proficient in recognizing these as spotted bass hangouts. They simply work along the length of the bluff and search for a ledge or irregularity in the rock formation that lies at the proper depth to attract Kentuckies. These ledges may be only a few feet in width, but they are one of the keys to locating spots. The fish will usually suspend just off them.

A less obvious, and usually more productive, area is what is known as bluff tailings. These occur at each end of a bluff where the river channel, which generally hugs a bluff, finally swings out away from the shore toward the center of the reservoir. In effect, a ledge or small flat is formed between the face of the bluff and the edge of the river channel. These bluff tailings are always potential hot spots and should be thoroughly checked for fish.

The best winter locations are short isolated bluffs where the main river channel swings by just touching the tip of an island bluff. If you can find an open-water island with a steep bluff near the channel, you are almost sure to locate fish. Ideally this bluff should be about 100 feet long. Longer bluffs, like those over a quarter of a mile, will hold winter bass, but the fish may be so scattered that they prove difficult to locate. Short bluffs, on the other hand,

"Here Bobby Murray demonstrates the proper position for casting when 'scraping the bluffs'."

narrow down the hunting area and make for better concentrations of fish. If you can't locate fish on island bluffs, then try a few mainland bluffs or even main creek bluffs. In either case, bluffs closest to the river or creek channel will usually be the best.

Another consideration when fishing winter spotted bass is to check out other types of structure similar to bluffs. Actually, almost any hard, vertical, isolated structure in open water will hold a few bass. This means that concrete bridge abutments should be checked out. Another underfished structure on highland reservoirs is the large concrete intake towers often located not far from the dam site. These isolated concrete structures may look barren, but bass seem to like them.

It would seem that fishing winter spots is a snap. We have a fairly simple locational pattern and a fish that is generally in a positive feeding mood. All we need to do is master a technique we call "scraping the bluffs" to put the final touches on this case study. And this is where the problems begin, for this particular method of presentation can be difficult. With bass tight up against the bluffs, jig presentation must be right on the money, and putting a 1/8-oz. jig on the money in 45 feet of water is no mean accomplishment.

Scraping the Bluffs

Typical equipment for fishing the bluffs is an open faced spinning reel, a light tipped rod, six-lb.-test line, and jigs between 1/8 and 1/16 oz. The secret of this method is to keep the jig as close to the bluff face as possible. These bluffs are so steep that for every foot you pull the jig away from the bluff you lose about 20% effectiveness of the cast. Winter spots won't more far to take a jig, and you almost have to hit them on the head to get a strike. That's the bad news. The good news is that once you locate fish they will be so tightly schooled that you can often take a limit in less than an hour.

The best way to approach the bluffs is to stay slightly off the bluff and cast right up to it. You want your jig to fall right next to it, "scraping" the bluff as it descends. Making your casts at about a 45 degree angle to the bluffs is the best approach. Casting directly to them tends to make it difficult to keep the jig on the rocks. Every time you move the jig it pulls away from the bluff. So be sure to cast to the bluff at an angle.

Try to place your cast as close to the face of the bluff as possible, no further than a foot away. When the lure hits the water, catch the line with your finger and lower the rod tip so the jig begins to tumble down the bluff. When the rod is parallel to the water, release your finger and quickly raise the rod tip, pulling off six to eight feet of line. Then catch the line with your finger again and continue to walk the jig down the bluff. Continue this process until you locate fish. There may be scattered fish from 15 feet on down, but the bulk of the bass will probably be in 45 feet of water.

During this time of year, do not expect the fish to attack your lure. The reason for keeping your finger on the line as the jig is dropping is to detect the light "tick" that signals a bass. Sometimes you will feel nothing and your only clue will be a slight twitch in the line. A

Scraping the Bluff Faces in Late Fall (water temp. 47°-42°F)

jig bounces and scrapes down rock ledges

—— 55' ——

strike zone

pause

—— 64' ——

high visibility line will help with the winter line-watching. With both your eyes and your finger on the line, you can react quickly and don't even need to engage the bail of your reel. At the slightest sign of anything unusual, set the hook. Even if the line simply stops dropping and doesn't move, set the hook. If you feel no resistance, make another cast; if the lure stops at the same depth, it has probably hit a small ledge. When this occurs, slowly crawl the jig off the ledge until it starts to free-fall. But be prepared. These ledges often hold the best concentrations of fish.

When you locate the depth at which there appears to be a concentration of fish, engage your reel and let the jig float out from the face of the bluff. Do not jig it. Do not swim it. Simply hold your rod, and the line that is in the water will help suspend the jig as it moves away from the bluff. During the winter period, some fish will suspend as far as 15 to 20 feet away from the bluff, and this floating technique will help you reach them. When the lure has worked its way back to the boat, make another cast and follow the same procedure. Often during this floating period you will feel or see nothing, but slowly the line will begin to feel heavy. When this occurs, set the hook. A heavy line usually means a bass.

The main difficulty with this technique is that most anglers tend to "overfish" the lure. They just can't resist giving the jig a little bouncing or swimming action. Certainly this makes the fishing a little more interesting for the angler, but the bass are unimpressed by this additional action.

Bobby Murray remembers a tournament he fished a few years ago, when he shared his bluff-scraping technique with his partner. Bobby was teamed with a woman basser, one of the best from her part of the country. She knew how to catch fish but had never tried this technique on winter spots. Bobby pulled his boat up to one of his favorite bluffs and struck it rich almost immediately. Within two hours he had fifteen bass and had culled a respectable limit for the tournament. His partner had nothing. Well, big-hearted Bobby set down his rod and explained his technique. Old habits are hard to break; after working the jig part of the way down the bluff, Ms. Basser engaged her reel and began tight-lining the jig. She then let it drop, but by that time it was well out of the fish-catching zone. On the next cast, Bobby told her to just peel off as much line as she could and leave it coiled on the bow of the boat. The cast was far enough from the bluff that the jig worked its way quickly down to the 40-foot level. Just as the line ran out, there was a slight twitch and Bobby's partner had her first bass of the day. Soon they both headed in with good limits of spots, and Bobby's partner had another valuable technique to improve her angling versatility.

Choosing the Right Tackle

Obviously a rod with a sensitive tip is necessary when fishing cold-water spots. The person who likes to use heavy tackle for hauling reservoir largemouth out of timber will have to make quite an adjustment. The combination of light lures with deep, clear, open water demands a light tackle approach. "Meat sticks" and heavy line are definitely out of place.

Light- to medium-action spinning rods are the ticket when it comes to spotted bass. Heavier casting tackle just doesn't handle light line and small lures

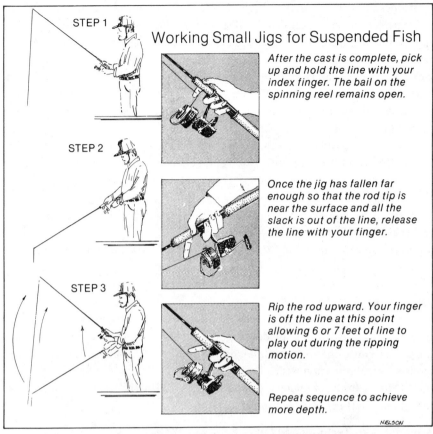

STEP 1
Working Small Jigs for Suspended Fish

After the cast is complete, pick up and hold the line with your index finger. The bail on the spinning reel remains open.

STEP 2

Once the jig has fallen far enough so that the rod tip is near the surface and all the slack is out of the line, release the line with your finger.

STEP 3

Rip the rod upward. Your finger is off the line at this point allowing 6 or 7 feet of line to play out during the ripping motion.

Repeat sequence to achieve more depth.

NELSON

effectively. A sensitive spinning rod, like the six-foot Skyline SKS 6007 graphite, enables you to feel what those tiny lures are doing, even in 60 or 70 feet of water. The strike of a spotted bass is often so light that it's easily missed, and the extra sensitivity of a graphite rod is a plus in detecting them. A graphite rod also provides the backbone needed to set the hook in deep water. An ultralight rig may sound like fun on cold-water spots, but it is too flexible to set the hook when the fish are 40 to 60 feet deep.

Most spotted bass fishing should be done with six-lb.-test line. It has the proper combination of sensitivity and low visibility and is strong enough for fighting spots in open water. Extra clear water may require lighter four-lb.-test line, but generally a premium six-lb.-test line like Berkley's Trilene, Du Pont's Stren, or Weller's Nitro will work fine. When this line is teamed with a quality spinning reel like a Shakespeare 2400, Daiwa G S 13X, or Zebco Cardinal 4, you'll have all the strength you need for handling Kentuckies.

Lure Selection for Scraping the Bluffs

If you examine a good spotted bass fisherman's tackle box, you'll find its contents to be amazingly similar to a crappie fisherman's assortment of goodies. You'd see a collection of small jigs, tiny wire hooks, and light sinkers. Small jigs are the rule, with 1/8 to 1/16 oz. usually the best weight. The actual type of jig head doesn't seem to make much difference. Banana-head, arrow-head, or ball-type jigs work equally well. The type of jig dressing, however, is very important, bucktail being preferred over other materials. Bobby Murray believes that a very sparse jig — 12 or 14 strands of bucktail — produces best for spots. He recommends keeping the physical bulk of the jig to a minimum. Remember, spots are a small fish and you don't need a monstrous lure. And the air trapped in natural bucktail assures that even a few strands will produce a temptingly slow dropping effect.

As for colors, Murray feels that spots show a definite preference toward either brown or gray, although yellow, white, and chartreuse are also effective. A new sorghum color, a combination of yellow and brown, has also been quite productive.

Maribou is a good second choice for winter jig-dressing material. Maribou is such a fine feather that it almost seems to breathe as it is retrieved through the water. It also drops more rapidly than bucktail, so a little bulkier dressing can be used to achieve the same slow-dropping effect.

While jigs are the most effective wintertime presentation, there are times when they present problems. Such is the case when sunken timber stands close to the base of a bluff. When this occurs, the best lure is a forked twin-spin. The forked wire that holds the spinner blades serves as a brush guard and can be used in the timber with little chance of hanging up. The best colors for twin spins are white, or white in combination with a green pork chunk. Of course, a heavier line — in the 10- to 12-lb. test category — and a stiffer rod work better in timber than traditional bluff-scraping equipment.

Adapting This Technique to Other Bodies of Water

Anyone who masters this technique of walking a jig down a bluff has solved one of the biggest problems confronting anglers who like to fish jigs. Most fishermen, no matter where they fish, rely on two methods of jig presentation, both of which are rather unsatisfactory. Many anglers simply cast out and engage their reel immediately. This permits them to be in touch with the jig at all times but also causes the jig to swing pendulum-like back toward the boat, thus missing most of the bottom and much of the fishable water. The other technique often used involves casting out, leaving the bail open until the jig hits bottom, and then beginning to retrieve. This allows anglers to cover more ground but leaves them unaware of any fish that might temporarily grab the jig while it is falling. Since bass most often hit a dropping jig, this technique is as unsatisfactory as the first. By using the "jig-walking" technique and keeping a finger in touch with the line, the angler always knows what is happening. This technique can be used on any steep structure and is effective in fishing rocky smallmouth lakes in Canada or any steep structure on any body of water. It can also be used when casting a jig to the edge of the weedline or in open water. Actually, the applicability of this technique is limited only by the imagination of the fisherman, and its effectiveness will increase angling versatility beyond belief.

CHAPTER 8-C
Live Bait Fishing for Spotted Bass

As the previous two chapters have illustrated, the spotted bass is such a naturally aggressive fish that anglers are seldom forced to teasing it with live bait. Jigs, grubs, tailspins, plastic worms and a few topwater baits will carry most anglers through the various calendar periods without any problem. Midday, during the fall period, is one of the few departures from this pattern. While spots will easily succumb to topwater lures when they are "running shad" early or late in the day, once the sun gets up and the fish drop down, live bait comes into its own. And about 90% of the time this means crayfish. We don't know why spotted bass exhibit such a strong preference for crawdads during the fall, but experience has proven this to be so. It could be that the annual fall migration of crayfish from the shallows to the mud bottoms, where they spend the winter, triggers a feeding spree. Whatever the reason, anglers who insist on fishing artificials during the fall midday are going to end up with very few spots.

Bass Location During the Fall Midday

When Bobby Murray first moved into the highland reservoir belt, he was pretty much an artificial lure angler. Naturally, he and the spotted bass hit it off immediately. It didn't take Bobby long to figure out the seasonal patterns or best lures, but he always seemed to strike out in late September or early October in between the early morning and dusk surface-feeding sprees. Most anglers were happy to take spots early or late and then shift to largemouth bass during the midday period. But Bobby was a guide. And sometimes a party wants to fish for spotted bass in midday. What to do?

After trying a lot of different tactics and locations, Bobby decided to take a lesson from another guide. One of the local guides, by the name of Jack Godfrey, seemed to have spotted bass figured out. He almost always brought in a limit for his party. At first Bobby thought that Jack had discovered a secret location for midday spots. Bobby usually did pretty well fishing creek mouths in the early morning. But when the fish went down, they just seemed to disappear. One day, when Bobby was crossing the reservoir, he saw Jack sitting in front of a creek mouth, on a timbered point, where Bobby had just fished the previous morning. Being the friendly type, and more than a little curious, Bobby pulled over to see how Jack was doing. As it turned out, Jack and his partner were just three fish shy of a 20-bass limit. Bobby asked if Jack minded his fishing in the same area; Jack said there were plenty of fish for everybody.

Old Bobby tied on his favorite jig and slowly began to work the area. He circled Jack's boat three times without a strike. He then picked up some fish on his depth finder and anchored about 15 feet from Jack. For 45 minutes Bobby worked just about every jig and spoon in his tackle box on those bass and never got a hit. Meanwhile, Jack continued to catch fish and cull out the smaller ones. Finally, in desperation, Bobby tossed his lure over to Jack and asked him to rig his line with what they were using.

Jack smiled. Slowly and methodically he reached into his tackle box, clipped off Bobby's jig, tied on a #6 hook, added one large split shot, and finally hooked a small crayfish through the tail. He then tossed the bait over the side of the boat and told Bobby to let it drop to the bottom. The crawdad had fallen about 25 feet when the line twitched and Bobby had a nice two-pound spot. Jack, meanwhile, gave Bobby the rest of his bait and headed in. On the next 15 drops Bobby caught 15 consecutive fish. But he wasn't satisfied. Now that he knew he was on active fish, Bobby began to experiment. He took another rod and dropped a jig down through the bass. Nothing happened. Next he tied on a small jigging spoon. No action. Finally, he eased another crawdad over the side and was fast to another spotted bass.

A strange story. Usually when fish are actively feeding they can be caught on more than one type of presentation, but not with midday spots. It was clear to Bobby that location was not the problem. The bass were still off the same points where he had caught them on surface plugs earlier in the day. The answer was *not* finding a new location, but changing presentation. When he realized that live bait was the answer, Bobby tried a few other locations and came up with similar results. Though the vast majority of spots are found near creek mouths in the fall, there are still a few fish relating to bluffs and open water reefs. When Bobby tried crayfish on these locations, he also caught fish.

Bobby also began to experiment with other types of live bait and found that leeches and crawlers, while not as effective as crayfish, would take bass. So the problem of midday spots was solved. But the mystery remains. Why should a fish so easy to catch on artificials during most of the year suddenly refuse these and accept only live bait? We still don't know why. And whenever we locate a school of spots during a fall midday, we try our jigs and spoons, but never with any luck. Maybe this is Mother Nature's way of reminding us that we still have a few things to learn about her creatures.

Tackle and Presentation for Live Bait Fishing

The tackle used in fishing live bait is the same as that described in the chapter on "scraping the bluffs." A medium-action spinning rod, teamed with an open-faced reel and six-lb.-test line, works just fine. If you should locate some bass in and around timber, it is best to move to eight- to ten-lb. test. Usually fall spots will take crayfish with such abandon that presentation doesn't have to be finicky.

The best crayfish size is two to three inches, and the best type is softshell crab. When a spot grabs a softshell, you can set the hook immediately. If you are using a hardshell crawdad, be prepared to wait a while. A spot will typically pick up a hard shell, crush it, and then spit it out to see if it is dead. The fish may do this

"*Spotted bass usually average only about a pound. Bobby Murray hefts a stringer that includes some real lunkers.*"

two or three times before actually swallowing its prey. When this happens, hold your rod at a 45 degree angle and let the fish bang the bait a few times. Drop the rod tip as the fish hits the crawdad. When the bass takes hold and starts to move off, slowly lower the rod tip 'til it just about touches the water and then set the hook. This takes patience, but if you try to set the hook immediately you will simply pull the bait away from the bass.

The actual rigging of the crayfish is simplicity itself. A #6 or #8 Aberdeen hook, in either black or bronze, is tied directly to the line, and then one large split shot is added about ten inches above the hook. Your best bet is to hook the crawdad up through the tail, about one-third of the way toward the body. Then, simply drop the bait to the bottom, counting all the way down. During the fall period, spotted bass may suspend off the bottom and it's only a matter of experimentation until you locate the right depth. When fishing on the bottom, try to keep some tension in your line so the crawdad does not crawl under a rock or log. This is particularly crucial when using softshell crabs. The softshell instinctively seeks cover because of its vulnerability. It if gets under an object, chances are your hook will tear free from the bait.

During the fall, live-bait fishing usually occurs in depths from 25 to 40 feet of water. There are occasions, however, before the spots start hitting shad on the surface, when you can take them in 12- to 15-foot depths. Under these conditions, take off the split shot and let the crawdad sink naturally to the bottom. There aren't many spots that can resist a sight like that.

Variations on a Theme

The live bait technique we have just described is exactly the same as that used on smallmouth bass in natural lakes. Its simplicity surprises many anglers, who are used to more sophisticated live-bait rigs, such as the slip sinker and bottom-walker. Of course, other rigs would probably work on spotted bass, but they just aren't necessary. Why go to a lot of extra work when the fish isn't that finicky? Remember, this isn't a touchy walleye, who will spit the bait at the slightest sign of resistance. You can have a real tug-of-war with a spotted bass before he will let go.

Northern anglers may be tempted, like Bobby was, to use other types of live bait. Our experiments have proved that leeches and worms will work. For some unexplained reason minnows don't seem to produce. Leeches are probably the best "backup" bait, though they are seldom used in the south and can be difficult to locate. Still, if you're a Yankee angler planning a fall trip south, slip a few dozen leeches into the cooler. Your southern guide may look twice, but you'll probably take some bass. Just be sure to take along a good supply of crawdads. The added versatility of crayfish is that at the end of the day when you return to the marina you can use Mr. Crawdad as an hors d'oeuvre. Just take your crawdads into the kitchen, pop off their tails, toss them into some boiling water and serve the tails with cocktail sauce — that's something you can't do with leeches.

CHAPTER 9
River Classification System

Throughout the ages, rivers and civilization have existed side by side. The annual flooding of the Nile turned desert sands into agricultural fields that nourished the first great empires of the world. Ancient civilization began along the Tigris and Euphrates Rivers.

In our own country, rivers provided the first highways for the Indians and early fur traders. From historical documents, we know that the fish population of America's rivers was incredible. Sadly, as towns and cities developed and as the industrial revolution dawned, rivers became open running sewers. Fish populations died off, and most anglers turned to lakes in search of game fish. The past decade, however, has seen a reversal of this trend. With more concern about the environment, and with the aid of federal legislation, rivers have begun to rejuvenate themselves. In fact, even environmental scientists have been amazed at the speed with which rivers can clean up their systems. With many fish populations at an all-time high, it is surprising how little fishing pressure most rivers receive.

Excluding the Great Lakes, rivers comprise approximately 20 per cent of the total surface area of inland fresh waters in the lower 48 states. In the continental United States, there are approximately 900,000 miles of streams. A Bureau of Sport Fisheries and Wildlife survey indicates that over 700,000 stream miles are productive for fishing, and only 100,000 miles of productive streams are in private ownership. American anglers should be very grateful for this. In England, Ireland, and Southern Europe, fishing streams are largely under private ownership.

Of our 700,000 miles of public fishing streams, about half are considered suitable for some variety of cool- or warm-water species, such as walleyes, bass, pike, and panfish. Cold-water streams, the home of trout and salmon, have a combined surface area of over 1.5 million acres, compared to roughly 3.4 million surface acres for cool- or warm-water streams. Thus, well over twice as many streams shelter bass, walleye, etc., as shelter cold-water species such as trout and salmon.

In this chapter, we will naturally focus attention on cool- and warm-water rivers that contain populations of smallmouth and largemouth bass. In our classification system, we do not consider regional differences. To do so would unnecessarily complicate matters. It should be obvious, however, that regional variation is important.

Rivers in the state of Maine generally differ from those in Mississippi, Texas, or Florida. Mississippi streams produce largemouth bass, crappies, sunfish, white bass, and catfish, while in Maine the waters are more likely to have brown trout, native brookies, and rainbows. By the same token, rivers west of the Rocky Mountains host different species than those of the Midwest. Regional climatic conditions and fluctuating local geography create great diversity in rivers and fish species that inhabit them.

While the geographical make-up in some states is quite uniform, in others it varies greatly. Arkansas has cool/cold-water streams that harbor rainbow trout and smallmouth bass, as well as warm-water streams that support largemouth and catfish. Wisconsin rivers play host to almost every imaginable freshwater fish. The Sabine and Angelina in Texas have largemouth bass, alligator gar, and crappie, while rivers that pour into the ocean in the same region are the home of brackish saltwater species like striped bass.

The Classification System

Geologists refer to rivers as "young," "middle-aged," or "old." These terms describe the nature or condition of the landscape carved by the river more than the actual age of the river itself. On some big rivers, like the Mississippi, Missouri, Ohio, and the Arkansas, you can see huge, well-developed flood plains — good evidence of an old river. Here, the original banks may be miles away and hundreds of feet higher than the existing stream bed. The surrounding geography and shape of the riverbed are the main clues to a stream's age.

In its youth, a river plunges rapidly downhill, cutting through narrow valleys. As a river matures, it moves more slowly and meanders gently through broad valleys bounded by smoothly rounded hills. In old age, a river curves widely across level flood plains surrounded by worn-down hills. The major catalyst to aging is erosion.

The process of erosion actually carries the aging process upstream. This gradual upstream aging is what usually reduces waterfalls to rapids. Most rapids were former waterfalls. Holes gouged out under the waterfalls were forerunners of the pools that occur under rapids. Of course, these pools are now elongated and shallower. Little by little, through the aging process, rapids and pool areas wear away into flat river runs with occasional dips. Interestingly, St. Anthony Falls, near Minneapolis, Minnesota, receded quite a distance from the time when the city was first built. Given enough time, the falls would have eventually worn away into a fast plunging rapids and the gradient eventually reduced to a rapid flow instead of a falls. Of course, the construction of a dam halted the further movement of the falls upstream.

Many factors contribute to a river's changing character — width, depth, gradient, current flow, and chemical characteristics. Especially important are the geological rock formations the river flows through and over. During each step along its route to the sea, a river changes personality, resembling a virtual aquatic schizophrenic.

Indeed, it is unusual for a river to be the same throughout its entire course. The ability to classify a particular stretch is very important. Certain stretches,

"The number of lake anglers outnumbers river anglers by about ten to one. But with smallmouth bass like this to be had, the word on river angling is finally getting out."

depending on which category they fall into, are more conducive to some fish species than to others. You may find walleyes in one section, smallmouth bass a few hundred yards away, and largemouth bass in a nearby backwater area.

A particular section of a river can be young, old, or somewhere in between. For example, a stream might be quite shallow, taper slowly for several miles, and have a number of backwater areas with a soft bottom and aquatic weed growth. Here largemouth bass and/or northern pike might be able to find adequate habitat. But all of a sudden, the same stream might break into a sharp gradient as it shoots through a rocky cliff-like area, creating rapids and finally pouring into a boulder-based pool. This younger stretch, although further downstream, could house smallmouth bass and, possibly, stocked rainbow trout.

With all these variations in mind, let's take a look at some specific characteristics of the different types of rivers. The classification system on the chart that follows is intentionally simple. But we think it will provide a few clues helpful in psyching out a river's fishing potential.

Treating Moving Water and Current as Structure

To fish rivers effectively, you have to understand current. If you don't, not only will you fail to locate fish, your presentation will be inappropriate. Current dominates the life force of a river and is the key to fish movement and location. Whereas in lakes fish relate to structural breaks like weedlines and drop-offs, in rivers fish relate to breaks resulting from changes in current velocity. To a river fish, a knife-edged wall of fast water, bounded by slower or slack water, is just as real as a vertical hunk of rock or a sharp drop-off. Objects on the bottom also

RIVER STRETCH CLASSIFICATION	YOUNG	MIDDLE-AGED	OLD
GEOLOGICAL MAKEUP BOTTOM CONTENT	Cuts through rock quickly due to steep gradient. Stream bed composed of both solid sheets of rock and broken rubble. Silt absent. Little sand present. Usually little vegetation.	Main channel composed mostly of sand, with some gravel stretches and rock outcroppings. Siltation becomes a factor; wing dams constructed to control this. More vegetation present.	Little if any "cutting" through rock. River tends to meander back and forth across old flood plain. Stream bed flows over sand or silt. Often dredging is necessary to keep channel open.
KEY IDENTIFYING FEATURES	Lots of rapids, with pools at head and foot of rapids and plenty of shallow water stretches in between. Some sections may dry up during summer.	Few, if any, true rapids. Some riffles and fast water in narrows. Man-made structure more prevalent; wing dams, bridges, runoff culverts, etc.	Flat, slow water with natural levees and man-made levees. Some sections may resemble lakes and often are treated like lakes by anglers.
CROSS SECTION OF STREAM BED	Very Little Vegetation Some Timber. Banks Rounded. Channel Bottom Begins to Round-Out with Rock Deposits	Flood Plain. Sand and Gravel Deposits	Natural Levees. Bluffs may Form. Channel may be Dredged
GRADIENT AND DEPTH	Gradient varies greatly for different sections but averages three to four feet per mile. Depths generally from three to six feet, with some pools 10 to 12 feet deep.	Gradient usually one and one-half to two feet per mile. Depths average eight to 10 feet. Some shallow stretches will be four to five feet. Deeper holes can be 15 to 20 feet deep.	Gradient extremely slow, between one-half and one foot per mile. Depth often a function of dredging. Main channel depths of 20 feet not uncommon.

RIVER STRETCH CLASSIFICATION	YOUNG	MIDDLE-AGED	OLD
PROBABLE SPECIES OF FISH PRESENT	Brook trout, stocked browns and rainbow, northern pike and in eastern U.S., chain pickerel. Sturgeon and suckers.	Smallmouth, walleye, sauger, northern pike, muskie, chain pickerel, catfish, silver bass, sturgeon, carp, perch, crappie, rock bass, buffalo, some largemouth in backwaters.	Largemouth and some northerns or pickerel if temperature remain low. Carp, white bass.
WATER QUALITY	Water is very clear and clean, except during times of high water. Some young streams stained as they drain through tamarack swamps.	Water color semi-clear to murky. Can be very turbid during high water, especially in agricultural areas. Water quality degrades quickly in industrial and agricultural areas.	Water is constantly turbid, but can clear considerably in lake-like areas where suspended material settles. Quality also improves where younger tributaries enter.
SOURCE AND DRAINAGE AREA	Springs and freshets from highland source. Often drains mixed pine and hardwood forests and areas of lumbering activity.	River flows through mixed hardwood forests and farming land. Many tributaries at this stage. Drains farmland and some urban areas.	Usually associated with main urban areas. A broad flood plain is prized as farming land. Few tributaries and often considerable pollution.
TYPICAL ILLUSTRATIONS	Hilly regions of Arkansas, tributaries of Buffalo, the Brule in Wisconsin, the North Shore rivers of Minnesota, Michigan's upper peninsula, White Mountains of Vermont, Shenandoah Valley tributaries, and salmon rivers of Maine.	Susquehanna in Pennsylvania, many smaller tributaries of the Mississippi, St. Croix in Minnesota, lower Buffalo in Arkansas, lower Black in Wisconsin.	Larger rivers in lower stretches, such as the Missouri, Ohio, Arkansas, and Mississippi.

slow, reverse, stop, or alter the flow of current, and river fish are extremely sensitive to all these changes.

Unfortunately, changes in current are not so obvious to anglers. Although some graph recorders indicate water turbulence, river fishermen must rely primarily on their eyes to locate current breaks. While it may be impossible to see a submerged boulder, its presence is revealed by a "boil" on the surface downstream from the actual location. Eddy currents, which circle back upstream, often occur below a point bar or any obstruction that breaks the surface. To a river rat, an eddy is as obvious as standing timber is to a reservoir angler. Of course, in slow rivers, where largemouth bass are dominant, there are often large sections with almost no current. Such a widening in a river often resembles a lake and should be fished accordingly.

"Even small boulders like this one can hold one or two river smallies."

How Rivers and Lakes Differ

From an ecological point of view, a lake is considered a "closed" system, while a river is an "open" system. What does this mean?

In general, the materials of life (plankton, vegetation, nutrients) remain within a lake and may be used over and over again. In contrast, a river receives most of its nourishment from without, and while life supporting materials may remain for a time lodged somewhere in a plant or animal, they all eventually pass downstream never to return directly. Thus, a river continuously receives new water and nourishment from the surrounding terrain. Even those life forms which develop within the river eventually work their way toward the sea, through the food chain, and out of the river's ecosystem.

River fishermen face more sudden and dramatic changes in water conditions than a lake fisherman can imagine. Most lakes are "a piece of cake" when compared with rivers. Water levels in natural lakes remain relatively stable over long periods of time. It usually takes a long-term drought or heavy rainfall to bring about severely high or low water levels in a lake. Yet river anglers are always fighting rising or falling water levels. They also have to adjust to bottom structure that is constantly changing. Sandbars and holes come and go and can change with a shift of the stream's course or increase in current.

Changing water levels will also affect fish location. As rapidly as water levels rise and fall, a good fish-holding current can suddenly appear or completely vanish. A pile of submerged rocks that might hold smallmouth bass during a spring flood could be high and dry a week later. Time on the river is the best way to learn to read currents and identify fish-holding structure, but the following examples from a middle-aged river should give anglers a good head start.

Channels

Main channels are the highways of river fish and are used during major migrations. The main channels, as well as side and feeder channels, all meander to some degree. A stream bed can shift rapidly, depending on the force and volume of the water. For example, a gravel tongue on an inside bend that was there one year may not be present the next. While channels are the primary migration routes, there are times when fish may avoid them because of the speed of the current. Thus, during periods when a river is flooding, most fish move out of the main channel and seek calmer side-water sloughs.

Point Bars on the Inside Bends of Rivers

Point bars are formed by the cutting action of the current. They are excellent holding areas for all fish. The river cuts the outside bend of a meander and deposits sand or gravel on the inside turn where there's reduced current. In the process, a tongue-like structure resembling a point is formed. Point bars also create eddy currents as water flows around them. Fish are attracted to such an area because the slower eddy current provides relief from the stronger current of the main channel and its reverse current pulls food into the eddy.

Sloughs

Sloughs are connected with the main river channel. As water levels in the main channel drop, so do water levels in the sloughs. Sometimes sloughs dry up completely. Due to the lack of current, these areas provide an attractive habitat for many warm-water species of fish, since they need expend little energy to maintain position. Sloughs maintain good oxygen levels throughout the year because of their connection to the main channel. Usually warmer than the main river, they are more desirable for warm-water fish such as largemouth bass. While smallmouth bass may often be found at the entrance or exit of a slough, they seldom move into the slough except during periods of high water.

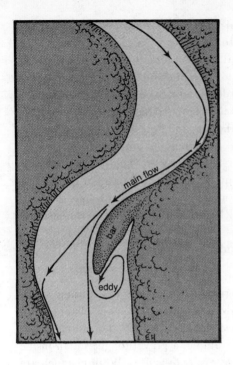

This diagram illustrates the formation of a point bar and the resulting eddy.

Natural Levees of Hard Material Left by Floods

These areas usually contain water only during floods and dry up as the river returns to normal. During floods, the current in the main channel is at its highest and carries large particles of sand in suspension. As the current drops, the particles in suspension begin to fall out and form a gravel or coarse sand bed near the river bank. During normal water levels, these areas are usually very shallow. But if there is some cover in the form of large rocks or logs, smallmouth or largemouth could use them for spring spawning.

Man-made Structures

Man-made structures are widespread on most rivers. Bridges, levees, concrete or sheet-steel sea walls, mooring posts, dams and spillways are all examples. Of all man-made structures, one of the most important is the wing dam. Although constructed for utilitarian purposes, wing dams are highly attractive to fish. These tangled structures of wood and rock attract smaller bait fish as smaller life forms are dropped into the calmer eddy waters. By funneling the water, wing dams also increase the current and thus keep the water cooler and more oxygenated.

Fish generally lie on the downstream side using the wing dam as a current breaker. As depth and velocity change, so do the currents and fish location. During high water, smallmouth bass would be below the wing dam and toward the shore on the eddy side of the main current. As the water level drops and currents change, they could be expected to move out toward the tip of the dam. During low water levels, the fish will hold on the downstream side of the

The diagram below indicates the typical construction and pattern of water flow of a wing dam. The interlaced rows of saplings and rocks provide both a hiding place and food source for baitfish and gamefish. Most anglers focus on the downstream side, but some wing dams have washout holes on the upstream side that will hold bass.

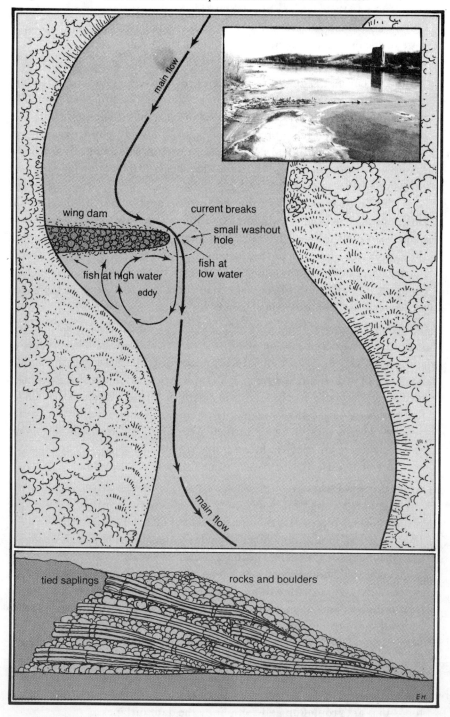

wing dam, on the upstream side, or they might abandon this structure altogether.

Depending on sufficient water level, wing dams could be fished most of the year. Brush on the banks, or brush interwoven within the dam itself, makes an even more attractive spot. If the wing dam continues out quite far and gets close to the main river channel, it becomes a super fish magnet.

Sandbars

Sand is constantly deposited and eroded in rivers. Thus, sandbars are always shifting and are the least permanent structural features of a river. The importance of sandbars for anglers lies in the current breaks they create and how fish relate to those breaks. Though not always uniform in shape, sandbars usually are tapered slowly on the upstream side and drop steeply on the downstream. In navigable rivers, the constant formation of sandbars necessitates regular dredging.

A long sandbar extending from the downstream tip of an island will hold smallmouth. The sandbar will often be about one to three feet deep, but will quickly drop off into the main channel, and will have a harder bottom than the side channel because of the flushing action of the current. A noticeable current break will form alongside of and downstream from the bar. Sometimes smallmouth will be right on top of it, next to the edge of the weeds that extend out from the side channel.

Tributary Entrances

In many rivers this can be one of the best fishing spots. The process of erosion builds up a host of structural elements at these junctions. The intersection of a tributary stream can vary a great deal in makeup, so it may take some time and effort to figure out a pattern. Usually there is a distinct lip that builds up on the downstream side where the tributary enters. The better defined the structure, the more attractive to fish. If it is made up of rock or gravel and there are snags or brush along with it, the spot is even better. It's a good bet that you will usually take some fish here year-round.

Areas Below a Dam

The concrete wing walls which form the sides of the apron of the dam are very important pieces of structure, provided you can fish close to the dam. The important thing to remember is that the water along the wall flows slower than the main stream of flow, forming a current break.

The edge of the underwater apron also attracts fish, especially when the water is low. On a smaller dam, this area will have vegetation and tend to hold minnows and other bait fish. Other fish locations are where the two edges of the apron join the wing walls.

Immediately below the rim of a dam's concrete apron is a deep washout area that usually holds good quantities of fish in summer. Big boulders and other structures on the bottom provide excellent slack water for all types of fish. This super-oxygenated water is a natural settling hole for all the fish foods that are ground up and spit out by the dam turbines.

While many anglers tend to associate dam fishing with walleyes or catfish, most fail to realize that some of these areas host large populations of bass. After the walleyes move out at the end of spring spawning, it is not unusual to catch smallmouth bass near dams in exactly the same area. Of course smallmouth need a little different type of structure. When seeking spring smallies, look for areas below dams where a large rock offers a break from the current and a convenient nesting place.

Of course there are other fish locations on rivers than those we've discussed. You'll discover different ones as you become familiar with river currents. Almost any obstacle in the current's path provides a potential resting and ambush point for river gamefish. By learning to read the surface of the water, you'll soon learn where these current breaks are located — and on a smallmouth river, current breaks and fish often go hand in hand.

River fishing offers one of the last frontiers in the angling world. One reason this frontier still remains is that river rats have been keeping their mouths shut and the fishing all to themselves. Rivers differ from lakes in that current itself becomes a structural consideration. Rivers are also less affected by cold fronts than are lakes. And, finally, river fish feed more often and fight better than their lake cousins. On the negative side, we must admit that rivers are more difficult to fish than lakes. Presentation is much more problematical, and fluctuating water levels can drive a lake angler crazy. In the chapters that follow, we will help you learn how to overcome the negative and accentuate the positive.

CHAPTER 10-A
Case Study: Smallmouth Bass in Middle-aged Rivers

The river rat is a breed apart. While many lake anglers ply their waters in streamlined, powerful, electronically equipped bass boats, the river rat climbs into his rusty old johnboat, cranks up a 150, 10-horsepower Johnson, and uses a paddle when he needs a depth finder. While the bassin' boys like to effect a professional aura with their color-coordinated jump suits, bass tournaments, and fancy language, the river rat wears what he pleases, fishes alone, and keeps his mouth shut. Perhaps the difference between these two stereotypes is appropriate, for the waters they fish are equally as different.

Lakes are fairly predictable, once you understand their structural makeup and seasonal patterns. Rivers are not only more structurally complex, but their moods vary, rolling calmly along one day and the next day raging with a torrent that intimidates man and beast alike. Presentation on a lake is usually simple, except in heavy weeds, sunken timber, or over rocky shoals. But all these elements are present in rivers, with the added complication of current. We have known more than a few competent lake anglers who just couldn't cope with the twisting, turning, ever-changing nature of river currents. Trying to keep a jig moving slowly downstream without hanging up, or learning to present live bait naturally in deep, fast pools, can test the skill and determination of the best. With all these difficulties, it is not surprising that rivers remain an untapped fishing resource. But once a few skills are mastered, fishing rivers can become one of the great joys of angling, particularly for the fisherman who loves the high leaping antics of the smallmouth bass.

Current as Structure

The life of a river smallmouth is one of constant movement. Every day of its life, even before it is able to swim, a bass must contend with the force, turbulence, and fluctuations of river currents. This constant battle creates a bass that is a little leaner than a lake or reservoir cousin. It also creates a muscular fish that knows how and when to use the force of the river to its advantage.

When analyzing the fishing potential of a lake, we usually focus on its structural makeup, both natural and man-made. In rivers, physical structure is also important, but equally important is the recognition that *current itself* becomes structure. In rivers, fish spend most of their time in what are called holding stations, areas of relative calm not far from the main current. Sometimes a small area of only a few square feet, behind a rock, can serve as a holding station. As the water breaks over the rock, it produces turbulence that has the effect of creating a calm-water pocket. This pocket becomes structure. Another classic example of current as structure occurs whenever water breaks around an object, for example, a wing dam. During normal water level, when the force of the current strikes the dam, it breaks and forms a small whirlpool. The water actually circles back on itself, with a small area of calm water created behind the dam and a line of relatively calm water below the dam. Bass will relate to these current breaks, and the wise angler uses his eyes to note the resulting surface disturbance. Learning to read the surface of river waters as a clue to current breaks is a big part of river angling.

Another, and different, type of current as structure is created when two streams join together, or when a smaller stream enters a river. This type of current break can be particularly visible if, for example, one stream is clear and the other muddy. The confluence of the clear waters of the St. Croix River with the murky old Mississippi at Prescott, Wisconsin, is a good example. The current line from these two rivers sometimes remains distinct for 40 to 50 yards downstream. Bass and walleye relate to this mixing current, for here they have their choice of foods from two sources. We will look at a number of examples of river structure and current breaks in the case study that follows.

Danny Boy River

For our case study on river smallmouth, we have chosen a typical middle-aged river that could exist in just about any part of the smallmouth's natural range. We picked a middle-aged river because these rivers have perhaps the greatest structural variety. Once again, the seasonal patterns will depend on water temperature, for Danny Boy River could be in upper New England, the midwest, or as far south as Georgia. In choosing fish-holding structure, we have limited ourselves to a few of the more important examples that almost any river would exhibit.

Area A   A small wing dam of limestone rock and saplings. It sticks out into the river about ten yards and creates a nice eddy.

Area B   The inside bend of the river. It is covered with small gravel and a few large rocks about two feet in diameter.

Area C   A sunken log or tree that extends from the bank and has only its major branches intact (i.e., not sunken brush).

Area D   A gravel bar that extends out from the shore, creating an eddy and a scoop-out hole about seven feet deep.

Area E   The outside bend of the river, usually where the deeper water is.

Area F   The deeper main river channel, in this case about eight to ten feet deep, with some large rocks on the bottom.

As you can see from these examples, Danny Boy River, in this particular section, is not very deep. But don't be disappointed by a river's lack of depth. These sections are often the prime producers of smallmouth bass. Now let's take a look at the seasonal movements of river smallies and some suggestions for lures and baits.

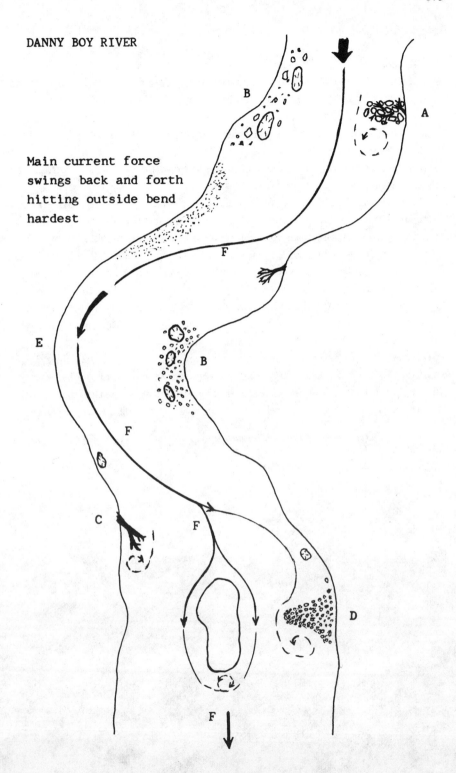

DANNY BOY RIVER

Main current force
swings back and forth
hitting outside bend
hardest

Pre-spawn	45°F - 55°F
Spawn	56°F - 60°F
Post-spawn	61°F - 65°F

Springtime Locational Patterns

In the northern sections of our country, spring often arrives with a rush. If the spring thaw is rapid and accompanied by warm rain, the rivers will exhibit their largest floods of the year. On these occasions, ice-out is a spectacular event, with gigantic masses of ice roaring downstream, tearing huge chunks of earth from the bank, and sometimes carrying away large trees and even a house or two. This is no time to fish, but rather a time to contemplate Mother Nature's power, and to stand in awe of it.

There are other years, however, when the ice slips slowly away. One day it's there and a few days later it's gone. When the ice is gone, the river quickly warms, generating the spawning urge, first in northerns, then walleyes and later bass. The walleye spawn usually peaks at about 44°F to 48°F. Because temperatures fluctuate so rapidly in rivers, the smallmouth bass could spawn anywhere from one week to a month later than the walleyes. Warm sunny days or a warm rain can turn the bass on quickly, so it's wise to carry a thermometer and keep close tabs on water temperature. When the walleyes have finished spawning, Mr. Smallie is usually waiting in the wings.

During the pre-spawn, while the walleyes are "doing their thing," the smallmouth are biding their time in deep, relatively calm water. This is a tough time to catch bass. When water temperatures are below 50°F, the smallmouth's metabolism is slow and they prefer the deeper water zone near the main channel.

"This is what a typical stretch of smallmouth spawning water looks like in the fall during low water."

Usually they can be found in the central one-third of the river, in water eight to 12 feet deep. They seek this deep, calmer water because they simply don't have enough energy to hold in fast water. Many anglers believe that the fastest current is in the middle of the river. While this is often true, it only holds for the top layer of water. River current grades fast to slow, from top to bottom. So Mr. Smallmouth can be pretty comfortable resting in the middle of a river on the bottom. A classic pre-spawn location is about 100 feet below a small rapids, or below gravel bars (area D) in the deepest part of the pool. About the only presentation that is effective during the pre-spawn is live bait, with crawlers, surprisingly, working better than minnows. Of course if the river is flooding, don't expect to find the bass in mid-channel. Under these circumstances, look for any available eddy with relatively calm water.

With widely fluctuating water temperatures in the early spring, smallmouth can be lethargic one day and show a flurry of activity the next. As water temperatures begin to stabilize in the mid-50's, however, the smallmouth will move out of deeper water and being looking for a nesting place in the shallows. 56°F seems to be a pivotal temperature for this movement. The fish instinctively avoids the calm backwater areas that many anglers logically look to for spawning bass. The smallie knows that a slight current is necessary in order to keep its eggs aerated and free from silt. Thus, the bass seek an area away from the main current but with enough current to do the job. Usually the inside bend of a river (area B) is a good prospecting place. As water courses around a bend, the inside bend receives the least flow. Here bass like to drop their eggs behind rocks or logs. The best size rocks always seem to be about two feet in diameter. Rocks that are completely submerged work better than those that are partially exposed. Unless you know these rocks are around, they are tough to spot. But an underwater boulder always gives away its presence by a telltale "boil" that comes to the surface a few feet *below* the rock. Once you locate good smallmouth spawning rocks, you will find fish there year after year, if the water level is sufficient.

If rocks are not available, the bass will use other obstructions, such as sunken logs, dock pilings, or even old tires. They will usually nest in water less than two feet deep, but seldom will you be able to spot their nests. The constant movement of the current prevents the construction of a nice tail-swept, symmetrical bed, such as a largemouth might construct. Instead, the action of water flowing around an obstruction must do the nest building. Other natural spawning areas include places where tiny spring rivulets enter the river, flooded standing timber, and flooded grass beds.

During the spawn, brightly colored lures or flashy spoons seem to produce the best. Silver crankbaits and jig-spinners work very well. You can also take fish on small jigs, tipped with a little piece of crawler. The best time of day in the spring seems to be between 9 a.m. and 2 p.m. However, water temperatures can fluctuate quite a bit, with cold evenings and warm sunny days. If the nights are particularly cold, the bass might not "turn on" until after 10 or 11 o'clock the next afternoon.

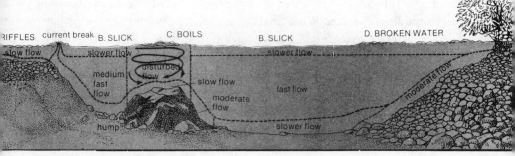

Typical Current Flow Patterns

Current velocity (speed) is not the same in all parts of a river channel. Friction on the sides, around obstructions and along the bottom slows the water's speed and results in different surface patterns.

*The surface **riffles** at A are produced by shallow water running over rocks. At the drop-off, the change in water speed results in a visible disturbance on the water's surface known as a **current break**. The **slick** surface at B is formed when water runs over a smooth bottom like silt or sand. But as soon as a rock or similar object interrupts the water's flow, you'll see **broken water** as shown at D or highly disturbed water like the **boils** at C. These surface disturbances are your "eyes" to the bottom and help you to locate fish.*

The post-spawn can provide some good fishing, but very few large bass are taken. Large females, just like their largemouth cousins, drop back into deeper water to recuperate from the rigors of spawning. They usually move to the same areas used during the pre-spawn, but this time even live bait won't tempt them. It takes about ten days to two weeks before the females are willing to feed once again. Meanwhile, the males freely roam the shallows. They are scattered, and every shallow rock or tree holds one or two. For these fellows, spinners, such as Mepps, Abu Reflex, or Panther Martin, work well. Jigs and jig-spinners also produce, as do small crankbaits. To tell the truth, it's hard not to catch little smallies at this time of year. Just about anything works.

Early Summer 65° F - 72° F
Mid-summer   73° F - 78° F

Summertime Locational Patterns   (higher than 78° F, depending on region)

The summer locational patterns of smallmouth bass are fairly predictable, so long as water levels remain constant. A heavy summer rain usually triggers a sudden feeding spree, followed by periods of inactivity as fish drop back into available calm water. During most of the summer, however, bass will spend much of their time in water five to eight feet deep. These bass will be in small schools of eight to ten fish and will hold below wing dams (area A), below gravel bars (area D), on the upstream end of outside river bends (area E), and in the deeper channel (area F).

Though river fish are seldom in a negative feeding mood, there will be periods of intense feeding activity. When these occur, the smallies always seem to move up-river as they feed and then drop back down-river once feeding is completed. During these feeding sprees they also move from deep water into the shallows. A clue to these movements is the sight of frantic baitfish skipping over the surface in the shallows. A skipping baitfish is seldom jumping for joy but, most often, looking at a pair of tonsils. When the bass are in the shallows, shallow diving crankbaits, like a Cordell Little O or a floating Rapala, are proven killers.

During neutral periods, when the bass are in deeper water, live bait or a jig in combination with live bait will catch fish. We like to use bottom-walking sinkers, like Gapen's or Mr. Twister's, for presenting crawlers or minnows to deep-feeding smallies. The typical slip sinker just doesn't seem to be able to cope with river currents and is forever hanging up. The bait walker skips along with nary a care. In Chapter 10-B, when we focus on how to "slip" a river, we will go over this method of presentation in more detail.

Fish behavior in the summer differs from that of the spring in that the fish are now schooled by size — the bigger the fish, the smaller the school. When bass get to be four or five pounds, there are usually only three or four fish in a school. Of course the really big bass are almost always loners. Two- to three-pound fish will form schools of between eight and 12 fish. And smaller bass will be in bigger schools yet. Though most summer bass are schooled, there will always be a few singles. A good place to prospect for these stragglers is behind rocks that held spawning bass in the spring. These rocks are now partially exposed, but if there is enough water behind them you'll usually find a smallmouth ready to pounce on your lure.

Toward the hot summer "dog days," smallmouth will remain in the same stretch of river they inhabited earlier but will inevitably drop down into the cooler pools. The mid-channel locations that held fish in the pre-spawn and post-spawn will once again pull fish. The best mid-summer holding areas are what we refer to as "slicks." A slick is the smooth water just below large eddies or the head of rapids. This area is not immediately below the rapids, which typically has choppy, standing waves, but below the standing waves where the water surface is smooth and the river bottom starts to slope upwards. A few large rocks to help create holding stations will make a slick the perfect place for mid-summer smallies. The best depth for a slick is between eight and 12 feet.

During the hottest part of the summer, many anglers naturally look for bass in the deepest holes available. And while many middle-aged rivers have holes 15 to 20 feet deep, these areas seldom hold smallmouth. The reason for the lack of game fish in deep river holes is that they have silt-covered bottoms and no food.

If you fail to locate fish in the mid-depth slicks, there will always be a few scattered fish on the outside edges of eddies and near current breaks below gravel bars and other obstructions. Another spot that may hold a few isolated bass is where a cool-water spring enters the river. These springs often trickle down from limestone or other sedimentary rock outcroppings. One way to locate springs is to look for shoreline greenery, such as watercress, arrowhead, or other vegetation. When fishing near a spring, live bait is a good choice for presentation.

"A shot upstream indicates the small channel that allows boats to navigate through this wing dam. Smallmouth will hold below the channel, on the edges of the current breaks, and close to the wing dam."

Both crayfish and crawlers will produce, but the best choice is a little critter than lives in these springs, the spring lizard or salamander. The best time for fishing springs, or any other summer structure seems to be from 10 a.m. to about 1 p.m., and then once again toward sunset. For some reason we don't understand, rivers just don't produce well in the mid-afternoon.

	Early Fall	78° F - 60° F
Cold Water Locational Patterns	Late Fall	59° F - low 40's

There are no major locational changes for river smallmouth, no matter what the season. While a few bass will join the annual fall upstream migration of walleyes, most river smallies continue to stay in the same stretch of river they have inhabited all year. Fall often means rain and higher water levels. But before the fall rains, or with the first cold rain, there can be an incredible migration of frogs back to the rivers. Not all rivers experience such a frog migration, but if yours does, get ready for smallmouth fishing at its finest. Since frogs will enter the river from marshes and damp lowlands, it is best to search out these areas along the river's edge. Short grass, in clay or sandy soil, near seepage areas is a good bet. Keep an eye peeled for lots of green grass and jumping frogs. If you are ever driving during a rain in the early fall and see the road splattered with frogs, you'll know the migration is under way. Skip work the next day and get out on the river. And when you do, place your casts as close to the shore as possible. You'll be amazed how shallow a big smallmouth will lie, waiting for a meal of frog legs. The best choice of presentation under these circumstances is either a green crankbait or a jig tipped with a piece of crawler.

Rivers that experience frog migrations generally do so when the water is around 50° F. Later in the fall, bass activity tends to be very sporadic. On warm sunny days, the fish will move to the shallows, and, if water levels are up, partially covered grass beds are a good bet. The entrances to sloughs will also hold fish during high water, with some penetration into the sloughs during flooding. On cold days, or after a particularly cold night, the bass will move into deeper water. Toward the end of the fall, when water temperature is in the middle to low 40's, most of the smallies will be in the deeper wintering holes. Once again, this does not mean the deepest water available. If a location has produced fish throughout the summer and has water 10 to 12 feet deep, it will probably hold bass in the late fall. Because bass metabolism is so slow, this is one time of year when it pays to fish an area thoroughly and not to try to cover a lot of ground. Presentation is pretty much limited to live bait.

During the coldest part of the winter, when water temperatures are in the low 40's or low 30's (depending on your region) smallmouth bass are somewhere between lethargic and comatose. There is, however, one place on a river where late fall and winter fishing can be super. If your river has a power plant that discharges warm water into the river, put on your cold weather gear and head for the power plant. Warm water discharges encourage a continued growth of food and for this reason they can pull a large number of game and pan fish. Last fall, Chet Meyers and Dan Gapen hit the old Mississippi near Monticello, Minnesota, after a cold snap that had most river bass bundled down for the winter. They only fished for three hours but caught over a hundred fish, including thirty smallies. That's fast fishing! Since bass are so sensitive to changes in temperature, we are not sure how they cope with movements in and out of a warm water discharge, but move they did. The bass would hit for ten minutes and then disappear. Perhaps they move back out into the cooler water. We really don't know. All we know is that despite the cold blustery day, when the smallies were in the warm water, we didn't mind the weather at all.

Middle-aged rivers will have different seasonal patterns, depending on their geographical region. Some rivers ice over for four or five months, while others run free the entire year. No matter what the region or seasonal pattern, the smallmouth is pretty much of a homebody. Once you identify a pattern and location, the bass may stay in that general vicinity all year long. Of course, water in the 10- to 12-foot range is important in northern sections where the shallows freeze up. But while location is a fairly simple matter, presentation on middle-aged rivers is another story. If you have never fished a river before and never had to deal with river currents, you're in for a big surprise. Hopefully, the next two chapters can make that surprise a pleasant one.

Summary of Calendar Periods for Smallmouth Bass in Middle-aged Rivers

Calendar Period	General Fish Location	Fish Attitude	Most Effective Lures/Baits	Retrieve
Pre-spawn	Central 1/3 of river, 8 to 12 feet deep, below rapids, riffles, or gravel bars.	Neutral to negative	Dark jigs with live bait, minnows and crawlers	Slow
Spawn	Shallow inside bend of river. Nests behind rocks and logs in shallow, yet moving water.	Strike to protect nest	Bright colored lures and spoons, jig tipped with piece of crawler	Stop and go
Post-spawn	Females drop back to deeper water. Males freely roam the shallows.	Females - Males +	Females: live bait Males: spinners, jigs, floating Rapalas and small crankbaits	Medium
Early Summer	Current breaks near wing dams, gravel bars, deeper river bends.	Positive	Jigs, crankbaits, stick baits, crawfish and crawlers	Medium to fast
Mid-summer	Deeper mid-channel locations, slicks below rapids, below wing dams, near cool water springs.	Positive	Deep-diving crankbaits, jigs (smaller/lighter) in natural colors, crawfish, salamanders, and crawlers	Varied
Early Fall	Depends on weather and water level. Movement back and forth from deep to shallow.	Very Positive	Jig spinners, flashy spinners, surface lures, frogs and minnows	Fast-slow
Late Fall	Deeper water, with shallow water movements on sunny days. Usually 10- to 12-foot depths. Warm water discharges.	Changing	Jig and live bait, minnows, regular lures when fishing warm water discharges	Slow
Winter	Deeper holes and warm water discharges.	Very negative	Live bait	Stationary

CHAPTER 10-B
Slipping A River for Smallmouth Bass

"But Old Man River, he just keeps rollin' along." So says the song. So it is. Much of the literature about rivers, and many of the songs, conjure up images of blissful days of easy fishing. And there are blissful days, for those who know the secrets of river angling. But for those who don't, the currents that keep Old Man River rollin' along can drive a grown man to tears. The biggest difficulty novice river anglers face is learning how to keep their lures and baits close to the bottom and in line with the currents that bring river bass their food. The fish are there, and more often than not they are in a positive feeding mood. But if your presentation isn't right on target, you might as well be fishing in your bathtub.

Current on rivers can be compared with wind on a lake — it can destroy presentation if not handled properly. Fighting current the wrong way will result in constant hang-ups, improper depth control, or placement of lures too far from the fish. River fish are not chasers like their still-water cousins. Once they are in position at an ambush point along a current break, their prey must come downstream right to them. They will usually not move more than a foot or two, sometimes even less! Any lure or bait approaching from behind rarely gets a fish's attention. Even baits pulled close enough, but across current and at right angles to a fish, might be bypassed. For this reason, anglers fishing downstream will take more fish than those trolling upstream.

How To Slip a River

River-slipping is not a new technique. Old river rats have been using it for decades. We first learned about it from Dan Gapen, one of the midwest's finest river anglers. And he first learned it from his grandpa on the Nipigon River in Ontario's bush country.

River-slipping is similar to backtrolling — a system of exact boat control. It is particularly effective in the faster water of middle-aged rivers. Slipping allows you to correctly position your rig so you can make the most efficient use of each cast or troll. Just like backtrolling, the secret of slipping is that it keeps your bait in the fish zone as long as possible. And, as with backtrolling, you can hold your boat virtually motionless without anchoring or move with precision if the occasion calls for it. You can follow the current path of an eddy with the same ease as a leaf on the water's surface, or just as easily change directions and pull out. One of the primary strengths of this method, along with its speed and mobility, is that it allows for versatility of presentation. You can jig, cast plugs, or troll live bait, and do all this effectively.

The principle of slipping is fairly simple to master. Once you locate an area you want to fish, swing your boat around so the bow faces upstream and keep your

outboard in gear. The trick is to adjust the throttle so that you are drifting downstream a little slower than the surface current. We could go into all the complexities of thrust, power, and force vectors, but you don't have to know physics to slip a river. If the force of your motor is stronger than the current, your boat will move upstream. If it is the same as the current, you will not move at all. If your motor's force is less than the force of the river, you are slipping. You determine the speed of the slip. There are a number of advantages to slipping:

(1) It is an effective way to hold a consistent depth under fast current, to negotiate sharp turns along current breaks in eddies, or to fish behind rocks or among trees and other objects. This method allows you to work these areas without cross-casting, an invitation to snag.

(2) Light line and light tackle can be used in fairly strong current. This is important, not only because you can use small, lightweight lures and baits, but because the *clear* conditions of middle-aged rivers demand light line.

(3) Once you make contact with fish, you can immediately return to the same spot with little effort.

(4) Like backtrolling, slipping keeps time-consuming line and lure tangles to a minimum. Jigs can be cast upstream or live bait drifted downstream with no danger of lines under the motor. And, as in backtrolling, three people can fish in a boat with a minimum of confusion.

(5) Finally, slipping can eliminate the necessity for anchoring. Anchoring in a river always creates problems. Often the anchor won't hold where you want it to, or there simply isn't enough anchor line to get a good hold. By adjusting the throttle, you can use slipping to hover in place, without

any movement up or downstream. Of course, in very shallow water or when fishing small eddies, you may have no choice but to anchor.

Boats and Motors for River Fishing

In order to fish rivers effectively, you must be rigged properly. A runabout, big bass boat, or even most "V" type fishing boats are not designed to cope with fast flow, shallow water, or invisible obstructions. River fishing is a different ball game and should be approached as such.

Let's face it, a large boat with a deep draft and a long shaft motor cannot maneuver in current or make the quick turns necessary to pivot in and out of eddies. The shallow draft necessary to skim over riffles or through rapids requires a different boat. We have fished shallow rivers with high horse power and long-shafted 35-hp. motors. Last year, Al Lindner lost a lower unit from his 115-hp. motor in the river.

The ideal rig for river slipping is a johnboat. A bigger boat is not really necessary for most of the smaller and shallower river stretches. The flat-bottomed johnboat is perfect for control in current. These flat-bottomed rigs ride on top of the flow and have a wide beam and shallow sides — all of which make for easy river movement. We prefer a 14-footer. A live well under the seat is a great asset. Moving water through the live well keeps fish or minnows very lively, which is much better than dragging a stringer. Another reason for a live well is that it will prevent your fish from being crushed between river rocks and the boat.

Rapids, boulders, riffles, and trees are all potential hazards for your motor. There are times, too, when you must crawl over six inches of water. Therefore, proper choice of motor is very important. When asked what his choice of motor was, Dan Gapen commented, "A light motor such as a 5 hp. Johnson with reverse gears is ideal for maneuvering your boat through the many river obstructions. I've found on the shallower river stretches that a 10 hp. or larger is just too cumbersome, and most of the time unnecessary." Some motors rated at 6 hp. or less do not have reverse. Obviously you cannot "slip" properly without this all-important reverse gear.

Because there are so many shallow rocks, logs, and obstacles in many river stretches, the standard metal prop can be chewed up in a matter of hours. The best solution is to equip your motor with a plastic propeller, which will bend when it strikes an obstruction and prevent breaking of shear pins. Another alternative is a new prop shield developed by Johnson motors, which protects the prop from the rocks. You can also attach a pitchfork to the motor's lower unit. This is fine for forward movement, but a disadvantage when running in reverse. These items can save the river angler a lot of grief, time, and money.

There are other important items to consider when battling a river. Because there are times when you'll really want to zero in on a spot, an anchor is a necessity. The shape of the anchor should be such that it can hook over odd-shaped rocks on the river bottom, and it should weigh at least 15 lbs. The standard mushroom shape works very well. It is also important to have a lot of rope on hand — at least 150 feet — because the current will dislodge the anchor unless you let out a lot of rope. Always attach the anchor to the front of the boat. Boats anchored from the rear and into the current may swamp. Other important accessories are a couple of long canoe paddles and a long push-pole in case you get grounded in shallow water. Dan Gapen jokingly refers to his paddle as the "Gapen Depth Finder." Since much of a river is so shallow, all you have to do is use a paddle to give you the makeup and depth of the bottom.

Proper River Tackle

There are basically two methods of presentation that can be used while slipping. You can cast a jig upstream, toward obvious structure or current breaks, or you can fish a live bait rig downstream behind the boat. When using either approach, we recommend a spinning rod and an open-faced reel. A variety of rods can be used, but we like one with a fairly fast tip and a good medium action. That way we can cast light jigs and lures and still have enough backbone to wrestle in a fighting smallie. Most river rats like to have two rods, one rigged with a jig for casting and another with a bottom-walking sinker for live bait presentation. Reels should be of good quality, and a fast gear ratio of 5:1 can be a real blessing in fast current. Reels should also be spooled with a high visibility line, as you will often see the line twitch and not feel a thing. Line weight can vary, but 8-lb.-test is usually sufficient. For an added thrill, it's always fun to take along an ultralight rig with 4- or 6-lb.-test. Often the fishing is good enough that you can risk losing a few fish, and battling a two-pound river smallmouth on an ultralight rig is one of the highs of river fishing.

Casting a Jig Upstream and Retrieving Downstream

In this case, a picture is worth a thousand words. The diagram on the next page clearly illustrates the do's and don't of casting upstream. The key to this method of presentation is to keep your retrieve at about the same speed as the current. It takes practice but can be easily mastered. This is where a high-gear-ratio reel comes in handy. A 5:1 ratio will help you keep up with your jig without wearing you out. It is also crucial to keep a fairly tight line. The biggest mistake that novice river anglers make is allowing a slack bow to form in their line. Slack line not only means missing a lot of hits, it also means getting a lot of snags.

The jig/live bait combo is particularly well suited for upstream casting. Small eddies, a current break, an emergent rock, or a log jam can be cast with pinpoint accuracy. All sides of an obstruction can be fished.

There are so many types of jig designs available it is often hard for even the experienced fishing hand to choose the correct one for a specific fishing situation. The weight, head shape, overall balance, body dressing, and hook type must all be considered. Certain types will work better under one set of conditions than under others. This is especially true in rivers. One design glides with current, another plunges through it. One dances and swims better in slow current, another functions best in fast water.

The design of the jig's head determines its action. In current, the shape of a jig's head is critical. The wrong choice will tend to hang up, tumble and roll, or rise to the surface, rather than plunge to the bottom.

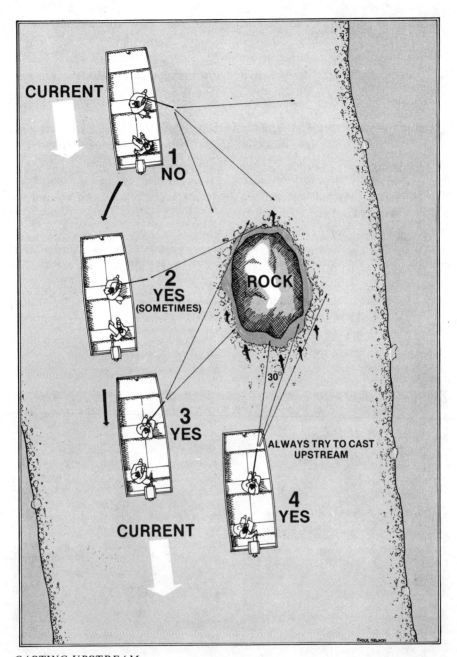

CASTING UPSTREAM

Hangups and river fishing do not have to go together. The best way to eliminate these problems is to cast upstream. Downstream casts are usually unproductive as the current quickly pulls the jig or bait off the bottom and out of the fish-catching zone. A better approach is to cast a jig upstream, at an angle of 30° or less, and let the current "ride" the jig back to you. Short casts work better than long casts, as it is easier to keep the slack out of your line with a short cast. Slack line is the biggest villain of river hangups, as the resulting bow in the line wedges both the lure and line between rocks, logs, and other obstructions.

Under most conditions, the type of jig head and weight are more important than the type of jig dressing. There are, however, some times when dressing is important. Marabou feathers perform well in quiet pool areas but tend to mat in fast waters. Marabou is also porous and absorbs substances like algae, oil, and scum, non-appetizing additions that can turn fish off or at least cause a quick rejection.

Certain types of feathers are not absorbent, particularly those from aquatic birds that have protective oils. Jigs made from this type of material are surprisingly productive; they actually pulsate in current. The feathers are tied with a thin but flexible feather shaft and are not "stripped" like the marabou. Consequently, they will not mat on the hook in current. Combinations of feathers and bucktail are also excellent river jigs, but they tend to be expensive, a definite consideration in snag-filled rivers.

While most river rats have their favorite type of jig or dressing, and these differ widely, there is unanimous agreement that a jig tipped with live bait will always outproduce one without. For summertime smallies, we like to use just an inch of crawler — a good way to economize, given the price of crawlers. In the spring and late fall, a small minnow or leech will also turn the trick. The most important thing to remember is not to overload your jig with too large a live bait attractor. In current this can throw the jig off-balance, cause it to tumble, and result in no fish!

"While a variety of jigs work on the river, in rocky stretches the Ugly Bug comes into its own (clockwise from the top: Ugly Bug, bullet head, muddler jig, bullet head with mylar and bucktail, ball head with maribou, and ball head with live rubber)."

Jig color can sometimes be an important factor when fishing lakes. In river fishing, however, there are few circumstances where specific color patterns are important. Because they eat more, river smallmouth are more aggressive feeders than their lake cousins. Maybe this is why color is less important in rivers than it is in lakes. If we had to pick one color combination that works well on river smallies, it would be brown and orange, the color of the most common prey, the crayfish.

The type of hook on a jig is an important feature, one that is too often overlooked by most fishermen. Some river stretches are so snag-infested you could lose a jig on every ten casts. The best remedy for this is to use a jig with a fine wire Aberdeen hook, one that will bend when snagged. If the jig snags, pull it free, then simply bend the hook back into place with pliers and cast again. In rocks, however, most hang-ups result when a bow in your line allows the jig head to lodge between rocks. In this case, it makes little difference what kind of hook you have. Usually, when slipping, you can simply run back and quickly dislodge a rock-bound jig. When choosing a jig with a light wire hook, make sure that it is stout enough to hold up under the strain of a three- or four-lb. smallie.

River Rigging with Live Bait

Although jigs are a river fisherman's "staple," don't underestimate straight live bait. Live bait works well on rivers, especially in open areas like the deeper sand and gravel slicks or deep pools. The same live bait that works well on lakes is equally effective on rivers. Various types of minnows, nightcrawlers, leeches, beavertails, crawdads, hellgramites, and salamanders are all dynamite on the river.

Nightcrawlers are an old standby and are available practically everywhere. Since most rivers do not house vast quantities of panfish, there is usually no problem with having your crawler ripped apart. A straight or air-injected crawler, rigged naturally, will work wonders on both walleyes and smallmouth. Though crawlers will take fish in the early or late coldwater periods, they are most effective in the summer warmer water period.

Minnows are also a favorite of many river buffs. They work well all year, but we have found them to be at their best in the spring. Certain breeds of minnows are more effective than others. Silver or golden shiners, fatheads, and, of course, red-tailed chubs, are all superior river baits. Generally speaking, smaller minnows like fatheads work best in spring and fall. During summer, the larger golden and silver shiners and redtails seem to work best.

Of course, no discussion of live bait would be complete without mention of the crayfish. Though crayfish form the bulk of a river smallie's diet, they are a difficult bait to fish, particularly in fast current. We usually use crayfish when fishing eddies or deeper pools. The crawdad can be rigged simply on a wire hook with a small splitshot. The current will supply most of the action. Just make sure friend crayfish doesn't crawl under a rock. By keeping a high rod tip and light line pressure, you can usually keep this lively bait out of the rocks.

The way you rig live bait for river fishing is critical. If you try to work a standard sliding live bait rig used in lake fishing, you are going to have problems. These sliding sinkers were not designed to be fished in swift current. The purpose of a slip rig is to feed the fish line as it runs, so there is no resistance. River fish are much more aggressive than lake fish, so this technique is unnecessary. It is best to work rivers with a stationary sinker rig so that you can pause momentarily and quickly set the hook.

The old reliable three-way drop sinker set-up is still a good choice for live-bait river fishing, having been used by veteran river rats for years. Relatively snagless, it consists of a three-way swivel, a drop line with a bell or pencil sinker attached, and, of course, another line with a hook. With this type of rig, you simply set the hook at any knock, bump, or hit.

A new stationary live-bait rig that works well in rivers is the Gapen "Bait Walker." Virtually snagless, it combines the best features of a three-way set-up in one efficient package. The keel-like weight is tapered and designed to dislodge easily from bottom snags. This rig is balanced perfectly to ride over the roughest of river bottoms, yet it trails the bait behind attractively. Its construction makes it easy to detect a strike. The curved wire design produces an "elevator effect" that holds the bait off the bottom. This is the first river rig that correctly presents live bait in almost all kinds of current. It can be trolled, drifted, slipped, cast and even still-fished in moving water.

One of the best places to slip with live bait is through a long, gently sloping pool. Often a pool in a middle-aged river will have a slight riffle of shallow water at its head. With the bow of the boat pointed upstream, you enter the pool and immediately drop your rigs over the side. The throttle is now adjusted so that the boat slips slowly downstream. Meanwhile, your live bait rig is moving more quickly downstream and your bait is actually backing down towards the upstream-facing fish. The main trick to live-bait slipping is to keep a tight line and continually lift the sinker slightly off the bottom. This allows the current to drift the bait downstream. If the line becomes slack, a giant bow will form in the line making it impossible to feel a hit or set the hook. When you come to the end of a pool, it's important to reel in the rig so it doesn't hang up on the rocks that form the foot of the pool. The illustration explains the basics of slipping a pool. If

SLIPPING A RIVER POOL
The diagram below illustrates proper boat and line position for "slipping" a river pool. Many fish will locate at the head or foot of a pool, but some fish will hold in the deepest water.

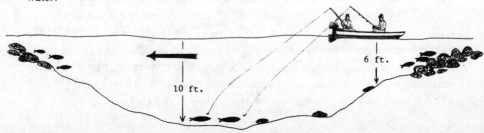

10 ft.

6 ft.

you've never tried this technique, you're in for a treat — you can kiss those snagged-on-the-bottom rivertime blues goodbye.

Rivers remain one of the greatest fishing resources in our country. The difficulties of fishing in current is one of the big reasons most anglers prefer to fish lakes. Yet with a few simple tricks anyone can successfully fish rivers. And the rewards in terms of leaping smallmouth and bonus walleyes, catfish, and white bass should provide the necessary incentive. Rivers can be frustrating, particularly when their level fluctuates after a downpour, but time on the river will teach the perceptive angler how to master even these difficult conditions. No! Rivers aren't easy. In fact, just like the little girl with the little curl, they can be horrid ... but they can also be very, very good. The next time your favorite lake or reservoir slows down, give your local river a try — you'll soon discover why river rats always have a smile on their face.

CHAPTER 10-C
Cranking Rivers for Smallmouth

It was a balmy August morning on the upper Mississippi River near Brainerd, Minnesota. Conditions were perfect for smallmouth fishing. In fact, they were better than most anglers encounter in a lifetime. A few weeks earlier, a large paper company had accidentally leaked a toxic chemical into the river that killed all the crayfish for a distance of fifteen river miles. The gamefish suffered no ill effect, only hunger pangs. The crayfish is the primary prey of river smallies, and a few days after the accident the bass were literally starved. Al Lindner discovered this fishing bonanza and called Chet Meyers to tip him off. The next day, Chet corralled his fishing buddy Cecil Underwood and drove north for a day of angling bliss.

Once on the river, both men began fishing a favorite river combination, a Gapen Ugly Bug tipped with a piece of crawler. They had hardly launched their canoe when both were fast to leaping smallies. It was like that the rest of the day. The only problem was a pleasant one. The jig/live bait combination was too slow a method of presentation. It took time to grab a crawler, pinch off an inch or two, and thread it on the hook. Chet, trying to make hay while the sun shone, tied on a crayfish-colored crankbait, and the fish pounced on it. The bass weren't monsters, but, after boating about 40 fish in a period of four hours, the anglers decided to take a lunch break and rest their weary arms. While Cecil broke out the sandwiches, Chet dug into his tackle box and tied on a large crankbait, one almost too large for even a big smallie. As they settled down to enjoy their lunch, Chet tossed his "hawg" crankbait toward a protruding 'deadhead'. The lure stopped, as if it had sunk into the old log, but then the water exploded and a five-lb. bass hung in mid-air with a very large crankbait embedded in its jaw. The smallmouth now hangs in Chet's den.

River cranking for smallmouth bass is a relatively new phenomenon. Fat-bodied crankbaits, or alphabet plugs, were first developed in the South and used with deadly results on largemouth bass. It took a while for northern anglers to adopt this lure, but, once they did, it wasn't long until river cranking caught on.

There are a number of advantages to using crankbaits on rivers. First, and foremost, cranking is a fast method of presentation that lets you cover a lot of ground and do so quickly. When you are drifting down a river, you need to make your casts as quickly and effectively as possible. If you want to get more than one cast as you float by a wing dam or sunken log, cranking is the only way to do it. Another advantage to cranking is that the vibrating noise of the lure attracts fish in naturally turbid river waters where bass initially locate their prey by sound rather than sight. Finally, cranking is a big fish method, often producing the larger fish when live bait and jigs will catch only smaller fish.

Locating Smallmouth Bass on Middle-aged Rivers

Fishing rivers for smallmouth is unique because it is so visual. As you drift a river you can actually locate structure by reading the telltale clues on the water's surface. Once you learn to "read the water" you'll be able to spot areas that could hold fish long before you come into casting range. Remember, river fish shelter themselves from the current whenever possible. They don't like fighting the current any more than you or I would want to run into a 60-m.p.h. wind. Most middle-aged rivers have enough rocks, logs, sand and gravel bars to create current breaks where fish can rest and enjoy the passing scene. As water breaks over and around these objects, the water's surface indicates their presence by forming boils, riffles, slicks, and eddies. Smallmouth bass love to gather along these current breaks during the summer months.

Most anglers unfamiliar with river smallmouth marvel at the shallowness of the water. While depths vary in middle-aged rivers, the best smallmouth stretches typically have water in the three- to 12-foot range. Often the bass will be working in even shallower water. Limestone, or any fractured sedimentary rock that provides habitat for crayfish, will only increase the fishing potential of a smallie river. Good examples of rivers ideal for river cranking are the upper Mississippi in Minnesota, the St. Croix in Wisconsin, the Tennessee River, the upper Allegheny and Susquehanna Rivers in Pennsylvania, and the St. Lawrence River in New York and Canada.

"The 'tiger stripe' markings on this river smallmouth's gill cover and its high-leaping acrobatics are two of its more distinguishing characteristics."

While crankbaits take bass at other times of year, we find them most effective during the summer. The depths to which crankbaits run coincide nicely with the general depths of the best smallmouth stretches. When river cranking we like to have two rods, one rigged with a lipped diving crankbait and the other with a sinking vibrating plug. A lipped crankbait, like a Cordell O, can be cast in shallow water and bounced off the rocky bottom — a dynamite way to turn on smallies. Sinking crankbaits, like a Hotspot, can be cast into the deeper eddies, allowed to sink toward the bottom, and then worked slowly back to the boat. Both lures are easy to operate. The only problem is getting them close enough to the fish.

Many novice river anglers fail to realize that river fish hold extremely tight on structure. While a lake largemouth in a positive feeding mood may move five or ten feet to take a lure, a river smallmouth seldom budges more than a foot from his holding station. This means that casting accuracy is an important part of river fishing. When you combine the need for pinpoint accuracy in casting with the speed of river currents as you drift by likely structure, it is easy to see why river fishing is relatively untapped. Let's take a look at a few suggestions that should help you cope with the complexities of river angling.

As we mentioned before, summer holding stations for bass are fairly easy to spot. Wing dams are one of the more productive fish locations. Sometimes they will be plainly visible above the surface and other times they may be partially or completely submerged. We suggest anchoring above the wing dam, casting below it, and then working a diving crankbait upstream as close to the rocks as possible. If the wing dam is above water, try using a shallow-diving crankbait and get your lure right up against it. If this doesn't work, tie on a deep-diving crankbait and work the lure along the current break below the tip of the dam. Another approach that works is casting right to the face of the dam and working a lipped crankbait the first few feet of the *upstream* side. Many anglers, new to river fishing, assume that fish always hold on the downstream side of structure. They fail to realize that the force of water striking an object creates a slack water pocket *in front* of that structure. On wing dams there is often a scooped-out trough on the upstream side that smallies like to lie in.

Other structure to consider includes large boulders. Once again, fish may hold on either the upstream or downstream side. Usually rocks only hold one or two fish, because the calm water pocket is so small. The current breaklines on the edges of eddies are a super location for summer smallmouth. These are best worked by positioning your boat upstream and cranking against the current. The larger calm water pockets in some eddies always looks inviting, and here is where a sinking vibrating plug works effectively. But if you are fishing a river in the northern part of our country, don't expect to find a lot of bass in the calm water. This is where old 'Jaws', the northern pike, likes to hang out.

Gravel bars and sandbars also provide good structure for river smallmouth. Often the downstream side is more productive, so we usually anchor above the bar. If you try to anchor below a river bar, your boat often gets caught in an upstream eddy current and you usually end up sitting right on top of the area you want to fish. Only time on the river and a good eye for changing river currents can solve this problem.

Be sure not to overlook man-made structure such as bridge abutments, old bridge pilings, culverts, sunken boats, or even old tires. If it looks as if it could hold a fish or two, it probably will. Also, don't be afraid to cast to likely structure in very shallow water. You'll be amazed how shallow you'll find some smallmouth, even on the sunniest days. Most of us have been indoctrinated to believe that fish only visit the shallows during the spawning season or fall feeding binge. We have also been taught that bright sunny days mean rotten fishing. Well, Mr. Smallmouth likes nothing better than shallow water, and he'll often lie there on days when the sun is directly overhead. Of course, he is usually near some type of cover, and most often on the shady side; but it is not uncommon to take fish out of a foot of water or less. Under these conditions, we like to use a floating Rapala or other minnow-type lure that only dives about a foot deep. We try to place our casts as close to the shore as possible and have often had a smallie nail the lure as soon as it touches the water. Be prepared. A river smallmouth can inhale and spit out a lure faster than any fish in the river.

The Effects of Changing Water Levels

Changing water levels have an important effect on the location of river fish. Areas that produce one day can be dry land the next. Such drastic fluctuations can be overcome by following a few simple guidelines.

"Al Lindner poses with a fine river smallmouth that just couldn't resist a crankbait."

During periods of high water, current breaks along the shoreline will hold most of the gamefish. The bass seem to move closer to shore to avoid the faster current and to take advantage of new cover created by the flood conditions. Extremely high and fast water can make areas in the center of the river that formerly held fish unproductive. The fish simply get "blown out" by the roaring current. As the water begins to drop, the fish will begin slowly moving away from the shore. And in periods of low water, they will concentrate in the center of the river, particularly in the pools. Under drought conditions, the vast majority of all river fish will pile into the few remaining holes and become extremely vulnerable to fishing pressure. If you should come across conditions like this, be a sport and don't take advantage of Mother Nature's critters.

As water levels fluctuate, fish will alter their location on a given piece of structure. A wing dam is a good example. During high water, bass will usually pull in close to the shore. Fish may even move into areas of flooded grass. As the water begins to drop, smallies will move out toward the tip of the wing dam. Some will move to the upstream side and others to the downstream side. During normal water levels, fish may be smack up against structure or drop down below it. And when water levels are low, bass will often begin locating on the current break below the wing dam.

High water levels are usually a spring and fall phenomenon. Except during periods of sustained rain, water levels during the summer are fairly stable or slowly dropping. If your river has a dam, the water levels may fluctuate daily, particularly if it is a power dam that regularly releases water to make electricity. No matter what the cause, water level changes on a river are normal. The fish know how to adapt to them, and in time so will you.

Equipment for Cranking Rivers

The equipment for river cranking is relatively simple. In fact, you can catch fish with no more than a rod, reel, crankbait, and a pair of wading sneakers. There is no question, however, that fishing from a boat will allow you to take maximum advantage of this system.

The motor and boat for river cranking is the same one we recommended in the last chapter. A johnboat, powered by a six- to ten-hp. motor, is just perfect. Many anglers are almost wedded to their bass boats. While the bass boat is unsurpassed on reservoirs and lakes, it just doesn't work on middle-aged rivers. Remember, eight to ten feet of water is *deep water* on a smallie river. There are plenty of places where rock and gravel bars are less than a foot deep. So leave the old bass boat at home and give the johnboat a try. Once you become accustomed to the simplicity and shallow-water maneuverability of this flat-bottomed craft, you'll understand why for hundreds of years river rats have stood by this boat.

Another benefit of leaving your bass boat at home is that you will rediscover the simplicity of angling. You might even learn to fish without a depth finder.

Many of the best river areas can be identified by simply looking at the river's surface. Once you understand the nature of current and how it reveals bottom contours and form, you'll be able to pick out most of the prime water with your eyes alone. A depth finder is most helpful on big, wider stretches of rivers where the bottom conditions are not always indicated by disturbances on the water's surface. However, since most smallmouth taken by the cranking method usually come from areas shallower than eight feet, a depth finder is not essential.

A six-foot canoe paddle can be a practical substitute for a depth finder. Placing it in the water will tell you not only the depth but the kind of bottom in the immediate area. If the water is deeper than four feet, it is usually capable of holding good quantities of smallmouth and maybe a few walleyes. Remember, deep water alone is not always of major importance in these types of rivers.

For most river cranking we prefer baitcasting tackle over spinning tackle. A baitcasting outfit gives you the best possible control of your lures, because you can "thumb" your reel and control the distance of each cast. This is important when you're pinpoint-casting to objects in the river. Spinning tackle works best with smaller crankbaits in shallow water and would be our second choice.

A bait-casting reel with five-to-one gear ratio will pick up the line quickly in the current without wearing out your arm and shoulder. Cranking a reel with a three-to-one gear ratio for an entire day can be exhausting. Finally, the extra speed of a five-to-one will keep your lures ahead of the current, even if you are quartering upstream.

For river cranking, we like a lightweight rod with a sensitive tip and plenty of backbone. The Skyline model SKC 5508 is an excellent choice and will transmit every vibration and bump of your crankbait.

Under most river conditions, 12- or 14-lb.-test line will be sufficient. Lighter line increases the chances of losing your expensive crankbaits on river snags. A line heavier than 12- or 14-lb.-test will not react as well because of increased current pull on a larger diameter line. Also, a heavier line will cause your crankbait to run shallower.

High-visibility line is as important in river fishing as it is in plastic worm or jig fishing. By watching your line, you will always have an idea of where your bait is in relation to the current and the bottom. Many times, by watching your line closely you will be able to detect a strike even before you feel it or before the vibration of the lure stops.

The first three feet of your line above the crankbait takes a terrible beating while cranking, as repeated contact with rocks and logs can fray the line in a very short time. Remember to check your knot and line every 15 minutes and break off a few feet of line so you won't lose that lunker bass when it hits.

Presentation

Fishing rivers for the first time can be a frustrating experience. Novice anglers usually have their biggest problem coping with current and keeping their lures or baits in the fish-catching zone. The beautiful thing about river cranking is that just about anyone can do it. Crankbaits can be cast across the current, at an angle, or directly down stream. About the only thing that won't work, except in extremely slow water, is casting upstream.

By far the easiest method is to cast a lipped crankbait downstream and retrieve it against the current. The speed of the retrieve is up to you. Because the force of the current itself forces the plug to dive, it is possible to simply hold the lure stationary, retrieve a short distance, and pause again. This stop-and-go method is sometimes deadly. Try to experiment with different approaches. If you are cranking too fast, your lure will let you know by rolling over and coming to the surface. We have even tried speed-trolling upstream and found it an effective way to checkout areas as we move up river.

As far as color goes, most of our experience indicates that it is not as big a factor in rivers as in lakes. This is because river fish are generally in a more positive feeding mood than lake fish. We do find that in the spring of the year silver or chrome works well, and in the summer a crayfish pattern of brown and hot orange turns the trick.

Adapting Cranking to Other Fishing Situations

As we mentioned earlier, crankbaits were originally designed for fishing largemouth bass in reservoirs and natural lakes. We assume that most anglers have used this method under these conditions and are well aware of its many advantages. Current is usually not a big factor in lake and reservoir angling, but when it is, it can drive even the most patient angler crazy. Rather than fighting the problems associated with fishing in the wind, why not adapt? The next time a strong wind comes up (assuming it's safe to continue fishing), try locating a windward shore that has hard clean bottom. Then tie on a deep-diving crankbait and troll with the wind, just bouncing your lure off the bottom. As long as the water is deep enough to prevent the bass from getting seasick, you might just strike it rich. Because the wind drives plankton and bait fish before it, the bass often lie just below the turbulence and feed on whatever blows their way. Why not add a crankbait to their menu?

"A wide selection of crankbaits will work on river smallies. We prefer a crawfish pattern in hot orange."

CHAPTER 11
How Weather Really Affects Bass Fishing

Except for brief periods of seasonal change in the spring and fall, the natural environment of the bass is fairly stable. Spring always signals a burst of activity and fall puts on the brakes, but during most of the year, the food chain progresses slowly, water levels are stable, and water temperatures fluctuate little. About the only dramatic changes in this rather placid underwater world are the result of daily weather conditions. In a period of only a few hours, a day can be brilliantly sunny, or dark and overcast, calm and peaceful, or raging and windswept. Beneath the water's surface, such changes in weather affect the amount of light penetration, the dissolved oxygen level, and the presence or absence of current. Bass are extremely sensitive to changes in their environment, and, although we do not know exactly *why* weather affects bass, we do know something about *how* they respond.

Bass have limited brain power and rely primarily on instinctual responses to guide their activity. Fish cannot change their environment, so they must adapt to it. The differences in these responses are striking. Anyone who has had the opportunity to observe bass underwater can immediately tell the difference between active and inactive fish. Active bass are alert and constantly on the lookout for prey, while inactive bass are dull and lethargic. Active bass may chase a lure quite a distance before nailing it with deadly accuracy. Inactive bass are sedentary, seldom moving even a foot to take the most tempting morsel. Active bass often ride high in the water, while inactive fish lie belly-to-the-bottom. In between these two extremes are a variety of dispositions, and it is often the weather that determines which of these moods fish will assume.

Weather Patterns in the United States

While bass have only limited instinctual responses to guide their activity, anglers can plot and reason. You don't have to be a meteorologist to be a good angler, but a few weather basics can help you make better use of those little grey cells in your brain.

Few anglers realize how important the topography of our North American terrain is in the determination of daily and seasonal weather patterns. Because of the earth's rotation, weather patterns generally move in a west-to-east direction across our continent. The major mountain ranges, the Rockies in the west and the Appalachians in the east, stretch north and south. While forming an effective buffer against weather coming off the Pacific Ocean (and to a lesser degree off the Atlantic), they leave the central part of our country wide open to a constant warfare between competing polar air masses from Canada and warm southern air from the Gulf of Mexico. The north central states take the brunt of this battle, but southern states are not completely immune.

The most classic confrontation is between a cool, dry, high-pressure system originating in Canada and a warm, moist system from the south. Cool air moves more quickly than warm, moist air, and, because cool air is also heavier than warm air, it slices under the warm air, forcing it aloft and triggering vigorous cloud development. This usually sets off wind squalls and thunderstorms, and the wise fisherman gets off the water as quickly as possible. As the storm passes, the sky clears, the air cools, and the sun shines with a blinding brilliance. This particular weather pattern is what most anglers refer to as a cold front — the most dreaded of all conditions to fish under.

Fishing Under Cold Front Conditions

Thank God for cold fronts! Without them many of us wouldn't have an excuse for not catching fish. In the past ten years it has become acceptable custom to blame the weather for poor fishing, particularly if that weather happens to be a cold front. And while it is true that cold fronts can put the damper on fishing, not all bodies of water are affected equally. Natural lakes, particularly clear-water lakes in the northern part of our country and in Florida, are the most adversely affected. In the upper midwest, cold fronts blow in every four to five days during the summer season. Florida experiences a lot of frontal activity during December through March. Since most of its lakes are shallow, the fish have no recourse but to burrow in the weeds. If you fish in these areas, your best bet is to choose the murkiest lake available and avoid clear water.

Reservoirs in the southern belt suffer less from cold front activity because the summer weather is much more stable. And for some strange reason not yet understood, rivers are little affected by cold fronts, no matter what their geographical location. Even fairly clear rivers in the upper midwest offer good fishing after the worst summer cold fronts. So if your lake or reservoir has the "cold front blues," let it rest and give your local river a lick.

Tactics for Fishing Cold Front Bass

While many anglers don't know the whys and wherefores, they accept as gospel that the "bluebird skies," blazing sun, and cool dry air indicating a cold front's passage mean poor fishing. We are still not sure why fish react so negatively to these conditions, but divers have confirmed that the "cold front blues" are not just a figment of anglers' imagination. Formerly active bass assume a negative feeding mood, and scattered schools tighten up and move closer to cover or head for deep water.

The most probable cause of this decreased activity is increased amounts of solar radiation. The cool dry air that follows a cold front is lacking in the humidity or water moisture that absorbs much of the solar rays poured forth on the earth's surface. Fish are generally sensitive to various forms of solar radiation and are not biologically equipped to handle the extra doses that come after a cold front. A fish's delicate skin apparatus is structured to serve other purposes than absorbing solar radiation.

"Fishing for bass can be super when a front is moving in, but those bright clear days the day after can spell tough fishing."

In most cases bass can respond to increased sunlight in two ways. They can seek cover or shade, or they can move into deeper water. In either case, they are seldom in a positive feeding mood. They tend to hold very close to available cover and divers have even seen bass buried in the weeds with only their tails exposed. Formerly active, high-riding bass will usually be as close to the bottom as possible. A school that might have occupied 50 square yards before a cold front might stack up in an area the size of a small card table. Under these conditions it is easy to see why some anglers stay home during a cold front. But fish can be caught if anglers will learn a few simple tricks and adapt their presentation accordingly.

The key to catching "cold front" bass is an awareness of different locational patterns. If a body of water has exceptional clarity and only sparse shallow water cover, the bass may have to move to deep water for protection from the sun's rays. If, on the other hand, a clear lake has sufficient shallow water cover, the bass may move only a few feet to the shade offered by thick weeds, brush, or rock slabs. Of course the darker the water color, the less severely bass are affected by cold front conditions.

A locational pattern that typifies cold front bass in natural lakes is a preference for dips and depressions in the lake bottom. While active bass prefer humps and rises, cold front bass like to lie belly-to-the-bottom in a small depression. While active bass congregate on points, whether they be cabbage beds, brushy points, or fingers of lily pads, cold front bass seek out pockets and the inside bend of weeds and brush. Finally, while active bass often relate to the outside edge of weeds, brush, and other cover following a cold front, inactive bass will move right into the thickest part of available cover.

Given these locational patterns and a neutral-to-negative feeding mood, the best approach to cold front bass is a slow methodical one. If you normally hit seven or eight spots when fishing active bass, stick with two or three after a cold front. If your boat control and casting are usually a little haphazard, polish both techniques. Under cold front conditions, quiet intelligent boat control and accurate casts are very important. Presentation has to be right in front of a fish's nose and even then might not arouse its interest. Cold front fish also spook easily and the angler who is "all thumbs" is bound to go fishless.

One of the best techniques is not unlike the one described for cold-water bass — slow, vertical jigging. The best choices of presentation are either live bait, a small Texas-rigged plastic worm, or a jig and minnow combination. Your choice depends on the type of cover, with Texas-rigged worms working best in heavy cover. Remember, cold front bass seldom chase their prey, so you may have to work your lure for a minute or two before the bass will strike. Make short accurate casts to the shady side of the cover and then slowly jig or even let the lure or bait remain motionless on the bottom. This technique, often referred to as the "dead worm," is extremely effective when fishing shallow Florida lakes under cold front conditions.

This type of angling takes time and patience, which is why most anglers have difficulty mastering it. Just convince yourself that there are some tight-lipped bass down there and stick with it. You may not catch your limit, but three or four cold front bass are worth a double limit under normal conditions.

Good Rain? Bad Rain?

Though most anglers don't enjoy fishing in the rain, the initial stages of a rainstorm can often make for excellent fishing. Of course, safety must be a major consideration. High winds and/or lightning have claimed the life of many an unwary angler. A good steady downpour, however, can sometimes create an explosion of bass feeding activity, particularly if it follows a long, hot dry spell. We have fished in rain so heavy that it was difficult to see ten feet in front of the boat — and caught fish on almost every cast.

But while an initial rain often signals good fishing, continued heavy rain usually means the opposite. Highland reservoirs can come up 10 to 20 feet; a flatland reservoir can more than double in area. Flooding rivers flush fish from the main channel and send them scurrying for calmer backwaters. While natural lakes seldom experience drastic water level changes, a prolonged rainy period often slows fish activity.

The worst possible fishing conditions after a rain are those that combine cold, high, muddy water. During a spring downpour, some southern reservoirs turn so red-brown with mud that even non-anglers could predict lousy fishing. The combination of cold and mud slows fish metabolism, limits a fish's range of vision, and desensitizes its lateral lines. The result? Comatose bass.

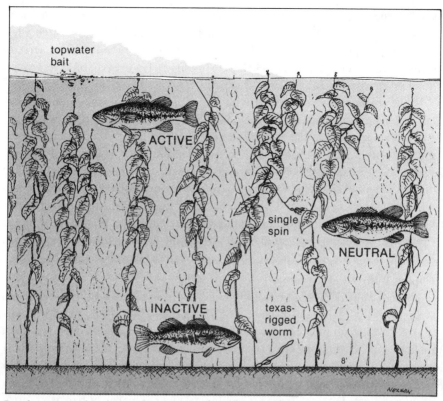

Bass location and corresponding presentation in the weeds depends on the activity level of the fish, often a function of weather conditions.

Lowland and flatland reservoirs suffer worst of all, not only due to cold, muddy water, but because their area can double or triple in size. In March of 1980, a bass tournament held at Sardis reservoir in Mississippi presented visiting pros with just these conditions. The results were predictable. During the three practice days prior to the tournament, 250 anglers, each fishing ten hours a day, caught 82 bass. That figures out to one bass for every 91.5 hours of fishing. During the actual tournament, the results were almost as bad. If you don't have to fish under these conditions, stay home and read a good book. It's just silly to bang your head against a wall.

If you want to try fishing reservoirs under these adverse conditions (they say adversity builds character), here are a few tips. Fishing will begin to improve once the rain ceases and the creeks start running clear. Begin prospecting for bass in small narrow creek channels and look for fish where clear and muddy water mix. In many instances, the breakline between the two is so distinct that you can have the bow of your boat in clearing water and the stern in muddy water. When you find this situation, the bass are nearby.

Bobby Murray and Chet Meyers once visited the Coosa River chain of reservoirs in Alabama after record-breaking rain had brought some of the reservoirs up 25 feet. Two days after the rain ceased, the smaller creek arms started running clear. While most anglers fishing the main reservoir body couldn't buy a bass, Bobby, Chet, and their host Robert Melvin located a few active fish where clear and muddy water mixed. Of the thousands of acres of water on the reservoir, the active fish were found in a few areas of often less than a hundred square yards.

While spring rains can create tough fishing, just the opposite conditions can occur during a long, hot summer. On ultraclear highland reservoirs, by the time August rolls around, the water can be so clear that the bass, particularly photosensitive spotted bass, head for the depths. With a nice solid summer storm, the creeks will begin to run muddy, but usually there is not enough rain to disturb the main reservoir. Once again, where the muddy water from the creeks hits the clear water is the best place to begin fishing. Now the fish are active, for water temperatures are up, and the muddy water provides protection from the sun and a good source of food. So the next time Mother Nature drops a load from the sky, keep an eye peeled for mixing water. The fish sure do.

Coping With Windy Weather

Though anglers debate lures and tactics endlessly, most readily agree that a strong wind is the most frustrating of all weather conditions. Wind not only makes for difficult boat control and erratic casting, it also has a dramatic effect on fish location. As with cold fronts, northern anglers suffer the most from windy weather. Not only do northern lakes experience more wind than lakes or reservoirs in other parts of the country, but the largemouth in northern lakes are usually restricted to a shallow water ecological niche. This can be bad news for, as we mentioned in Chapter 5-C, largemouth do not like getting tossed about in shallow windy water. They usually either move to deeper water or seek areas of relative calm. Even so, fish activity can be excellent during windy weather, for the wind brings with it increased levels of dissolved oxygen, decreased light penetration, and increased movements of plankton and bait fish. Once anglers learn a few strategies for coping with the wind, fishing can be super.

A strong wind creates surface currents in any body of water. These currents can be "read" just like currents in a river. And, like river currents, often the breakline between current and calm water creates a natural holding and feeding station for bass. Wind breaking around a point of land creates a definite current breakline between the windy and lee sides. You'll seldom find bass on the windy side unless the drop-off is sharp enough that they can lie beneath the tossing waves. Usually, the fish will locate right along the current breakline, awaiting windblown food and bait fish drawn into the eddy created by the point.

Al Lindner recalls how reading windy water helped him during a tournament on Table Rock Reservoir. During practice Al had located a school of bass in some sunken timber about 50 yards off a well-known point. He had taken the fish with a jig and a worm in about 30 feet of water. The first day of the tournament Al hit that point but the bass weren't home. Since this was well into the summer pattern, he was pretty sure the fish hadn't moved a great distance. As he was about to leave to check another area, Al noticed that the wind had shifted direction from the previous day. As the wind broke around the point, it formed a slight breakline between choppy and calm water. Even though the water was only five feet deep and very clear, Al moved his boat toward the point and dropped a small plastic worm right on the current breakline. In short order he had four nice bass and was well on his way to placing in the money.

Another condition that results in good fishing is when the waves "roil" shoreline waters of a normally clear highland reservoir. Waves hitting a rock and red clay bank can create off-color water for 20 to 30 yards offshore. Bass move into this colored water to feed on crayfish and other food blown into or flushed out of the rocks. The colored water also cuts down on the amount of light penetration, thus giving the fish a greater sense of security. Under these conditions bass normally locate not where the waves are crashing, but in the nearest available calm water. If the bank is fairly steep, they might hold close to shore, right beneath the wave action, while on a gradual bank they will hold further from shore. In either case, the feeding activity can be fast and furious. All anglers need do is learn to use the wind to their advantage.

"Rainy weather may dampen the body, but not the spirit."

Of course, one effective method for fishing in the wind is backtrolling. Developed by midwestern walleye anglers a number of years ago, backtrolling answers the problem of boat control. While developed primarily as a method of live bait presentation in deep water, it can easily be adapted to bass fishing. Very simply, backtrolling involves backing a boat stern-first into the wind. Splash guards attached to the stern prevent water from washing into the boat. This method can be used either to move slowly against the wind, to slip with the wind, or just to hold in place.

A good technique when moving against the wind in deeper water is to back-troll with a jig/eel, jig/grub, or jig/live bait combination. Lines are worked out the front of the boat so there is no problem getting them tangled in the motor. Three people can fish this method easily — one out the right side, one out the left, and the third directly over the bow. A heavier than normal jig must be used when back-trolling, as the biggest problem when fishing in the wind is maintaining contact with your lure. The heavier weight will keep a bow out of your line and let you know when Mr. Bass decides to give your lure a rap.

Another method used with backtrolling is casting downwind with a diving plug or jig and eel. This method works best with only two anglers, both casting their lures with the wind rather than casting into it. For a shallow-water approach, an electric motor can be used while casting and slipping with the wind. Naturally the strength of the wind will determine whether or nor an electric motor is sufficient. By experimenting you will discover other ways of coping with the wind. Just remember, the wind moves food and bait fish around and usually means actively feeding bass. It is always tempting to seek a quiet sheltered bay on a windy day, but the fish are usually somewhere near where wind and calm water meet.

Long Term Weather Conditions

While dramatic changes in weather conditions create equally dramatic changes in fish location, periods of calm stable weather comprise the day-to-day patterns most anglers deal with during the bulk of the fishing season. With stable, or gradually changing weather, fish feeding activity becomes fairly predictable. Sticking with one body of water long enough to learn to recognize these patterns is what separates competent anglers from weekend dabblers.

"Lookout, Kermit!"

While every body of water exhibits its own specific pattern, a few weather generalizations hold across the board. These are most observable during the spring and fall when water temperatures fluctuate dramatically. The first warming trend of the spring almost always signals good bass fishing. If water temperatures have reached the low 50's, a few bright, sunny days normally trigger a strong pre-spawn movement of bass. It is important to note, however, that it is sunlight and not simply warm air that is the crucial factor. During a warm, *overcast* spring it can take a long time for the water to warm — solar radiation is the key. At the same time, cold, overcast weather can quickly cool shallow water spawning areas and send pre-spawn bass back to deeper waters. This shallow-to-deep-to-shallow pattern is most noticeable in northern lakes, but will also occur in southern waters. Because there is often a lag time between the actual amount of sunlight or cool nights and their effect on water temperatures, look for the best fishing a day or two after a warming trend begins and the worst angling a half a day after a cooling trend.

During the summer months, particularly in the south, the weather can exhibit protracted hot, dry periods. When surface temperatures climb into the low 80's, bass fishing can begin to slow. At this time a *cooling* trend means good fishing. By keeping an eye to the weather map, anglers can observe cooling trends moving into their area. The best time to be on the water during the summer (if conditions are safe) is during the initial cooling wind or rain. The longer and hotter the preceding weather, the better the fishing when a new system moves in.

During the fall and winter, sunlight once again becomes a factor. When water temperatures are in the mid-40's, bass fishing slows down, but a bright sunny day can often pull fish up in a vertical migration toward the warming waters. This often occurs on southern reservoirs, where wintering fish may locate deep in standing timber and move toward the surface. As with spring fishing, the best time to fish is a day or two after the onset of warm fall or winter weather.

Besides these general seasonal weather patterns, there are other patterns not always evident to even the best anglers. The only way to discover these subtle daily patterns is by keeping a daily log book, noting how weather influences bass on your lake, river, or reservoir. We have learned a lot of "pattern secrets" by thumbing through our fishing logs on cold winter evenings. We suggest you do the same.

Of course, it would be nice if we could all wait for the best weather conditions to do our fishing, but, sadly, life isn't that way. Few of us have the luxury of timing our trips with the weather, unless we happen to live on a lake or reservoir. And often on a pre-planned trip we will encounter cold front conditions or a sudden heavy rain that disturbs the normal seasonal patterns. No matter. Just remember that even under poor weather conditions there are usually a few catchable bass. So use your brains, consider the conditions, select the best techniques, and give it a try. As one old timer said, "You sure ain't gonna catch any fish if your line ain't in the water."

CHAPTER 12
A Little Night Fishing

When the subject of night fishing comes up, the majority of anglers literally doze off. Why would anyone want to fish at night? It's difficult to see. The mosquitoes are intolerable. Chances are you will get lost. And the fish are all asleep anyway — right? Wrong — on all counts. At night the bass are often wide awake and prowling the shallows. You don't usually move around enough to get lost. After the first hour of darkness, the bugs all but disappear. And, with the aid of a flashlight, you can see amazingly well.

This is not to say that night fishing offers no challenges. Night anglers have to be especially quiet and well organized in their presentation. A snarled reel at night spells "bad news," and trying to feel a bass gently inhale a plastic worm, without the added assurance of seeing the line twitch, is a real challenge to most angler's confidence. But the rewards of night fishing are many — not the least of which is the special magic that surrounds the sloshing of lunker bass.

Where to Fish at Night

Not all lakes or reservoirs offer good night fishing. Our experience has shown that the clearer the water, the better the night fishing. Though bass can, under extreme conditions, feed without relying on their eyes, vision is normally a crucial part of fish feeding behavior. During the night, when light is minimal, the water must be clear enough for fish to be able to silhouette their prey against the surface. This works fine on crystal clear lakes that are often tough to fish during the day, but on murky water it's a different story. We have tried fishing some excellent but murky bass water and consistently found that fish activity was almost non-existent after dark. But on clear lakes, highland reservoirs, and strip pits, the bass are active and feeding on the darkest nights.

Highland reservoirs offer good examples of prime night fishing water. Because of the clarity of most highland reservoirs, daytime fishing during the summer months becomes difficult and the heat downright uncomfortable. Night fishing offers a better alternative. Other examples of good night fishing water are the clear natural lakes either near large metropolitan areas or surrounded by summer resorts. Both types see lots of human traffic in the form of water skiing, pleasure boating, and fishing. When any lake experiences extensive daytime use, the fish frequently adapt to nighttime feeding. It's much safer for a bass to move into a reed bed and feed at night than to do so during the day when some hot-rod Harry is trying out his new speedboat.

Heavy fishing pressure on both resort and metropolitan lakes can also make for good night fishing. Though this sounds a bit illogical, it does make sense.

Studies of fish behavior indicate that not all bass behave in the same way. Certain strains of fish are more aggressive and thus easier to catch than others. If a lake receives a lot of intelligent fishing pressure during the day, the aggressive bass will be selectively eliminated. At this point, the cautious night-feeding fish will continue to thrive, but most anglers won't know it.

A good case in point is Vermillion Lake in northern Minnesota. Vermillion is large by natural lake standards and has more miles of rocky shoreline than any lake in the state. It is also a very popular resort lake, its shoreline dotted with cabins and those cabins filled with avid walleye anglers. A few years ago, walleye anglers began catching increasing numbers of smallmouth bass. It wasn't long until bass anglers from around the midwest were pounding Vermillion and taking great catches of two- to four-lb. smallies. Their tactics were simple. Locate a sunken reef (most were plainly indicated by large floating buoys), toss a crankbait over the top, and bounce it back to the boat. For three or four years walleye fishing took a backseat while smallmouth angling became Vermillion's claim to fame.

Soon after this initial flurry of activity, however, smallmouth fishing dropped off and the usual claims that the lake was "fished out" began to surface. While it is true that many of the aggressive smallies had been *fished down,* other strains of smallmouth were relatively untouched. And many of these less aggressive fish were primarily night feeders. Though the word is not out yet, a few dedicated anglers are once again making excellent catches of smallmouth by fishing the same daytime reefs at night. So, if your favorite resort lake seems to have slacked off in recent years, and if its water is fairly clear, why not take a nap during the day and give that tired old lake a try at night? You may be pleasantly surprised.

Perhaps the best choice for night fishing water is strip pits. Most pits have extremely clear water, and anglers always report with frustration seeing big bass cruising around that "just can't be caught." In Appendix D we will discuss the specifics of pit fishing, but for now make a mental note to check out pits in your area at night. You'll be amazed how those "uncatchable bass" manage to end up on the end of your line.

How to Fish at Night

Because nighttime affords the bass the opportunity to freely roam the shallows, most angling is done in water 15 feet deep or less. As far as actual tactics go, these depend on the body of water, the type of cover present, the conditions of a given night, and the region that is fished.

One favorite springtime technique, used in highland reservoirs, is to locate a point that holds a concentration of bass during the day and work it over with a spinnerbait at night. Try to arrive about an hour before sundown and mark the point at about the 15-foot level, which is as deep as you normally need fish at night. Then, anchor your boat so that you can fancast the tip and both sides. Concentrate on the six- to ten-foot levels and slowly work the entire area with ⅜-oz. single-spin spinnerbait. Because line watching is difficult at night, you will have to rely on your sense of touch and be very sensitive to the slight tap that signals the presence of a bass. Don't expect the bone-jarring strikes that you might get during the daytime hours. Most underwater nighttime strikes are seldom more than a very light tap — like a rain drop landing on the tip of your cap. To stay in touch with your lure, make your cast, immediately engage the reel, and then either tightline the lure or feather it down to the bottom. As you lift and drop the lure, be sure to keep any slack out of the line. By feathering or riding the lure as it drops to the bottom, you will be able to detect even the slightest break in the rhythm of the lure's blade. If the blade misses even a single beat, set the hook, because Mr. Bass is on the other end.

Summertime angling on highland reservoirs involves fishing a little deeper, but once again, seldom deeper than 15 or 20 feet. As far as location goes, there won't

"Even after the sun sets there is plenty of light as far as Mr. Bass is concerned."

be a lot of furious action at the far end of the creek arms. Instead, the best fishing takes place on main channel points, sunken islands, or any main reservoir area where there is brush or sufficient cover.

An excellent summertime method that only a few anglers employ is what we call "dragging the worm." This approach works best on extended underwater ledges where the bottom drops from the ten- or 15-foot range down to about 20 or 30 feet. When casting perpendicular to such a ledge you necessarily miss a lot of bottom area. Dragging a worm the length of the ledge is much more effective. To begin, use your depth finder to map out a length of ledge approximately 100 yards long. Place marker buoys at either end and near small points or indentations. Then, start at one end, make one long cast behind your boat, and *slowly* troll the ledge using an electric motor. A Texas-rigged worm with a ¼-oz. slip sinker is a good choice, and black is the preferred nighttime color.

As with any night fishing, you will have to rely pretty much on your sense of touch. Keep the rod tip high so that when a bass picks up your worm you can immediately drop the tip. Then, let the trolling motor take any slack out of your line, and set the hook. Don't try to give the fish any line or attempt to feel the fish on your line. In a feeling match at night the bass always wins. Any good spinning or baitcasting reel will work, and light line need not be a consideration. A graphite rod, however, can make a world of difference. The added sensitivity of graphite is a real blessing when trying to get in touch with night-feeding bass. It's nice to be able to feel the fish breathing on your worm before he inhales it.

Of course the most popular method of night fishing is casting a noisemaking surface lure. This technique works extremely well on lowland reservoirs, natural lakes in Florida, northern natural lakes, or any body of water where there is an abundance of vegetation. Skittering a Jitterbug over the tops of weeds is a longstanding tradition in the bassin' world and has accounted for a lot of big bass down through the years. The biggest problem that most of us have with fishing surface lures at night is that our reactions are *too quick*. If you strike at the sound of the splash you usually miss the bass. Often a fish strikes behind a lure, and a quick reaction pulls the lure out of the fish's range of interest. The best approach is to wait until you actually feel tension on the line, then set the hook. Keep the rod tip low and slowly walk the lure over the surface. If you hear a splash, pause; and if you feel any pressure on your line, set the hook. If there is no tension, let the lure rest quietly for a few moments and then continue the retrieve. Most strikes will occur just as the lure begins to move.

Nighttime is a good time to fish extensive weedy flats that often abound in natural lakes. Flats are frustrating to fish during the day. The fish are usually present, but tempting them to strike when they are buried in three or four feet of weeds takes more patience than most of us possess. At night the bass leave their weedy burrows and freely roam the flats. A good approach is to position your boat in the middle of a weed-studded flat and then begin fancasting all the way around the boat. Bass on the flats are tought to pattern and "blind-casting" is a good way to cover a lot of ground quickly. Jitterbugs work well, as do buzzbaits and big-bladed spinnerbaits. We find that a large #6 Colorado blade calls up more fish than the smaller-bladed models.

When to Fish At Night

The best time to begin night fishing is an hour or two before sunset. Use this time to get to know the lay of the land. We suggest fishing a body of water that you are already familiar with. When fishing at night it doesn't pay to move around a lot. The best approach is to choose an area that you are sure holds bass during the day and then work it over thoroughly. Look for areas that offer good shallow water feeding, such as weeds, rocks, or brush piles. Often such an area may not be far from a public access area. After the sun sets, begin looking for lights you can use to find your way home. Most public access or resort lights stay on all night long. A few marker buoys strategically placed will help remind you where the breaks or weeds are. Recently, market buoys with small flashlight batteries have come on the market, and these are super for night angling purposes.

Not all nights offer equally good fishing. Because there are a few added complications to night fishing, the best nights are calm and windless. Luckily, Mother Nature often cooperates. Normally the wind dies down after sunset and calm nights are a fisherman's dream.

Fish movements at night are difficult to predict, but typically there will be two. One can occur at any time during the evening and the other will happen just before sunup. The controversy rages on about the effects of the moon on angling, and particularly on night fishing. Many southern anglers swear that night fishing is always best as the moon is increasing towards a full moon. They contend that after the moon is full fishing drops off noticeably. Other anglers prefer to do their night fishing during the dark of the moon. During a given night, some anglers believe fishing is best before the moon sets. We won't try to resolve the controversy here. Maybe after you have spent some time fishing at night you'll come up with a theory of your own.

Safety at Night

Night fishing has a charm all its own. During the calm of evening, with the tree

"Bobby Murray sets up for fishing before dark actually settles . . . a good tip for nighttime anglers."

toads gently peeping, it is easy to get lulled into a false sense of security. While there is nothing inherently dangerous about night fishing, it does pay to take extra precautions.

Always make sure your running lights are in good order, both bow and stern. Also, be sure to carry a large flashlight or spotlight so that if another boat approaches you can gently remind folks of your presence. Another precaution that *must* be followed when fishing at night is *to make sure you wear your life jacket at all times.* Anything can happen at night and an errant cast from your buddy in the bow or a careless boater who doesn't see your boat can quickly send you into the drink. Though a bit uncomfortable on warm evenings, don't take your preserver off.

To simplify things on a night fishing venture, try to have everything organized in your boat *before* you start. You will be fishing shallow water, so silence is a prime consideration. Hang a few lures on a styrofoam strip on the side of your boat so you don't have to continually open and close your tackle box. Clean out any unnecessary equipment and have two rods rigged and ready to go. An anchor will help, should a slight breeze come up, and a knife should always be handy in case you get tangled in a trot line or have to cut loose from something. Finally, always carry a little mosquito repellent just in case those early evening bugs get pesky.

For light, a small flashlight should be sufficient for most tackle changes. Recently the introduction of *black light* has made line watching a possibility on the darkest night. Black light (the kind kids use to make those psychodelic posters glow) has the ability to make fluorescent monofilament line glow in the dark. A black light system mounted so it pans up and out toward the water will make your line glow like a torch and gives additional security if you are a "line watcher." Some tackle stores have demonstration exhibits set up so you can see the results for yourself. Tackle stores also have available "moon glow" fluorescent lights that mount on the bow of a boat and throw a soft diffuse light against the shore for easier nighttime casting.

If you make sufficient preparations before your first night fishing trip, things should run smoothly and you can relax and enjoy the fishing. As we mentioned earlier, choose an area carefully and then try not to move around too much. An hour or two may go by without a strike and then, in the next half hour, you may limit out. That's the way night fishing is. Anyway, give it a try. You'll find that you have the water and the bass pretty much to yourself. And you just may find yourself having a midnight tug-of-war with the lunker of a lifetime.

APPENDIX A
Tidal Rivers

If rivers in general remain an untapped fishery, then tidal rivers provide the almost unheard of opportunity for virgin largemouth bass fishing. Starting in Virginia and working down the eastern shore through the Carolinas, Georgia, and Florida, there are a number of underfished and unfished tidal areas just waiting for the splash of a spinnerbait. Continuing around Florida, there is also an excellent bass population in the tidal rivers of Alabama, Mississippi, Louisiana, and Texas. Some of these waters, like Albemarle Sound, Currituck Sound, and the St. Johns River, may be familiar to bass anglers, but there are numerous lesser known tidal rivers and backwater areas that possibly provide the biggest bass bonanza this side of Cuba. While bass in tidal waters seldom reach "hawg" size (except in the St. Johns River), there are an abundance of fish in the five- to eight-lb. category, and for most of us that's "hawg" enough.

One of the added thrills of fishing tidal water is that fresh and salt water species mix. It is not uncommon to catch a bass on one cast and to be fast to a tarpon or speckled trout on the next. Be prepared for the unexpected and take along a good strong baitcasting outfit when venturing into rivers that flow to the sea.

In tidal waters most of the fishing is done in shallow water, with depths seldom exceeding nine feet. But if the water lacks depth, it doesn't lack irregularity, with channels twisting and turning in complex serpentine patterns. If you have never fished a tidal river before, it pays to take along a guide until you become familiar with the lay of the land. On large rivers it is particularly easy to get turned around and, with a guide, you're sure to find the way home. Even some of the smaller rivers have confusing side channels and backwater areas, so if you do go it alone be sure to take along a map and compass to help you keep your bearings.

Angling in tidal rivers usually focuses on two main areas: (1) backwater areas, and (2) main river current flows. When working the backwater areas, you may run into some flooded timber. If the water is very shallow, you may be fishing around the bases of flooded timber, like cypress. Cypress trees have strange expanded bases with lots of protruding knees; working as close as possible to this type of structure usually pays good dividends. On occasions where timber is more deeply flooded, the same tactics used on reservoirs will suffice. More than likely, however, it will be vegetation, not timber, that greets the tidal angler. Lily pads, hydrilla, and a variety of water grasses can create conditions not unlike those of a "slop" bay in a natural lake. In heavy cover like this, the tactics described in Chapter 5-B will often work. Of course when fishing in heavy vegetation, it is wise to use a 15- to 20-lb. test line. Backwater areas are no place for ultralight tackle.

Selection of lures for backwater areas varies seasonally, just as it does on any body of water. In the spring, spinnerbaits are deadly. In the summer, keep using spinnerbaits, but add plastic worms and buzzbaits to your repertoire. In mid- to late summer, topwater plugs and topwater spoons become a good choice. And in the fall, buzzbaits, worms, and topwater lures work extremely well. Fishing is usually pretty good in backwater areas from late spring through the fall and can be excellent during the hottest part of the summer, when reservoir fishing gets tough. About the only time these waters fail to produce with regularity is during the winter. Because the water is so shallow, cold winter nights play havoc with bass metabolism. For this reason, fish are hard to pattern and the fishing is difficult.

The normal pattern of fish location in backwaters is that of fish scattered in twos or threes close to heavy cover, while out in the main river areas of current flow there are larger concentrations of schooled fish. In the main river areas most of the fish relate to slack water sections, such as eddies created by old pier pilings, sunken barges, points, man-made canals, or smaller entering streams. Fishing the main river channel, away from the eddies, is often a waste of time. The direction of the water's flow is an important consideration when fishing river eddies. This sounds like common sense, until one realizes that in tidal rivers *the water flows both ways*. During a rising tide, river waters reverse and flow upstream. On an outgoing tide, they flow toward the sea. Certain pieces of structure, like an old sunken barge, can provide good fish-holding structure on an incoming tide and be "dead water" when the tide is going out. Unsuspecting anglers may write off a piece of structure on one trip, not realizing that nine or ten hours later the fish can be packed into that area like cordwood.

Lure selection in main current areas doesn't vary as much as it does when fishing the backwaters. Usually plastic worms, jig/grubs, and medium running crankbaits will work well from the spring through the fall in river eddies. Winter fishing here is just as slow as it is in the backwaters. But winter in the south is never long lasting, and before you know it the pre-spawn bass are once again moving in the bayous.

You probably won't read many fishing articles in magazines about this type of out-of-the-way angling, and it might take you a while to line up a guide who is willing to introduce you to this fishing paradise. But once you try it, you'll be back for more. The next time the family wants to head for the ocean on vacation, take along your bass tackle. Then, when you arrive, drop the folks at the beach for the day, hop into your car, and check out some of those meandering rivers that empty into the sea. Not far from where the salt water mixes with fresh water there's a bass waiting for you.

APPENDIX B
Smallmouth in Reservoirs

While most anglers think of the lakes and rivers of the southern Canadian Shield as the stronghold of the smallmouth bass, it is no accident that Dale Hollow Reservoir in Tennessee claims the world record. While Canadian lakes have a beauty all their own, the growing season for smallmouth is three to four months longer each year in southern reservoirs. Throughout the highland reservoir belt of Tennessee, Kentucky, and northern Arkansas, the smallmouth bass not only thrives but grows fat and sassy. Deep, clear reservoirs, like Bull Shoals, Center Hill, Lake Cumberland, and Lake Norris, not only provide the proper temperature range, their rocky bluffs and points are a natural production area for the smallmouth's favorite forage — Mr. Crayfish.

Locational patterns for smallmouth in reservoirs are very similar to those of the spotted bass. Both species prefer rocky shorelines and neither roams about as much as the wandering largemouth. In the spring the smallmouth seeks out mud and gravel spawning banks and, if the water is clear, will usually spawn deeper than either the largemouth or the spot. If, however, a spring shower muddies the water, you will find smallies spawning in three or four feet of water on a rocky shore. The best spring baits seem to be medium- to deep-running crankbaits in crayfish color, or small single-spin spinnerbaits.

As the summer approaches, the smallmouth moves out of the spawning creeks and bays and begins to locate on long points and rounded bluff points on the main reservoir. Here they can be caught on small, ⅛- to ¼-oz. jigs or small slider jigs with a four-inch plastic worm. The best summer fishing for smallmouth, however, is done at night when they move into the rocky shallows to feed on crayfish. Due to extreme water clarity of summertime highland reservoirs and the nature of the smallmouth, most fish suspend out from bluff points in 20 to 25 feet of water during the middle of the day. Catching suspended smallmouth is not easy, but can be done by locating them with a depth finder and then fishing through them with live bait.

Another summertime locational pattern is a combination of a steep rocky bank with one or two isolated fallen trees. This pattern differs quite a bit from most reservoir largemouth. While the largemouth likes vast expanses of standing timber toward the back ends of coves, the smallmouth prefers an isolated timber that has fallen down a steep bank in 15 to 25 feet of water. This situation will usually hold a small school of smallies all summer long.

In the fall of the year, when surface temperatures are in the low 70's to mid 60's, water clarity in highland reservoirs remains clear and nighttime smallmouth fishing is even better than the summer. At this time the fish abandon the longer points and activity focuses on the short rounded points that either have good rock structure or a combination of rocks and a few fallen timbers. The fall usually sees smaller looser schools of fish, and you will seldom pull into a point and take a limit from a concentrated area. Rather, you'll probably take one or two fish, move 50 feet, and then pick up another fish.

Normal depth for smallmouth in September and October is 10 to 15 feet, and the best lures include either small jigs or large single-spin spinnerbaits. Black is always a good nighttime color and ½- to 1-oz. spinnerbaits cast parallel to a bank and yo-yo'd in about the 12-foot range work well. Another good fall approach is to cast a twin-spin perpendicular to the bank and then work it slowly down the bank, as we described in "Scraping the Bluffs." Small jigs and plastic worms will also take a few smallies during the fall period, but the single- and twin-spins will usually take the bigger fish.

As winter approaches and water temperatures get into the mid 50's, you will once again start catching smallmouth during the day. The best winter locations seem to be the short steep bluffs and the small bluffs back in the creek channels. The best baits are small jigs and medium- to deep-diving crankbaits. Jigs in the ⅛- to ¼-oz. size work well, and yellow or white jigs with a small pork rind are preferred. Brown and black would be a second choice, also with a pork rind trailer. The best colors for crankbaits are reds and browns in a crayfish pattern. Remember, water temperatures in the mid 50's mean slow presentation. A good tactic is to parallel the bank with a deep-diving crankbait (plastic, as opposed to the more bouyant balsa). Quickly crank the lure down and then slowly walk it across the bottom back to the boat.

Once the water temperatures get into the mid 40's, smallmouth fishing slows down, but good catches can still be made by concentrating on the little cuts or coves with a sharp drop to 25 feet. These small cuts may extend only 20 or 30 yards into the bank and each may hold one or two fish. A ⅜-oz. black or brown jig with a pork frog to slow the fall of the lure is a good choice of bait. Fishing small cuts is a big fish pattern and smaller fish can be taken off the rock bluffs.

One of the big advantages of fall and winter smallmouth fishing is that the fishing pressure is considerably less than during the summer and fall months. And this is your chance to land a really big fish.

No, Virginia, all the big smallmouth aren't in Canada. Your next "wallhanger" is probably prowling the depths of a southern reservoir right now. Next winter why not give it a try?

APPENDIX C
Farm Ponds

Most anglers would be surprised not only at the number and variety of farm ponds in our country, but also at the size of the bass that inhabit these tiny fishing gems. Farm pond angling often recalls childhood memories. Many of us cut our angling teeth on a farm pond. And, though bluegills and catfish were probably our first quarry, farm ponds harbor some amazingly big bass. In fact, a state record largemouth from Ohio came out of a farm pond.

Farm ponds vary in size from less than an acre to over 100 acres. Size is an important consideration when planning a fishing strategy. Most small ponds are either scooped out by a bulldozer or are the result of damming a small depression in the land. In either case, the bottom is usually lacking in drop-offs, breaks, or other noticeable structure. For this reason the bass relate to shoreline weeds, stumps, overhanging trees, or other available cover.

In approaching a small pond you need to be aware of how the vibrations of your footsteps can alert fish. Try to approach the pond as slowly and quietly as possible. Also be aware of shadows you may cast on the pond's surface. Fish in small ponds are very spooky, so take your time plotting your approach. Your first casts should be made parallel to the shoreline, two casts to the left and two to the right. Then look for any visible cover and slowly work your way around the pond with the sun in your face. By keeping your eyes peeled for fish movement you can sometimes spot-cast to your quarry.

Larger ponds can be fished from shore, waded, or even fished from an inner tube, but most anglers prefer some type of boat. Because bass boats are not feasible, a small cartop johnboat or canoe equipped with an electric trolling motor is the best bet. Large ponds can often be treated like mini-reservoirs. They will have greater structural variety than smaller ponds and may have creek beds, sunken timber, and even small islands. Since no maps are available for farm ponds, anglers must either use a portable depth finder or simply probe the depths with jigs and deep-diving crankbaits to determine bottom structure.

The configuration of a pond is usually a good clue to different types of bottom structure. Round or egg-shaped ponds tend to have bottoms that are rather featureless. Ponds with irregular shorelines, including small bays, fingers, and islands, will have a good variety of bottom structure. Both large and small ponds often have a dam at one end that indicate the deepest water. But deep water in a farm pond may only be 10 or 15 feet. If you fish farm ponds in the northern U.S., be sure to check with the owner to see if there has been a "freeze-out" in recent years. Every six or seven years we have unseasonably cold winters, and a hard winter can wipe out the entire population in some ponds and necessitate restocking. Last year's favorite pond could be "dead water" by the next spring.

Another idiosyncracy of farm ponds is that the calendar periods are greatly accelerated in the spring and fall. This is due to the general shallow-water structure of these ponds and is particularly true of northern ponds. Waters can warm so quickly in a small pond that fish will be active the same day the ice goes out. There are usually two big fish movements on small ponds, one right after ice-out and the other just prior to freeze-up. You have to time things perfectly, but if you can be on your favorite pond during one of these periods, you'll be pleasantly surprised at the size of some of the bass "you never knew were there."

During the summer period on farm ponds, the typical feeding patterns are at daybreak and again at dusk. On extremely small ponds of only a few acres, once the feeding period is over you might as well pack your bags and go home til the next one. On larger ponds there will be a shallow water movement early and late in the day, but during midday the fish will drop down into creek channels or other deep water areas and can be dredged up with a plastic worm.

Tackle preparations for pond fishing should be as simple as possible. Usually a few spinners, floating and diving minnow-type lures, and an assortment of plastic worms will suffice. There is no need to bring along the foot locker-size tackle box, as often everything you need can be fit into a small pocket box. On farm ponds devoid of timber and heavy weeds, ultralight tackle works best. There is a special thrill approaching a small pond in morning's early light, casting a floating plug down the shoreline, and waiting for the telltale slurp of a farm pond bass.

One final consideration — always be sure to ask permission of the landowner and leave a fish or two as payment for your fishing pleasure. This builds good will and can make for long-term access to your own private fishing wonderland.

APPENDIX D
Fishing Pits

In a country where virgin bass fishing is almost unheard of, it is encouraging to know that untouched waters still exist. Most pits are either so obvious, as with "borrow pits" near cloverleafs on major interstate highways, or so remote, as with strip pits in old mining areas, that few anglers have ever sampled this fantastic fishery. Borrow pits are so named because highway construction crews excavate, or borrow, gravel and sand from an area in order to build up cloverleaf entrances, exits, and overpasses. The resulting pits are most common near major metropolitan areas and are bypassed by literally millions of anglers every day on their way to and from work. True "strip pits," on the other hand, usually exist in remote hinterlands where either coal or iron has been mined. In either case, pits receive even less fishing pressure than farm ponds — and that's not much.

Pits are normally very small in size, usually ranging from one to 20 acres. Though small in size, many pits have surprisingly deep water. It is not uncommon for a pit, particularly a mining pit, to have water from 50 to over 150 feet deep. Because pits have been excavated, their basins are almost totally lacking in bottom structure. Given this scooped-out shape and steep dropping sides, pits create a habitat in which bass exhibit two classic location patterns. Bass in pits either relate to available shoreline cover, such as weeds, brush, or standing timber, or they suspend. Often fish may exhibit both patterns in the same pit. However, bass are more likely to spend their time suspended if the pit is a gravel or sand pit with little shoreline cover. These different patterns often confuse anglers new to pit fishing.

The best way to learn to fish pits is to begin by understanding the idiosyncracies of their seasonal patterns. Without a doubt, the best time to fish pits is during the cold-water periods of the spring and fall. When water temperatures are in the mid 50's, pit fishing is hard to beat. One difference between pits and other bodies of water is the incredible clarity of the water. Extremely clear water frustrates many anglers, particularly in pits, where it is not uncommon to see schools of bass lazily drifting along — bass that behave as if their mouths have been permanently wired shut. A quick look at seasonal patterns of a typical pit helps explain why pit bass behave the way they do.

On northern pits the ice goes out much earlier than it does on natural lakes. Even though pits have deep water, shoreline areas warm quickly and it may be a matter of only a day or two before a strong pre-spawn movement is underway. Since there is little available spawning habitat, the majority of spawning bass in a pit may be crammed into a relatively small space. On strip pits the bass often spawn right along the original roadbed that trucks once used to haul out their loads of coal or iron ore. The clearer the water, the deeper the bass will spawn. Small spinners or live rubber jigs are good cold-water lures, and spinners, small crankbaits, and top-water work well during the spawn.

During the bulk of the summer, fishing can be tough. Pits in the north central part of our country can be especially difficult because of the combination of clear

"Here's a selection of small lures that are just about right for finicky strip pit bass."

water and cold front weather conditions. Here are a few clues for summer pit fishing.

1. If the pit has little timber or brush, use four- to six-lb.-test line and light tackle.
2. Live bait, particularly minnows, rigged with a small hook and splitshot will work wonders on spooky pit bass.
3. Fish early or late in the day, or on overcast days during low light conditions.
4. Always try to fish the shady side of the pit. Look for small washout areas or other tiny cuts in the bank, as these will often hold active single fish.
5. During the day use small baits, such as four-inch worms with ⅛-oz. jig heads, or ⅛- to ¼-oz. safety-spin spinners.
6. Whenever possible fish at night. Use large surface lures like a Jitterbug or Hula Popper and don't limit yourself to casting the shoreline. Remember those suspended bass? Well, during the night those bass drift toward the surface and it is possible to catch fish on surface plugs in the middle of a pit where the water is over 100 feet deep.

As the fall cold-water period approaches and water temperatures once again get into the mid 50's, change back to live rubber jigs or a jig and eel and begin working the shoreline. Most anglers make the mistake of casting to the shoreline and then immediately beginning their retrieve. This causes the jig to drop 20 or 30 feet and misses a lot of bass. A better method is to retrieve the jig only a few inches and walk it down the steep-sloping sides. This technique is similar to "scraping the bluffs" for spotted bass. If your pit has lots of standing timber, work the edges of the trees with Texas-rigged worms or jigs with brush guards.

One of the pleasant benefits of pit fishing is the size of the bass. A number of the biggest bass in a number of states, including the present state record in Illinois, come from pits. There is excellent pit fishing in Indiana, Minnesota, south central Illinois, Wisconsin, southern Iowa, Arkansas, Oklahoma, Kansas, Nebraska, Missouri, Pennsylvania, Kentucky, Tennessee, Virginia, and West Virginia. That's almost one third of the United States.

When was the last time you went pit fishing?

APPENDIX E
What You Need to Know About Electronic Equipment

In a decade that has witnessed a proliferation of electronic fishing equipment, it would be possible to spend an entire book explaining the different types of equipment and their uses. While anglers of old relied on a lead weight and marking line, modern bassers can choose from a number of different types and styles of depth finders. And thirty years ago, who would have foreseen the advent of oxygen meters, light meters, ph meters, aerated live wells, and electronic thermometers?

The choice as to which of this equipment you actually need should be dictated by the amount of time you spend fishing and the type of water you fish. In most cases, most anglers can get along with a few basics.

Depth Finders

Shore fishermen or anglers who fish small ponds or small rivers have little need of depth finders, but for everyone else who spends a lot of time on the water a depth finder is indispensable. There are basically two types of depth finders on the market, flasher units and graphing units. The flasher units indicate depth, weed growth, and other bottom structure on a circular dial through a combination of sonar and rotating light bulb. Graphing units record bottom contours by tracing a line over straight-line graph paper. Of these two, the flasher unit is sufficient for most fishing needs.

One consideration before purchasing a flasher unit is the depth of the bodies of water you will be fishing. Flasher units come with different depth ranges on their dials. Reservoir anglers, fishing deep-water spotted bass in highland reservoirs, would want at least a 60-foot dial, while anglers fishing shallow natural lakes might do best with a 30-foot dial. The advantage of a 30-foot dial on shallow water is its ability to pick up small two- and three-foot drop-offs that would be difficult to notice on the 60-foot dial. In either case, both models will measure over the range indicated on the dial by simply making a second revolution of the light to pick up deeper water. Thus, the second time around, the 10-foot mark on a 30-foot dial actually measures 40 feet of water. Similarly, the second revolution on a 60-foot dial measures 70 feet when flashing at the 10-foot level.

Graphing units are even more expensive than flasher units and are more of a specialty tool for the professional guide or serious angler. The advantage of these units is that they clearly indicate the presence of fish and make it easy to distinguish between weeds, timber, drop-offs, and other types of bottom structure. A graphing unit would be of assistance to anglers fishing suspended bass in southern reservoirs or to midwest anglers who fish walleyes and northern pike as well as bass. Whether or not fish spend a lot of time suspended depends on the body of water and the type of prey present. A graphing unit is reassuring to use, particularly when you know those blips you might see on a flasher unit are actually fish. The frustration comes with sitting over a school of fish and trying to catch them. Seeing and catching are two different things, particularly when fish are in a negative feeding mood. Then you might wish you had an old flasher unit that didn't indicate fish so obviously. Once you see a school of lunkers on your graph paper it takes a lot of self discipline to leave them and accept the fact that they just won't bite.

Thermometers

Because of the important role water temperature plays in the changing calendar periods for all members of the bass family, every angler should have at least an inexpensive surface temperature thermometer in his tackle box. In fact, during the early spring and fall, a thermometer can be as important as a depth finder in locating bass. There are a number of relatively inexpensive, non-electronic thermometers that can be used. One that we like is the type used by professional photographers in preparing their developing solutions. These thermostatic thermometers register water temperature on a small dial and give an almost instantaneous readout. They cost about fifteen dollars.

Guides and fishing pros like to have electronic digital surface thermometers mounted under the hull of their boats so they can be constantly aware of changing surface temperatures. This type of thermometer can be extremely helpful in the spring, when fluctuating air temperatures and wind can move water around on a big lake or reservoir. It is not uncommon to find a cove at one end of a reservoir with surface temperature readings in the low 60's, while in a cove at the other end of the same reservoir temperatures could be in the low 50's. Such a temperature differential often spells the difference between active and inactive bass.

Subsurface temperature readings are best taken with a "drop" thermometer. This style operates on a small penlight battery and a reeled cable with a temperature sensor on its tip. The sensing unit is lowered over the side of the boat and, as the cable runs out, the depth either is recorded on the main unit or is marked on the cable. With this unit you can read temperatures at different depths, a helpful capability once water stratifies and a thermocline is established. During the spring and fall, however, the action of wind and rain usually homogenizes a lake's waters, so the surface temperature is often a good indication of water temperature both in the shallows and mid-depths.

Meters, Meters, and More Meters

A good flasher depth finder and an inexpensive surface thermometer are about as far as most anglers need go in the realm of fishing electronics. There are, however, other pieces of equipment available.

Light-sensing units have been developed that indicate on a meter the amount of available light at any given depth. Such a device could be of assistance to anglers pursuing spotted bass in clear highland reservoirs, or might help midwest anglers who enjoy fishing for walleyes as well as bass. Most anglers, however, can simply use their eyes to get an indication of the general water clarity.

Ph meters have recently been developed that give a readout of the relative acidity or alkalinity of the water. We have yet to see conclusive evidence that ph levels provide an effective guide to bass location on a given lake. Of course, fish cannot successfully spawn when the water is highly acid. As we discover more about acid rain, ph meters may help us analyze the fishing potential of a body of water.

Oxygen meters indicate the amount of dissolved O_2 in the water and can help anglers eliminate unproductive water during hot, calm periods when a lake develops a thermocline. Oxygen meters are probably of more use to southern anglers where such conditions often exist during the summer months. Midwest anglers usually have enough wind action so that the lack of dissolved O_2 is seldom a big problem.

Undoubtedly, additional sophisticated electronic equipment will soon be on the market, promising anglers easy answers to their fishing frustrations. Just remember, every additional piece of equipment in your boat means one more fishing tool that can take time away from actual fishing. While the appropriate electronic equipment can help solve some angling problems, improved technology is never the final answer. Choose your equipment carefully, but remember that the real key to successful angling involves a lot of common sense and hard work.

APPENDIX F
What You Need to Know About Boats

A few decades ago there really wasn't much choice in suitable boats for bass fishing. Most of us just made do with what we had. The sixties and seventies, however, witnessed such a boom in fishing boat production that there are now hundreds of different styles to choose from. To make sense of all these possibilities we have broken boats down into a few simple categories.

The primary consideration in choosing a boat should be the type of water that you most frequently fish. This is really a matter of both safety and comfort. On a large body of water where wind, high waves, and frequent storms are common occurrences, a big boat and large motor are pretty much a necessity. On smaller lakes, many public accesses won't accommodate a large boat, and in shallow water they are impractical. Since most of us have a preference for a certain type of water, or are limited to what is available, it is best to select a boat with that water in mind. If you like to fish other bodies of water you can always rent a boat when the occasion calls for it.

"Here's an 18' 8" Ranger bass boat that can comfortably fish three anglers without any difficulty."

The Big Bass Boats

Big bass boats do everything but fly — and at 60 m.p.h. they almost do that. They are fast, stable, and have plenty of room to move about in safety. These boats are designed primarily for large reservoirs or natural lakes, where it is not uncommon to run ten or 20 miles between fishing spots. They are made of impact resistant fiberglass and, more recently, of lightweight kelvar. Most big boats come equipped with a prewired electrical system that allows the angler to quickly add depth finders, surface thermometers, lights, anchor winches, and other fishing niceties. Anglers that enjoy slow trolling often add a smaller 25-hp. motor alongside a 75- or 100-hp. motor so that they have both speed and maneuverability.

The Versatility Rig

Boats that are small enough to control with tiller-handle outboards make good versatility rigs for small to mid-sized water. You can cast, troll, drift, and move into fairly shallow water with these rigs. A bow-mounted electric motor makes shallow water angling a breeze. Of course you do sacrifice some of the speed of the larger boats, as 35- 50-hp. motors are usually sufficient for the job. Weather safety is always a concern when fishing from a small boat. Since it is difficult to outrun a storm, you need time to keep an eye peeled for bad weather and head for shore.

"This smaller 15′ craft is just about right for two anglers."

Aluminum V-Hulls

A recent innovation in bass fishing is the aluminum V-hull boat that features flat floors and pedestal bass seats. Of course this boat has long been a favorite of walleye anglers in the midwest, but the addition of a flat floor makes it more than suitable for bass fishing. V-hulls are similar to the aforementioned versatility rigs and combine a medium sized outboard and an electric motor with a comfortable casting platform.

The V-hull is designed for anglers who fish a variety of species and spend a lot of time on big lakes. The deep V-hull combined with high sides is designed to handle large waves with ease. These boats will handle windy water even better than a large bass boat. There are, however, a few drawbacks. You have to put up with a lot of wind resistance due to the high sides; because of this, a V-hull is more difficult to control than a low-profile bass boat. Because of its shape, the V-hull is also not quite as stable when anglers are standing and casting. Still it makes an excellent choice for mixed species fishing on large natural lakes.

Flat-Bottomed Boats

The granddaddy of them all, the old johnboat, still has its place in the modern bassin' world. Flat-bottomed boats are great on small lakes, farm ponds, swamps, or rivers — anywhere you don't have lots of open water exposed to the wind. For puddle jumping and car topping, a johnboat is excellent, but in a wind and big waves it can be a disaster.

For years the johnboat was made of wood. Though they were sturdy, they sure lacked comfort. Now you can purchase carpeted aluminum models with live wells and pedestal seats. These models are still relatively inexpensive and are great for anglers who like the solitude of fishing small, out-of-the-way water.

Whazzits

You figure a name for them. In the last few years several versions of lightweight fiberglass cartoppers have hit the market. Some look like the small paddle boats, the kind you used to rent at amusement parks. Others are simply small modified duck boats. These tiny one- and two-man rigs are perfect for popping in and out of small strip pits and farm ponds.

In this category you will also find canoes, inflatable craft, and inner tubes, and by the time this book is out there will doubtless be five or ten new models. They certainly have their place on tiny ponds and small streams.

— — — — — — — — — —

What all this boils down to is an awareness that no boat is perfect for all conditions. Shop around, consider the alternatives, compare prices, and then pick the type that best suits your needs. Make sure the motor you get is the proper size for your boat and then rig it up to match your own comforts.